Taste of Home
Contest Winning
ANNUAL RECIPES

Taste of Home
Contest Winning
ANNUAL RECIPES

EDITORIAL

EDITOR-IN-CHIEF	Catherine Cassidy
CREATIVE DIRECTOR	Howard Greenberg
EDITORIAL OPERATIONS DIRECTOR	Kerri Balliet

MANAGING EDITOR/PRINT & DIGITAL BOOKS	Mark Hagen
ASSOCIATE CREATIVE DIRECTOR	Edwin Robles Jr.

EDITORS	Christine Rukavena, Heather Ray
ART DIRECTOR	Jessie Sharon
CONTRIBUTING LAYOUT DESIGNER	Siya Motamedi
EDITORIAL PRODUCTION MANAGER	Dena Ahlers
COPY CHIEF	Deb Warlaumont Mulvey
COPY EDITORS	Mary C. Hanson, Mary-Liz Shaw
CONTRIBUTING COPY EDITOR	Erica Walburg

CHIEF FOOD EDITOR	Karen Berner
FOOD EDITORS	James Schend; Peggy Woodward, RD
ASSOCIATE FOOD EDITOR	Krista Lanphier
RECIPE EDITORS	Mary King; Annie Rundle; Jenni Sharp, RD; Irene Yeh
CONTENT OPERATIONS MANAGER	Colleen King
CONTENT OPERATIONS ASSISTANT	Shannon Stroud
EXECUTIVE ASSISTANT	Marie Brannon

TEST KITCHEN AND FOOD STYLING MANAGER	Sarah Thompson
TEST COOKS	Nicholas Iverson (lead), Matthew Hass, Lauren Knoelke
FOOD STYLISTS	Kathryn Conrad (senior), Shannon Roum, Leah Rekau
PREP COOKS	Megumi Garcia, Melissa Hansen, Bethany Van Jacobson

PHOTOGRAPHY DIRECTOR	Stephanie Marchese
PHOTOGRAPHERS	Dan Roberts, Jim Wieland
PHOTOGRAPHER/SET STYLIST	Grace Natoli Sheldon
SET STYLISTS	Stacey Genaw, Melissa Haberman, Dee Dee Jacq

BUSINESS ANALYST	Kristy Martin
BILLING SPECIALIST	Mary Ann Koebernik

BUSINESS

VICE PRESIDENT, CHIEF SALES OFFICER	Mark S. Josephson
VICE PRESIDENT, BUSINESS DEVELOPMENT & MARKETING	Alain Begun
GENERAL MANAGER, TASTE OF HOME COOKING SCHOOL	Erin Puariea

VICE PRESIDENT, DIGITAL EXPERIENCE & E-COMMERCE	Jennifer Smith
VICE PRESIDENT, DIRECT TO CONSUMER MARKETING	Dave Fiegel

THE READER'S DIGEST ASSOCIATION, INC.

PRESIDENT AND CHIEF EXECUTIVE OFFICER	Robert E. Guth
VICE PRESIDENT, CHIEF OPERATING OFFICER, NORTH AMERICA	Howard Halligan
PRESIDENT & PUBLISHER, BOOKS	Harold Clarke
VICE PRESIDENT, NORTH AMERICAN OPERATIONS	Philippe Cloutier
VICE PRESIDENT, CHIEF MARKETING OFFICER	Leslie Doty
VICE PRESIDENT, NORTH AMERICAN HUMAN RESOURCES	Phyllis E. Gebhardt, SPHR
VICE PRESIDENT, CHIEF TECHNOLOGY OFFICER	Rob Hilliard
VICE PRESIDENT, CONSUMER MARKETING PLANNING	Jim Woods

COVER PHOTOGRAPHY

PHOTOGRAPHER	Jim Wieland
FOOD STYLIST	Kathryn Conrad
SET STYLIST	Stephanie Marchese

© 2014 RDA ENTHUSIAST BRANDS, LLC
5400 S. 60TH ST., GREENDALE WI 53129

INTERNATIONAL STANDARD BOOK NUMBER:	978-1-61765-289-9
INTERNATIONAL STANDARD SERIAL NUMBER:	1548-4157
COMPONENT NUMBER:	118400028H00

PICTURED ON THE FRONT COVER: Chocolate Raspberry Tunnel Cake, page 192.
PICTURED ON THE BACK COVER: Bacon Vegetable Quiche, page 88; Strawberry & Wine Sorbet, page 211; Hungarian Nut Rolls, page 218; Orange Spinach Salad, page 45.

TABLE OF CONTENTS

Introduction 4

Snacks & Appetizers 6

Special Salads 26

Soups & Sandwiches 48

Breakfast & Brunch 72

Beef Entrees 92

Pork Entrees 106

Poultry Entrees 122

Seafood & Meatless Entrees 142

Sides, Breads & Condiments 156

Cookies, Bars & Candy 176

Cakes & Pies 190

Just Desserts 206

The Cook's Quick Reference 228

Indexes 230

MORE THAN 350
PRIZEWINNING
RECIPES & TIPS!

Every year, thousands of home cooks from across the country enter their cherished recipes in a *Taste of Home* contest. Now you can enjoy our judges' favorites with the latest edition of *Contest Winning Annual Recipes*.

You're sure to love sampling these amazing winners as much as our judging panel did. This brand-new edition is bursting with 27 grand-prize recipes and hundreds of runners-up. And because the recipes are from *Taste of Home*, each award-winner uses everyday, easy-to-find ingredients. So gather your loved ones around to discover a new dish to cherish today. When you cook from this collection of treasured recipes, everybody wins!

This cookbook brings you the winners of dozens of contests published in *Taste of Home* and her sister publications. You'll even find the winners of our best and biggest contest, America's Best-Loved Recipe, with cash prizes totaling $27,000.

From more than 10,000 entries, George Schroeder's Penne Gorgonzola with Chicken (page 140) was singled out for top honors. George's 30-minute pasta dinner quickly rose to the top in our contest's Time Saver category, and then went on to take the whopping $25,000 grand prize!

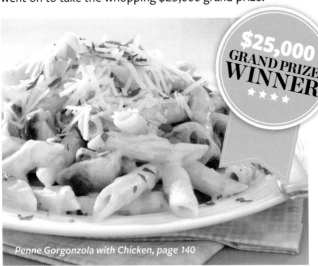

$25,000
GRAND PRIZE
WINNER

Penne Gorgonzola with Chicken, page 140

Other fabulous winners in this celebrated competition include:

- **CLASSIC CATEGORY:** Sandy Blessing's magnificent Italian Meatball Tortes (page 96)

- **SERVES 2 CATEGORY:** Esther Danielson's grilled Asian-Style Baby Back Ribs (page 115)

- **LIGHT CATEGORY:** Christine Vaught's produce-packed Mango Chicken with Plum Sauce (page 125)

Winners from Dozens of Contests

The contests found here span a variety of topics, from brunch favorites to home-baked holiday specialties; prizewinning salads to over-the-top chocolate treats. Whether you need a quick summer meal that won't heat up the kitchen or a surefire hit at the next potluck, look no further than this beautiful volume.

Here's a taste-tempting preview of the grand-prize winners you will find inside.

GO NUTS
What's not to love about crunchy candied pecans layered atop savory cream cheese? Heidi Blaine Hadburg's French Quarter Cheese Spread (page 22) offers up an irresistible taste of the Big Easy!

BEAT THE HEAT
California reader Terri McCarty keeps the kitchen cool with fresh and simple Balsamic Chicken Pasta Salad (page 33). Terri's quick recipe teams up summery tomatoes and basil with leftover chicken or grilled shrimp.

YOU SAY TOMATO
For a sensational spin on the classic tomato-mozzarella-basil salad, don't miss South-of-the-Border Caprese Salad (page 40). It pairs cilantro vinaigrette and Mexican cheese with heirloom tomatoes for a flavor that pops!

SPECTACULAR SALADS
Homemade poppy seed dressing, smoky bacon and loads of satisfying Swiss cheese pushed Jennifer Rytting's Orange Spinach Salad (page 45) above all the rest. This high-yield recipe is great for potlucks.

SUMMER POTLUCKS
Bursting with garden-fresh flavor, Summer Veggie Subs (page 50) are perfect for a block party, baseball outing or family reunion. The recipe makes two giant sandwiches that are easy to share.

SPECTACULAR SANDWICHES
A succulent chutney that's surprisingly quick to prepare helped Georgia cook Lily Julow earn the grand prize. Her Roast Pork Sandwiches with Peach Chutney (page 56) are both simple and sophisticated.

BOUNTIFUL BEANS
Hearty Shaker Bean Soup (page 63) is filled with the slow-simmered goodness of smoky ham, fresh vegetables and buttery great northern beans. Florida's Deborah Amrine took top honors with this blue-ribbon favorite.

MUSHROOMS EVERY DAY, EVERY WAY

No one will miss the meat when Portobello Burgers with Pear-Walnut Mayonnaise (page 67) are on the menu. Zesty mushroom burgers are piled high with creamy melted Gorgonzola cheese and peppery arugula. It's a must-try vegetarian meal.

WE'RE TALKING TURKEY

Cheeseburgers get an irresistible makeover with Lisa Hundley's sassy Turkey Sliders with Chili Cheese Mayo (page 68). The cheesy, bacony bites are ideal for any party! Bet you can't eat just one.

POWER FOODS

Good nutrition has never tasted better than with Rosemarie Weleski's Baked Blueberry & Peach Oatmeal (page 78). This wholesome creation packs heart-healthy oats, walnuts and antioxidant-rich blueberries into every bite.

BREAKFAST & BRUNCH

Rise and shine with golden, flaky Ham & Cheese Breakfast Strudels (page 85). Serve the easy-prep pastries for brunch or pop them in the freezer for quick handheld meals on the go. Either way, you win with these savory bundles.

SIMMERED ALL DAY

Pot roast and hearty winter vegetables slow-cook to perfection with Patricia Kile's recipe for succulent Gone-All-Day Stew (page 104). The stick-to-your-ribs dish is a classic pairing with hot, buttery noodles.

5-INGREDIENT

North Carolina's Tanya Reid took top prize with Secret's in the Sauce BBQ Ribs (page 112). Bottled barbecue sauce tastes homemade with the addition of Dijon, garlic and cherry preserves. Poured on thickly over baby back ribs and slow-cooked, it's sensational.

LOTSA PASTA

Penne pasta gets a fanciful twist with Barbecue Pork and Penne Skillet (page 119). Shredded barbecue pork, cheddar cheese and green onions make a fun skillet pasta the whole family will love.

LIGHTENED-UP RECIPES

You really can have it all with Heather O'Neill's surprisingly low-fat, low-calorie Lasagna Deliziosa (page 126). For anyone trying to eat more healthfully, this magnificent dish is a reason to rejoice!

FOR THE BIRDS

Simple enough for a weeknight yet company-special, Prosciutto Chicken in Wine Sauce (page 133) simmers up quickly on the stovetop. Just add starch and a green vegetable for a satisfying dinner that's good for you, too.

AMERICA'S BEST-LOVED RECIPE

New Jersey's George Schroeder captured the $25,000 prize in *Taste of Home*'s first mega-contest searching for the very best recipe in the U.S.A. See for yourself why George's Penne Gorgonzola with Chicken (page 140) stole our judges' hearts!

SAY CHEESE

Mac 'n' cheese gets a grown-up take thanks to fresh spinach and shrimp in Michael Cohen's luscious baked Shrimp & Macaroni Casserole (page 147). It's perfect for serving two or three. Or, bake it up just for yourself and enjoy the leftovers the next day.

MAKE IT IN 10

With three teens constantly on the go, Connecticut reader Veronica Callaghan needs tasty recipes that come together in a snap. Veronica's Peachy Shrimp Tacos (page 150) are sure to be a go-to dinner in your house, too.

STANDOUT QUICK BREADS

You really can put a golden loaf of bread on the table in just one hour! Peppery Cheese Bread (page 165) is studded with green onions, cheddar cheese and cracked black pepper for a fabulous, family-pleasing taste.

PEPPER UPPERS

Sweet, sour, salty and a little bit hot, Bread & Butter Peppers (page 172) are can't-stop-eating-them good. Making them just might become a summer tradition in your house. No canning equipment required!

KIDDIN' AROUND

For wholesome cookies that will thrill the kid in all of us, don't miss Rebecca Clark's Oatmeal Surprise Cookies (page 186). The Alabama baker uses chocolate-covered raisins and pumpkin pie spice to create a new cookie-jar classic.

HOME-BAKED FOR THE HOLIDAYS

Loaded with walnuts and iced with a decadent cream cheese frosting, Holiday Walnut Torte (page 197) is a showstopping addition to any holiday table. Reader Eileen Korecko took first prize with her grandmother's beloved recipe.

BERRY BONANZA

A shortbread cookie crust, creamy lemon filling and a layer of sweet blueberry topping added up to victory for New York's Erin Chilcoat. Everybody wins when they try Erin's blue-ribbon Lemon Blueberry Tart (page 208).

SMALL-BATCH BAKING

Cute and creamy with a candy surprise tucked inside, Miniature Peanut Butter Cheesecakes (page 215) are destined to become a favorite wherever they go. One little batch makes six of the treats in about half an hour.

CHOCOLATE LOVERS'

With their intense mocha flavor and rich molten centers, Warm Chocolate Melting Cups (page 220) are as scrumptious as they sound! You won't believe these dinner-party desserts tip the scales at just 197 calories each.

FRUIT FEST

Savor a fresh bite of summer when you serve Sally Sibthorpe's Dessert Bruschetta with Nectarine Salsa (page 227). She livens up sliced pound cake with fresh fruit, rich mascarpone and a kiss of honey for a treat that's ready in just 15 minutes.

Chocolate Chip Dip, page 14

9

17

25

Snacks & Appetizers

These **blue-ribbon munchies** will shine at your next party or potluck. From twice-baked **mini** potatoes to **decadent** cheese bites, **addictive** snack mixes and **smoky** stuffed peppers, each recipe is a guaranteed winner.

Spinach & Black Bean Egg Rolls

Black beans and spinach provide lots of healthy nutrients in these delicious baked egg rolls. Rolling them up is a cinch, too.
—**MELANIE SCOTT** AMARILLO, TX

START TO FINISH: 30 MIN. • **MAKES:** 20 EGG ROLLS

- 2 **cups frozen corn, thawed**
- 1 **can (15 ounces) black beans, rinsed and drained**
- 1 **package (10 ounces) frozen chopped spinach, thawed and squeezed dry**
- 1 **cup (4 ounces) shredded reduced-fat Mexican cheese blend**
- 1 **can (4 ounces) chopped green chilies, drained**
- 4 **green onions, chopped**
- 1 **teaspoon ground cumin**
- ½ **teaspoon chili powder**
- ½ **teaspoon pepper**
- 20 **egg roll wrappers**
  Cooking spray
  Salsa and reduced-fat ranch salad dressing, optional

1. In a large bowl, combine the first nine ingredients. Place ¼ cup of mixture in the center of one egg roll wrapper. (Keep remaining wrappers covered with a damp paper towel until ready to use.) Fold bottom corner over filling. Fold sides toward center over filling. Moisten remaining corner with water; roll up tightly to seal. Repeat.
2. Place seam side down on baking sheets coated with cooking spray. Spray tops of egg rolls with cooking spray. Bake at 425° for 10-15 minutes or until lightly browned. Serve warm with salsa and dressing if desired. Refrigerate leftovers.
FREEZE OPTION *Freeze cooled egg rolls in a freezer container, separating layers with waxed paper. To use, reheat rolls on a baking sheet in a preheated 350° oven until crisp and heated through.*
PER SERVING *147 cal., 2 g fat (1 g sat. fat), 7 mg chol., 298 mg sodium, 26 g carb., 2 g fiber, 7 g pro.* **Diabetic Exchanges:** *1½ starch, 1 lean meat.*

Tomato-Jalapeno Granita

Everyone will say "Wow!" after one taste of this refreshing, icy appetizer. Even my grandchildren enjoy the cool combination of tomato, mint and lime.
—**PAULA MARCHESI** LENHARTSVILLE, PA

PREP: 15 MIN. + FREEZING • **MAKES:** 6 SERVINGS

- 2 **cups tomato juice**
- ⅓ **cup sugar**
- 4 **mint sprigs**
- 1 **jalapeno pepper, sliced**
- 2 **tablespoons lime juice**
  Fresh mint leaves, optional

1. In a small saucepan, bring the tomato juice, sugar, mint sprigs and jalapeno to a boil. Cook and stir until sugar is dissolved. Remove from the heat; cover and let stand for 15 minutes.
2. Strain and discard solids. Stir in lime juice. Transfer to a 1-qt. dish; cool to room temperature. Freeze for 1 hour; stir with a fork.
3. Freeze 2-3 hours longer or until completely frozen, stirring every 30 minutes. Scrape granita with a fork just before serving; spoon into dessert dishes. Garnish with additional mint if desired.
NOTE *Wear disposable gloves when cutting hot peppers; the oils can burn skin. Avoid touching your face.*
PER SERVING *59 cal., trace fat (trace sat. fat), 0 chol., 218 mg sodium, 15 g carb., trace fiber, 1 g pro.* **Diabetic Exchange:** *1 starch.*

Mediterranean Tomato Bites

My friend Mary served these lovely appetizers at a summer gathering several years ago, and I adapted the recipe a bit to my own taste. It's a great summer recipe when tomatoes and herbs are at their freshest.

—SUSAN WILSON MILWAUKEE, WI

PREP: 20 MIN. • **BAKE:** 15 MIN. • **MAKES:** 32 APPETIZERS

  1 **package (17.3 ounces) frozen puff pastry, thawed**
1½ **cups (6 ounces) shredded Gouda cheese**
  6 **plum tomatoes, cut into ¼-inch slices**
 ¼ **cup pitted ripe olives, coarsely chopped**
  1 **cup (4 ounces) crumbled feta cheese**
    Minced fresh basil and oregano

1. Unfold puff pastry; cut each sheet into 16 squares. Transfer squares to greased baking sheets. Sprinkle with Gouda cheese; top with tomatoes, olives and feta cheese.
2. Bake at 400° for 14-18 minutes or until golden brown; sprinkle with herbs. Serve the appetizers warm or at room temperature.
FREEZE OPTION *Cover and freeze assembled unbaked pastry squares on waxed paper-lined baking sheets until firm. Transfer appetizers to freezer containers, separating the layers with waxed paper; return to freezer. To use, remove desired number of pastries from freezer 30 minutes before baking and place on greased baking sheets. Bake and serve as directed.*

Stuffed Asiago-Basil Mushrooms

Don't like mushrooms? You will now! These pretty appetizers taste divine. For a meatless main dish, double the filling and use large portobellos.

—LORRAINE CALAND SHUNIAH, ON

PREP: 25 MIN. • **BAKE:** 10 MIN. • **MAKES:** 2 DOZEN

 24 **baby portobello mushrooms, stems removed**
 ½ **cup reduced-fat mayonnaise**
 ¾ **cup shredded Asiago cheese**
 ½ **cup loosely packed basil leaves, stems removed**
 ¼ **teaspoon white pepper**
 12 **cherry tomatoes, halved**
  2 **tablespoons grated Parmesan cheese, optional**

1. Place mushrooms on a greased 15-in. x 10-in. x 1-in. baking pan. Bake at 375° for 10 minutes. Drain liquid from mushrooms.
2. Meanwhile, place mayonnaise, Asiago cheese, basil and pepper in a food processor; cover and process until blended.
3. Fill mushrooms with a heaping teaspoonful mayonnaise mixture; top with tomato. Bake 8-10 minutes or until lightly browned. Sprinkle with Parmesan cheese if desired.
ITALIAN SAUSAGE MUSHROOMS *Prepare mushrooms as directed. In a large skillet, cook 1 pound bulk Italian sausage over medium heat until no longer pink; drain. In a bowl, combine 6 ounces softened cream cheese, 3 tablespoons minced fresh parsley and sausage. Spoon into mushroom caps. Bake as directed. Sprinkle with an additional 1 tablespoon minced fresh parsley.*

Stuffed Baby Red Potatoes

This recipe just says "party!" These fun appetizers look like you worked a lot harder than you did.

—CAROLE BESS WHITE PORTLAND, OR

PREP: 45 MIN. • **BAKE:** 15 MIN.
MAKES: 2 DOZEN

- 24 **small red potatoes (about 2½ pounds)**
- ¼ **cup butter, cubed**
- ½ **cup shredded Parmesan cheese, divided**
- ½ **cup crumbled cooked bacon, divided**
- ⅔ **cup sour cream**
- 1 **egg, lightly beaten**
- ½ **teaspoon salt**
- ⅛ **teaspoon pepper**
- ⅛ **teaspoon paprika**

1. Scrub potatoes; place in a large saucepan and cover with water. Bring to a boil. Reduce heat; cover and cook 15-20 minutes or until tender. Drain.

2. When cool enough to handle, cut a thin slice off the top of each potato. Scoop out pulp, leaving a thin shell. (Cut thin slices from potato bottoms to level if necessary.)

3. Mash potato tops and pulp with butter. Set aside 2 tablespoons each of cheese and bacon for garnish; add remaining cheese and bacon to potatoes. Stir in sour cream, egg, salt and pepper. Spoon mixture into shells. Top with remaining cheese and bacon; sprinkle with paprika.

Place in an ungreased 15-in. x 10-in. x 1-in. baking pan. Bake at 375° for 12-18 minutes or until a thermometer reads 160°.

FROM THE WEB

These are so delicious and cute. I used a good shredded Parm cheese, and it added great flavor. Everyone loved these. I served them as a side dish to bourbon salmon and Caesar salad (to use the shredded Parm again). I will definitely make them again!

—WOLFENLION TASTEOFHOME.COM

Gorgonzola & Cranberry Cheese Ball

A cheese ball is a classic appetizer to take to any gathering, and it's so easy to make. Studded with tangy dried cranberries, this version is a holiday hit.

—**KATHY HAHN** POLLOCK PINES, CA

PREP: 15 MIN. + CHILLING • **MAKES:** 2 CUPS

- 1 package (8 ounces) cream cheese, softened
- 1 cup (4 ounces) crumbled Gorgonzola cheese
- 1 cup dried cranberries
- 2 tablespoons each finely chopped onion, celery, green pepper and sweet red pepper
- ¼ teaspoon hot pepper sauce
- ¾ cup chopped pecans
  Assorted crackers

In a small bowl, combine cheeses. Stir in the cranberries, vegetables and pepper sauce. Shape into a ball; wrap in plastic wrap. Refigerate for 1 hour or until firm. Roll cheese ball in pecans. Serve with crackers.

Secret-Ingredient Stuffed Eggs

My take on deviled eggs is full of surprises. The down-home appetizer Mom used to make gets an instant upgrade with chutney, goat cheese and pecans. People love these treats.

—**BETH SATTERFIELD** DOVER, DE

START TO FINISH: 15 MIN. • **MAKES:** 1 DOZEN

- 6 hard-cooked eggs
- 4 tablespoons crumbled goat cheese, divided
- 3 tablespoons finely chopped pecans, divided
- 3 tablespoons mayonnaise
- 2 tablespoons finely chopped celery
- 2 tablespoons mango chutney
- ¼ teaspoon salt
- ⅛ teaspoon pepper

1. Cut eggs in half lengthwise. Remove yolk; set whites aside. In a small bowl, mash yolks. Add 3 tablespoons goat cheese, 2 tablespoons pecans, mayonnaise, celery, chutney, salt and pepper; mix well. Stuff into egg whites.
2. Just before serving, sprinkle with remaining goat cheese and pecans.

Fresh Peach Salsa

Scooped on a chip or in a taco, peach salsa makes everything taste like summer. It's also great served with chicken or fish, and since it comes together in a food processor, it takes hardly any time to make.
—**SHAWNA LAUFER** FORT MYERS, FL

PREP: 15 MIN. + CHILLING • **MAKES:** 4 CUPS

- 4 **medium peaches, peeled and pitted**
- 2 **large tomatoes, cut into wedges and seeded**
- ½ **sweet onion, cut into wedges**
- ½ **cup fresh cilantro leaves**
- 2 **garlic cloves, peeled and crushed**
- 2 **cans (4 ounces each) chopped green chilies**
- 4 **teaspoons cider vinegar**
- 1 **teaspoon lime juice**
- ¼ **teaspoon pepper**
  Baked tortilla chip scoops

In a food processor, combine the first five ingredients; cover and pulse until coarsely chopped. Add the chilies, vinegar, lime juice and pepper; cover and pulse just until blended. Transfer to a serving bowl; chill until serving. Serve with chips.
PER (¼ -CUP) SERVING *20 cal., trace fat (trace sat. fat), 0 chol., 58 mg sodium, 5 g carb., 1 g fiber, 1 g pro.* **Diabetic Exchange:** *Free food.*

Greek Pinwheels

I really like Greek-style food and appetizers, so I created this recipe for a baby shower. It's a simple combination of puff pastry, cream cheese and a tasty filling. I just love sharing it!
—**VERONICA WORLUND** PASCO, WA

START TO FINISH: 30 MIN. • **MAKES:** 20 APPETIZERS

- 1 **sheet frozen puff pastry, thawed**
- 1 **tablespoon beaten egg**
- ¾ **teaspoon water**
- ½ **cup cream cheese, softened**
- ⅓ **cup marinated quartered artichoke hearts, drained and finely chopped**
- ¼ **cup crumbled feta cheese**
- 1 **tablespoon finely chopped drained oil-packed sun-dried tomatoes**
- 3 **Greek olives, finely chopped**
- 1 **teaspoon Greek seasoning**

1. Unfold puff pastry. Whisk egg and water; brush over pastry. Combine the remaining ingredients; spread over pastry to within ½ in. of edges. Roll up jelly-roll style. Cut into twenty ½-in. slices.
2. Place appetizers 2 in. apart on greased baking sheets. Bake at 425° for 9-11 minutes or until puffed and golden brown. Serve warm.

Sesame Chicken Dip

A co-worker made this dip for one of our many parties, and it went over so well that I adopted the recipe as my own. I can't get enough of it.

—DAWN SCHUTTE SHEBOYGAN, WI

PREP: 35 MIN. + CHILLING • **MAKES:** 36 SERVINGS (¼ CUP EACH)

- 2 tablespoons reduced-sodium soy sauce
- 4 teaspoons sesame oil
- 2 garlic cloves, minced
- 4 cups shredded cooked chicken breast
- 3 packages (8 ounces each) reduced-fat cream cheese
- 8 green onions, thinly sliced
- ½ cup chopped salted peanuts
- 2 cups chopped fresh baby spinach
- 1 jar (10 ounces) sweet-and-sour sauce
  Sesame rice crackers

1. In a large resealable plastic bag, combine the soy sauce, sesame oil and garlic; add chicken. Seal bag and turn to coat; refrigerate for at least 1 hour.
2. Spread cream cheese onto a large serving platter; top with chicken mixture. Sprinkle with onions, peanuts and spinach. Drizzle with sweet-and-sour sauce. Cover and refrigerate for at least 2 hours. Serve with crackers.

Olive & Roasted Pepper Bruschetta

I've tried many versions of bruschetta, but I think this recipe contains the perfect blend of ingredients. It's super-easy, and you can prepare the topping in advance.

—JENNIFER MATHIS HILTON HEAD, SC

START TO FINISH: 15 MIN. • **MAKES:** 16 APPETIZERS

- ½ cup grated Romano cheese
- ½ cup chopped pitted green olives
- ½ cup chopped roasted sweet red peppers
- 2 teaspoons olive oil
- ½ teaspoon dried basil
- 16 slices French bread baguette (½ inch thick), toasted

In a small bowl, combine the first five ingredients. Top each bread slice with 1 tablespoon olive mixture.
PER SERVING *62 cal., 3 g fat (1 g sat. fat), 4 mg chol., 251 mg sodium, 7 g carb., trace fiber, 3 g pro.* **Diabetic Exchanges:** *½ starch, ½ fat.*

BRUSCHETTA KNOW-HOW

Try rubbing the bread for this classic Italian appetizer with garlic or lightly brushing it with a garlic-olive oil blend before toasting. In the summer, top the bread with shredded Parmesan, garden tomatoes and basil.

Chocolate Chip Dip

Is there a kid alive (or a kid at heart) who wouldn't gobble up this creamy dip for graham crackers? It beats dunking them in milk, hands down! You can also try it with apple wedges.
—**HEATHER KOENIG** PRAIRIE DU CHIEN, WI

START TO FINISH: 15 MIN. • **MAKES:** 2 CUPS

- 1 **package (8 ounces) cream cheese, softened**
- ½ **cup butter, softened**
- ¾ **cup confectioners' sugar**
- 2 **tablespoons brown sugar**
- 1 **teaspoon vanilla extract**
- 1 **cup (6 ounces) miniature semisweet chocolate chips**
  Graham cracker sticks

In a small bowl, beat cream cheese and butter until light and fluffy. Add the sugars and vanilla; beat until smooth. Stir in chocolate chips. Serve with graham cracker sticks.

Sun-Dried Tomato Dip

I love to serve this dip for just about any occasion. It's so quick and easy to pull together and just full of flavor!
—**ANDREA REYNOLDS** ROCKY RIVER, OH

START TO FINISH: 10 MIN. • **MAKES:** 2 CUPS

- 1 **package (8 ounces) cream cheese, softened**
- ½ **cup sour cream**
- ½ **cup mayonnaise**
- ¼ **cup oil-packed sun-dried tomatoes, drained and patted dry**
- ½ **teaspoon salt**
- ¼ **teaspoon pepper**
- ¼ **teaspoon hot pepper sauce**
- 2 **green onions, sliced**
  Assorted crackers and/or fresh vegetables

Place the first seven ingredients in a food processor; cover and process until blended. Add green onions; cover and pulse until finely chopped. Serve with crackers and/or vegetables.

Grilled Stuffed Jalapenos

These cheese-stuffed jalapenos are always popular when my husband and I host a tapas party. There's a flavor explosion in each crisp and tender pepper.
—**MARY J. POTTER** STERLING HEIGHTS, MI

START TO FINISH: 30 MIN.
MAKES: 10 APPETIZERS

4	ounces cream cheese, softened
½	cup shredded Monterey Jack cheese
½	teaspoon garlic powder
½	teaspoon ground cumin
½	teaspoon chili powder
¼	teaspoon salt
¼	teaspoon smoked paprika or paprika
10	jalapeno peppers

1. In a small bowl, combine the first seven ingredients. Cut a lengthwise slit down each pepper, leaving the stem intact; remove membranes and seeds. Fill each pepper with 1 tablespoon cheese mixture.
2. Prepare grill for indirect heat. Place peppers in a disposable foil pan. Grill, covered, over indirect medium heat for 8-10 minutes or until peppers are tender and the cheese is melted. Serve warm.
NOTE *Wear disposable gloves when cutting hot peppers; the oils can burn skin. Avoid touching your face.*

SMOKED PAPRIKA

If you're an avid home cook, smoked paprika may be a worthwhile investment. Its rich and smoky flavor adds complexity to many dishes. The spice is especially good in lentil and bean soups, where it lends a robust, meaty flavor. You could also use smoked paprika in recipes that call for ground chipotle pepper. Just add cayenne or chili powder if needed to boost the heat.

Tomato & Brie Focaccia

Combine tender yeast bread with creamy Brie cheese and tomatoes, and you've got an appetizer that guests will line up for. The focaccia is also nice with a bowl of soup.

—**LAURIE FIGONE** PETALUMA, CA

PREP: 20 MIN. + RISING • **BAKE:** 25 MIN. • **MAKES:** 12 SERVINGS

2½ to 3 cups all-purpose flour
 2 packages (¼ ounce each) quick-rise yeast
 1 teaspoon sugar
 1 teaspoon salt
 1 cup water
 ¼ cup plus 1 tablespoon olive oil, divided
 1 can (14½ ounces) diced tomatoes, drained
 2 garlic cloves, minced
 1 teaspoon Italian seasoning
 6 ounces Brie cheese, cut into ½-inch cubes

1. In a large bowl, combine 2 cups flour, yeast, sugar and salt. In a small saucepan, heat the water and ¼ cup oil to 120°-130°. Add to dry ingredients; beat just until moistened. Stir in enough remaining flour to form a soft dough.
2. Turn onto a floured surface; knead until smooth and elastic, about 6-8 minutes. Place in a greased bowl, turning once to grease the top. Cover and let rise for 20 minutes.
3. Punch dough down. Press into a greased 13-in. x 9-in. baking pan. Cover and let rest for 10 minutes.
4. In a small bowl, combine the tomatoes, garlic, Italian seasoning and remaining oil. Spread over dough; top with cheese. Bake at 375° for 25-30 minutes or until golden brown. Place pan on a wire rack.

Nacho Party Cheesecake

Always fun to present at parties, this playful cheesecake appetizer features a tortilla chip crust with a savory cream cheese filling and colorful taco toppings.

—**MELINDA MESSER** BENSON, NC

PREP: 25 MIN. • **BAKE:** 70 MIN. + CHILLING • **MAKES:** 24 SERVINGS

1¾ cups crushed nacho tortilla chips
 ⅓ cup butter, melted
 3 packages (8 ounces each) cream cheese, softened
 ½ cup mayonnaise
 1 envelope taco seasoning
 2 tablespoons all-purpose flour
 4 eggs, lightly beaten
1½ cups finely chopped cooked chicken breasts
1½ cups (6 ounces) shredded Mexican cheese blend
 ⅓ cup finely chopped green onions
 1 cup (8 ounces) sour cream
    Whole kernel corn, cubed avocado, chopped tomato and
      sliced ripe olives
    Salsa, optional
    Assorted crackers or additional nacho tortilla chips,
      optional

1. Combine crushed tortilla chips and butter; press onto the bottom of a greased 9-in. springform pan.
2. In a large bowl, beat the cream cheese, mayonnaise, taco seasoning and flour until smooth. Add eggs; beat on low speed just until combined. Stir in the chicken, cheese blend and onions. Pour over crust. Place pan on a baking sheet.
3. Bake at 325° for 60-70 minutes or until center is almost set. Gently spread sour cream over the top; bake 10 minutes longer or until set.
4. Cool on a wire rack for 10 minutes. Carefully run a knife around edge of pan to loosen; cool 1 hour longer. Refrigerate for 8 hours or overnight.
5. Just before serving, remove sides of pan. Garnish with corn, avocado, tomato and olives. Serve with salsa and crackers if desired.

Cheeseburger Cups

START TO FINISH: 30 MIN. • **MAKES:** 5 SERVINGS

- 1 **pound ground beef**
- ½ **cup ketchup**
- 2 **tablespoons brown sugar**
- 1 **tablespoon prepared mustard**
- 1½ **teaspoons Worcestershire sauce**
- 1 **tube (12 ounces) refrigerated buttermilk biscuits**
- ½ **cup cubed process cheese (Velveeta)**

1. In a large skillet, cook beef over medium heat until no longer pink; drain. Stir in the ketchup, brown sugar, mustard and Worcestershire sauce. Remove from the heat; set aside.

2. Press each biscuit onto the bottom and up the sides of a greased muffin cup. Spoon beef mixture into cups; top with cheese cubes. Bake at 400° for 14-16 minutes or until golden brown.

> "A terrific recipe for moms with young kids and busy lives, this simple, inexpensive dish takes just a short time. Best of all, kids will go absolutely crazy for these darling dinner bites!"
>
> —**JERI MILLHOUSE** ASHLAND, OH

Sweet & Spicy Nuts

Hot and spicy with a hint of brown sugar sweetness, these snacking nuts are simply sensational. You and your guests will not be able to stop munching!

—**PATTY LOK** SHERMAN OAKS, CA

PREP: 25 MIN. + COOLING • **MAKES:** 2 CUPS

- ½ **teaspoon salt**
- ¼ **teaspoon ground cinnamon**
- ¼ **teaspoon ground cumin**
- ¼ **teaspoon cayenne pepper**
- ¼ **teaspoon chili powder**
- ¼ **teaspoon ground chipotle powder**
- ⅛ **teaspoon ground nutmeg**
- 3 **tablespoons unsalted butter**
- 1 **cup shelled walnuts**
- 1 **cup pecan halves**
- ¼ **cup packed brown sugar**
- 1 **tablespoon water**
- 1½ **teaspoons Worcestershire sauce**
  Dash Louisiana-style hot sauce

1. In a small bowl, combine the salt and spices; set aside. In a large heavy skillet, melt butter. Add the walnuts and pecans; cook over medium heat until nuts are toasted, about 4 minutes.

2. Sprinkle with spice mixture. Add the brown sugar, water, Worcestershire and hot sauce. Cook and stir for 1-2 minutes or until sugar is melted. Spread on foil to cool. Store in an airtight container.

Mini Muffuletta

Everyone likes the bold flavors in these easy sandwich wedges. The recipe is great for parties or taking along to sporting events.
—**GARETH CRANER** MINDEN, NV

PREP: 25 MIN. + CHILLING • **MAKES:** 3 DOZEN

- 1 jar (10 ounces) pimiento-stuffed olives, drained and chopped
- 2 cans (4¼ ounces each) chopped ripe olives
- 2 tablespoons balsamic vinegar
- 1 tablespoon red wine vinegar
- 1 tablespoon olive oil
- 3 garlic cloves, minced
- 1 teaspoon dried basil
- 1 teaspoon dried oregano
- 6 French rolls, split
- ½ pound thinly sliced hard salami
- ¼ pound sliced provolone cheese
- ½ pound thinly sliced cotto salami
- ¼ pound sliced part-skim mozzarella cheese

1. In a large bowl, combine the first eight ingredients; set aside. Hollow out tops and bottoms of rolls, leaving ¾-in. shells (discard removed bread or save for another use).
2. Spread olive mixture over tops and bottoms of rolls. On roll bottoms, layer with hard salami, provolone cheese, cotto salami and mozzarella cheese. Replace tops.
3. Wrap tightly in plastic wrap. Refrigerate overnight. Cut each into six wedges; secure with toothpicks.

Hot Pepper Pleasers

You get just a little heat from these banana peppers, as well as some spice from the pepperoni—a perfect combination with cool cream cheese.
—**DARIUS KOVACINA** ACME, PA

PREP: 20 MIN. • **BAKE:** 25 MIN. • **MAKES:** 20 APPETIZERS

- 10 banana peppers
- 1 package (8 ounces) cream cheese, softened
- 1 egg
- 1 cup (4 ounces) shredded cheddar cheese
- ½ cup shredded part-skim mozzarella cheese
- 1 small onion, finely chopped
- ½ cup finely chopped pepperoni
- 2 tablespoons olive oil

1. Cut peppers in half lengthwise; open and lay flat. Remove seeds if desired.
2. In a small bowl, beat cream cheese and egg until blended. Stir in the cheddar, mozzarella, onion and pepperoni. Spoon into peppers.
3. Place in two 15-in. x 10-in. x 1-in. baking pans and drizzle with oil. Bake at 350° for 25-30 minutes or until lightly browned.
NOTE *Wear disposable gloves when cutting hot peppers; the oils can burn skin. Avoid touching your face.*

Kickin' Snack Mix

Ranch salad dressing mix, buttery pistachios and a kick of cayenne put a zesty spin on a traditional snack mix. This makes a terrific gift. It will have everyone reaching for more.

—**KIM VOGT** CREIGHTON, NE

PREP: 20 MIN. • **BAKE:** 45 MIN. + COOLING • **MAKES:** 3 QUARTS

- 3 **cups Crispix**
- 3 **cups Wheat Chex**
- 2 **cups cheddar-flavored snack crackers**
- 1 **cup pretzel sticks**
- 1 **cup almonds**
- 1 **cup mixed nuts**
- 1 **cup pistachios**
- ½ **cup butter-flavored popcorn oil**
- 1 **envelope ranch salad dressing mix**
- 1 **teaspoon dill weed**
- 1 **teaspoon garlic powder**
- 1 **teaspoon cayenne pepper**

1. In a large bowl, combine the first seven ingredients. In a small bowl, combine the oil, dressing mix, dill, garlic powder and cayenne. Drizzle over cereal mixture; toss to coat.
2. Transfer to two greased 15-in. x 10-in. x 1-in. baking pans. Bake at 250° for 45-55 minutes, stirring every 15 minutes. Cool on wire racks.
3. Store in an airtight container.

Roasted Garlic & Tomato Spread

Bold flavors and a creamy consistency make this spread a real crowd-pleaser. Serve it warm or chilled with pita chips, crackers or breads.

—**TARA MCDONALD** KANSAS CITY, MO

PREP: 45 MIN. + COOLING • **MAKES:** 1½ CUPS

- 2 **whole garlic bulbs**
- 3 **teaspoons olive oil, divided**
- 3 **plum tomatoes, quartered**
- 1 **carton (8 ounces) spreadable chive and onion cream cheese**
- ¼ **teaspoon Italian seasoning**
- ¼ **teaspoon salt**
  Crackers or snack breads

1. Remove papery outer skin from garlic (do not peel or separate cloves). Cut tops off of garlic bulbs; brush each with ½ teaspoon oil. Wrap each bulb in heavy-duty foil. Place garlic and tomatoes in a foil-lined 9-in. square baking pan. Brush tomatoes with remaining oil.
2. Bake at 425° for 30-35 minutes or until garlic is softened. Cool for 10-15 minutes; squeeze garlic into a small bowl. Drain any liquid from tomatoes; chop and add to garlic. Stir in the cream cheese, Italian seasoning and salt. Serve with your favorite crackers or snack breads.

Marinated Cheese

This special appetizer always makes it to our neighborhood parties and is the first to disappear at the buffet table. It's attractive, delicious—and easy!

—LAURIE CASPER CORAOPOLIS, PA

PREP: 30 MIN. + MARINATING
MAKES: ABOUT 2 POUNDS

- 2 **blocks (8 ounces each) white cheddar cheese**
- 2 **packages (8 ounces each) cream cheese, softened**
- ¾ **cup chopped roasted sweet red peppers**
- ½ **cup olive oil**
- ¼ **cup white wine vinegar**
- ¼ **cup balsamic vinegar**
- 3 **tablespoons chopped green onions**
- 3 **tablespoons minced fresh parsley**
- 2 **tablespoons minced fresh basil**
- 1 **tablespoon sugar**
- 3 **garlic cloves, minced**
- ½ **teaspoon salt**
- ½ **teaspoon pepper**
  Toasted sliced French bread or assorted crackers

1. Slice each block of cheddar cheese into twenty ¼-in. slices. Cut each block of cream cheese into 18 slices; sandwich between cheddar slices, using a knife to spread evenly. Create four 6-in.-long blocks of cheese; place blocks in a 13x9-in. dish.

2. In a small bowl, combine the roasted peppers, oil, vinegars, onions, herbs, sugar, garlic, salt and pepper; pour over the cheese.

3. Cover and refrigerate overnight, turning once. Drain excess marinade. Serve cheese with bread or crackers.

FROM THE WEB

Absolutely delicious! Works well with thin crackers or baguette bread. I made it the day before so it had plenty of time to marinate. A real hit at parties.

—MCCINC2 TASTEOFHOME.COM

Southwest Egg Rolls & Avocado Dip

A friend of mine prepared these egg rolls for my birthday treat several years ago. They are the best I have ever eaten.
—**BECKY AYLOR** SISTERS, OR

PREP: 35 MIN. • **COOK:** 5 MIN./BATCH
MAKES: 20 EGG ROLLS (1½ CUPS SAUCE)

2½ cups shredded cooked chicken
1½ cups (6 ounces) shredded Mexican cheese blend
⅔ cup frozen corn, thawed
⅔ cup canned black beans, rinsed and drained
5 green onions, chopped
¼ cup minced fresh cilantro
1 teaspoon salt
1 teaspoon ground cumin
1 teaspoon grated lime peel
¼ teaspoon cayenne pepper
20 egg roll wrappers
  Oil for deep-fat frying

DIP
1 cup ranch salad dressing
1 medium ripe avocado, peeled and mashed
1 tablespoon minced fresh cilantro
1 teaspoon grated lime peel

1. In a large bowl, combine the first 10 ingredients. Place ¼ cup of chicken mixture in the center of one egg roll wrapper. (Keep remaining wrappers covered with a damp paper towel until ready to use.) Fold bottom corner over filling. Fold sides toward center over filling. Moisten remaining corner with water; roll up tightly to seal. Repeat.
2. In an electric skillet or deep-fat fryer, heat oil to 375°. Fry egg rolls, a few at a time, for 2 minutes on each side or until golden brown. Drain on paper towels.
3. Meanwhile, combine the dip ingredients. Serve with the egg rolls.

Corn Cakes with Shrimp & Guacamole

Corn cakes are one of my favorite appetizers to make, especially in summer when corn is fresh. You could also used canned corn to save time, and use store-bought guacamole if you don't want to make your own.
—**CARLA DEVELDER** MISHAWAKA, IN

PREP: 30 MIN. • **COOK:** 5 MIN./BATCH • **MAKES:** 2 DOZEN

½ cup fresh or frozen corn
1¼ cups water, divided
1 cup complete buttermilk pancake mix
2 tablespoons grated Parmesan cheese
⅛ teaspoon hot pepper sauce
2 tablespoons finely chopped sweet red pepper
1 green onion, chopped
1 tablespoon minced fresh cilantro
1 medium ripe avocado, peeled and pitted
2 tablespoons finely chopped onion
1 tablespoon chopped seeded jalapeno pepper
1 tablespoon lime juice
⅛ teaspoon salt
24 cooked small shrimp, peeled and deveined
  Small strips green onion and/or fresh cilantro leaves

1. In a small saucepan, bring the corn and ½ cup water to a boil. Reduce heat; cover and simmer for 4-6 minutes or until tender. Drain.
2. In a large bowl, combine pancake mix and cheese. Add pepper sauce and remaining water; stir just until moistened. Fold in corn, red pepper, green onion and minced cilantro.
3. Pour batter by tablespoonfuls onto a greased hot griddle; turn when bubbles form on top. Cook until the second side is golden brown. Set aside.
4. In a small bowl, mash avocado with onion, jalapeno, lime juice and salt. Top each pancake with a teaspoonful of guacamole and a shrimp. Garnish with green onion and/or cilantro. Serve immediately.
NOTE *Wear disposable gloves when cutting hot peppers; the oils can burn skin. Avoid touching your face..*

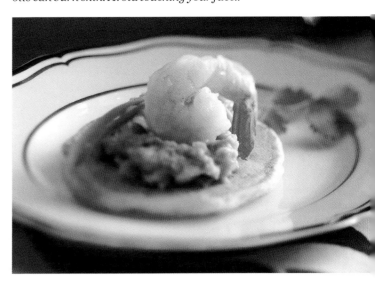

Sparkling Kiwi Lemonade

Keep some kiwi ice cubes in the freezer so they're ready whenever you crave a tall glass of this dressed-up summertime favorite.

—EMILY SEIDEL AINSWORTH, NE

PREP: 20 MIN. + FREEZING • **MAKES:** 6 SERVINGS

- 8 **medium kiwifruit, peeled, divided**
- ¾ **cup sugar**
- ¾ **cup lemon juice**
- 1 **liter carbonated water, chilled**

1. Slice two kiwi into small pieces. Place in ice cube trays and fill with water. Freeze.

2. Cut remaining kiwi into large pieces; place in a food processor. Cover and process until smooth. Strain; discard pulp. In a 2-qt. pitcher, stir sugar and lemon juice until sugar is dissolved. Stir in kiwi puree. Refrigerate until chilled. Just before serving, stir in carbonated water. Serve over kiwi ice cubes.

French Quarter Cheese Spread

Topped with toasty pecans, this sweet-and-savory cheese is simply a hit. Make it ahead of time for convenience, then bring to room temperature and serve.

—HEIDI BLAINE HADBURG SAFETY HARBOR, FL

START TO FINISH: 20 MIN. • **MAKES:** 8 SERVINGS

- 1 **package (8 ounces) cream cheese, softened**
- 1 **tablespoon grated onion**
- 1 **garlic clove, minced**
- ¼ **cup butter, cubed**
- ¼ **cup packed dark brown sugar**
- 1 **teaspoon Worcestershire sauce**
- ½ **teaspoon prepared mustard**
- 1 **cup finely chopped pecans, toasted**
  Assorted crackers

1. In a small bowl, combine the cream cheese, onion and garlic. Transfer to a serving plate; shape into a 6-in. disk. Set aside.

2. In a small saucepan, combine the butter, brown sugar, Worcestershire sauce and mustard. Cook and stir over medium heat for 4-5 minutes or until sugar is dissolved. Remove from the heat; stir in pecans.

3. Cool slightly. Spoon over the cheese mixture. Serve with crackers.

Easily peel a kiwifruit with either of these methods.

1 Cut both ends from fruit. Using a spoon, scoop out the flesh.

2 Cut both ends from fruit. Using a vegetable peeler, peel off fuzzy brown skin. Cut into slices, wedges or chunks with a sharp knife.

GO NUTS
GRAND PRIZE
WINNER
★ ★ ★ ★

Chicken, Pear & Gorgonzola Tarts

I was experimenting with candied bacon and tried incorporating it into some of my favorite recipes. These little bites were created during the holiday season and were gobbled up by friends and family.

—**KATHLEEN BOULANGER** WILLISTON, VT

PREP: 30 MIN. • **COOK:** 5 MIN. • **MAKES:** 2½ DOZEN

- 8 bacon strips
- 1½ teaspoons brown sugar
- ¼ teaspoon ground cinnamon
- ¾ cup finely chopped cooked chicken breast
- ⅓ cup pear nectar
- ¼ cup finely chopped dried pears
- 3 tablespoons apricot preserves
- 2 teaspoons butter
- ¼ teaspoon salt
- ¼ teaspoon pepper
- 2 packages (1.9 ounces each) frozen miniature phyllo tart shells
- ⅓ cup crumbled Gorgonzola cheese

1. Place bacon in a 15-in. x 10-in. x 1-in. baking pan; broil 4 in. from the heat for 4-6 minutes on each side or until crisp. Combine brown sugar and cinnamon; sprinkle over bacon. Broil 1 minute longer or until bacon is glazed and bubbly. Drain on paper towels. Cool slightly and crumble.
2. In a small skillet, combine the chicken, pear nectar, pears, preserves, butter, salt and pepper. Bring to a boil; cook, stirring occasionally, for 3-4 minutes or until thickened. Spoon about 1 teaspoonful of filling into each tart shell; place tarts on a baking sheet. Sprinkle with bacon and cheese.
3. Bake at 350° for 5-7 minutes or until heated through. Serve warm.

Spinach & Crab Dip

We love this recipe! I've lightened it up considerably without losing any of the original's richness, and no one can tell the difference. I also serve it as a potato topping.

—**SANDIE HEINDEL** LIBERTY, MO

START TO FINISH: 25 MIN. • **MAKES:** 4 CUPS

- 1 package (10 ounces) frozen chopped spinach, thawed and squeezed dry
- 1 package (8 ounces) reduced-fat cream cheese, cubed
- 1 cup (8 ounces) plain yogurt
- ½ cup grated Parmesan cheese
- ½ cup Miracle Whip Light
- 2 garlic cloves, minced
- 1 teaspoon crushed red pepper flakes
- ¼ teaspoon salt
- ¼ teaspoon pepper
- 1 can (6 ounces) lump crabmeat, drained
  Assorted crackers or baked tortilla chip scoops

1. In a large saucepan over low heat, combine the first nine ingredients. Cook and stir until cream cheese is melted. Stir in crab; heat through.
2. Transfer to a serving bowl; serve with crackers. Refrigerate leftovers.

Crab Cakes with Red Chili Mayo

This has to be one of the most popular appetizers I've made, and it's so attractive for a party. The spicy mayo is just the right accent for the crab cakes.

—TIFFANY ANDERSON-TAYLOR

GULFPORT, FL

PREP: 35 MIN. + CHILLING
COOK: 10 MIN./BATCH
MAKES: 2 DOZEN (1 CUP SAUCE)

- 1⅓ cups mayonnaise
- 2 tablespoons Thai chili sauce
- 2 teaspoons lemon juice, divided
- ¼ cup each finely chopped celery, red onion and sweet red pepper
- 1 jalapeno pepper, seeded and finely chopped
- 4 tablespoons olive oil, divided
- ½ cup soft bread crumbs
- 1 egg, lightly beaten
- 1 pound fresh crabmeat
- ¼ cup all-purpose flour

1. In a small bowl, combine the mayonnaise, chili sauce and 1¼ teaspoons lemon juice. Set aside.
2. In a small skillet, saute the celery, onion, red pepper and jalapeno in 1 tablespoon of oil until tender. Transfer to a large bowl; stir in the bread crumbs, egg, ½ cup of reserved mayonnaise mixture and remaining lemon juice. Fold in crab. Cover and refrigerate for at least 2 hours. Cover and refrigerate remaining mayonnaise mixture for sauce.
3. Place flour in a shallow bowl. Drop crab mixture by 2 tablespoonfuls into flour. Gently coat and shape into a ½-in.-thick patty. Repeat with remaining mixture.
4. In a large skillet over medium-high heat, cook patties in remaining oil in batches for 3-4 minutes on each side or until golden brown. Serve with reserved sauce.
NOTE *Wear disposable gloves when cutting hot peppers; the oils can burn skin. Avoid touching your face.*

Fruited Turkey Salads, page 40

31

39

45

Special Salads

Cool, **crispy**, nutritious salads are a swift way to a complete, healthy meal. This **fresh crop** of prizewinning recipes is **brimming** with luscious fruit salads, **summery** sides and quick-to-prep main dishes.

Chicken Tostada Salad

If I don't have tostada shells on hand for this recipe, I just heat taco shells, break them in half and lay them flat on the plates. Either way, this Southwestern salad is a winner.
—**EDIE DESPAIN** LOGAN, UT

START TO FINISH: 10 MIN. • **MAKES:** 4 SERVINGS

- 4 **cups shredded lettuce**
- 1 **medium tomato, cut into wedges**
- ½ **cup reduced-fat ranch salad dressing**
- ¼ **cup sliced ripe olives**
- 2 **tablespoons taco sauce**
- 4 **tostada shells**
- 2 **packages (6 ounces each) ready-to-use Southwestern chicken strips**
- ½ **cup shredded Mexican cheese blend**

In a large bowl, combine the first five ingredients. Divide among shells. Top with chicken; sprinkle with cheese.

Zesty Crouton Salad

It takes no time at all to prepare this simple recipe. And everyone loves the resulting combination of tastes and textures. The salad pairs well with everything from grilled entrees to pasta.
—**VALERIE G. SMITH** ASTON, PA

START TO FINISH: 10 MIN. • **MAKES:** 5 SERVINGS

- 2 **cups grape tomatoes, halved**
- 1½ **cups salad croutons**
- 4 **pieces string cheese, cut into ½-inch pieces**
- 8 **fresh basil leaves, thinly sliced**
- 2 **tablespoons red wine vinegar**
- 1 **tablespoon olive oil**
- ½ **teaspoon minced garlic**

In a large bowl, combine all ingredients.

Turkey Waldorf Salad

This hearty salad is is a great use of leftover Thanksgiving turkey. Crunchy apples, walnuts and dried cranberries make it taste like fall. Also stuff it in pita bread for an on-the-go lunch.
—TRISHA KRUSE EAGLE, ID

PREP: 20 MIN. + CHILLING
MAKES: 4 SERVINGS

- ¼ cup sour cream
- ¼ cup mayonnaise
- 1 tablespoon rice vinegar
- 2 teaspoons brown sugar
- 1 teaspoon reduced-sodium soy sauce
- ¼ teaspoon salt
- ¼ teaspoon lemon-pepper seasoning
- 2 cups cubed cooked turkey breast
- 2 celery ribs, thinly sliced
- ¼ cup dried cranberries
- 1 large apple, diced
- ⅔ cup chopped walnuts, toasted
- 4 Bibb lettuce leaves

1. In a small bowl, whisk together the first seven ingredients.
2. In a large bowl, combine the turkey, celery and cranberries. Pour dressing over mixture; toss to coat. Cover and refrigerate for at least 1 hour.
3. Just before serving, stir in apple and walnuts. Serve on lettuce leaves.

WALDORF SALAD

Created in New York's famed Waldorf-Astoria Hotel over a century ago, the salad originally contained just three ingredients: celery, apples and mayonnaise. Walnuts became a standard ingredient later on. Today, there are many variations of Waldorf salad. Common add-ins include raisins or other dried fruit, seedless grapes, orange segments and shredded carrots. Pecans are sometimes used instead of walnuts.

Refreshing Grilled Chicken Salad

This recipe is light, zippy and flavorful. It's a nice healthy salad that's great for a luncheon with friends.

—DENISE RASMUSSEN SALINA, KS

PREP: 20 MIN. + MARINATING • **GRILL:** 10 MIN. • **MAKES:** 4 SERVINGS

- ½ cup lime juice
- 2 tablespoons honey
- 4 teaspoons olive oil
- ½ teaspoon salt
- ½ teaspoon pepper
- 4 boneless skinless chicken breast halves (4 ounces each)
- 6 cups spring mix salad greens
- 2 cups cubed seedless watermelon
- 1 cup fresh blueberries
- 1 medium sweet yellow pepper, cut into 1-inch pieces
- ⅓ cup chopped walnuts, toasted

1. In a small bowl, combine the lime juice, honey, oil, salt and pepper. Pour ⅓ cup into a large resealable plastic bag; add chicken. Seal bag and turn to coat; refrigerate for at least 1 hour. Cover and refrigerate remaining lime juice mixture for dressing.

2. Drain and discard marinade. Using long-handled tongs, moisten a paper towel with cooking oil and lightly coat the grill rack. Grill chicken, covered, over medium heat or broil 4 in. from the heat for 4-7 minutes on each side or until a thermometer reads 170°.

3. In a large bowl, combine the salad greens, watermelon, blueberries and yellow pepper; add reserved dressing and toss to coat. Divide among four serving plates. Slice chicken; serve with salads. Sprinkle each serving with 4 teaspoons walnuts.

PER SERVING *300 cal., 12 g fat (2 g sat. fat), 63 mg chol., 257 mg sodium, 25 g carb., 4 g fiber, 28 g pro.* **Diabetic Exchanges:** *3 lean meat, 2 fat, 1 vegetable, 1 fruit, ½ starch.*

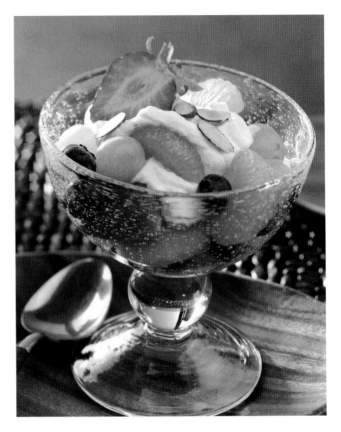

Fruit & Cream Layered Salad

Being from the South, I love salads—especially fruit salads. I also try to cook healthier foods now that everyone is trying to watch what they eat!

—APRIL LANE GREENEVILLE, TN

START TO FINISH: 25 MIN. • **MAKES:** 13 SERVINGS (¾ CUP EACH)

- 3 ounces reduced-fat cream cheese
- 1 tablespoon sugar
- 2 teaspoons lemon juice
- ¼ teaspoon almond extract
- ¾ cup (6 ounces) strawberry yogurt
- 2 cups reduced-fat whipped topping
- 3 medium peaches, peeled and sliced
- 2 cups halved fresh strawberries
- 2 cups fresh blueberries
- 2 cups green grapes
- 1 can (11 ounces) mandarin oranges, drained
- ¼ cup sliced almonds, toasted
  Fresh strawberries, optional

1. In a small bowl, beat the cream cheese, sugar, lemon juice and extract until smooth. Add yogurt; beat until blended. Fold in whipped topping.

2. In a 3-qt. trifle bowl, layer the peaches, strawberries and blueberries. Top with half of the whipped topping mixture. Layer with grapes, oranges and remaining whipped topping mixture. Refrigerate until serving. Sprinkle with almonds just before serving. Garnish with strawberries if desired.

PER SERVING *124 cal., 4 g fat (2 g sat. fat), 5 mg chol., 37 mg sodium, 22 g carb., 2 g fiber, 2 g pro.* **Diabetic Exchanges:** *1 fruit, ½ starch, ½ fat.*

Alfresco Bean Salad

START TO FINISH: 25 MIN. • **MAKES:** 12 SERVINGS (⅔ CUP EACH)

- ¼ cup lime juice
- 4½ teaspoons olive oil
- ½ teaspoon chili powder
  Dash salt and pepper
- 1 can (16 ounces) red beans, rinsed and drained
- 1 can (15¼ ounces) whole kernel corn, drained
- 1 can (15 ounces) garbanzo beans or chickpeas, rinsed and drained
- 1 can (15 ounces) black beans, rinsed and drained
- 2 medium tomatoes, seeded and chopped
- 1 cup coarsely chopped fresh cilantro
- 1 small yellow onion, chopped
- 1 small red onion, chopped
- 1 jalapeno pepper, seeded and chopped

In a large bowl, whisk the lime juice, oil, chili powder, salt and pepper. Add the remaining ingredients and toss to coat. Chill until serving.

NOTE *Wear disposable gloves when cutting hot peppers; the oils can burn skin. Avoid touching your face.*

PER SERVING *146 cal., 3 g fat (trace sat. fat), 0 chol., 360 mg sodium, 23 g carb., 6 g fiber, 6 g pro.* **Diabetic Exchanges:** *1½ starch, 1 lean meat.*

"If you're bored with the usual greens, try this healthy version of classic three-bean salad. It's terrific as a side dish, but sometimes, I fill my plate and make it a meal."

—CRISTINA VIVES PALM BEACH GARDENS, FL

Chicken Pita Salad

I often take this popular salad to family get-togethers. It's simple and refreshing and always disappears in a blink.

—**CATHY SLUSSLER** MAGNOLIA, TX

PREP: 30 MIN. + CHILLING • **MAKES:** 16 SERVINGS (¾ CUP EACH)

- 3 pita breads (6 inches)
- ¼ cup olive oil
- ¼ cup balsamic vinegar
- 3 tablespoons lemon juice
- 1 tablespoon minced fresh oregano or 1 teaspoon dried oregano
- 2 garlic cloves, minced
- 2 teaspoons grated lemon peel
- 1 teaspoon sugar
- 1 teaspoon salt
- ¼ teaspoon pepper
- 2 cups shredded cooked chicken
- 1 can (15 ounces) garbanzo beans or chickpeas, rinsed and drained
- 1 English cucumber, halved and sliced
- 1 pint cherry tomatoes, halved
- 1 small red onion, quartered and sliced
- ½ cup crumbled feta cheese

1. Cut each pita bread into eight triangles; split in half. Place on a baking sheet. Bake at 350° for 10-12 minutes or until lightly toasted.
2. For dressing, in a small bowl, whisk the oil, vinegar, lemon juice, oregano, garlic, lemon peel, sugar, salt and pepper.
3. In a large bowl, combine the chicken, garbanzo beans, cucumber, tomatoes and onion. Stir in pita triangles. Drizzle with dressing and toss to coat.
4. Cover and refrigerate for at least 30 minutes. Just before serving, sprinkle with cheese.

PER SERVING *141 cal., 6 g fat (1 g sat. fat), 17 mg chol., 294 mg sodium, 14 g carb., 2 g fiber, 8 g pro.* **Diabetic Exchanges:** *1 starch, 1 lean meat, ½ fat.*

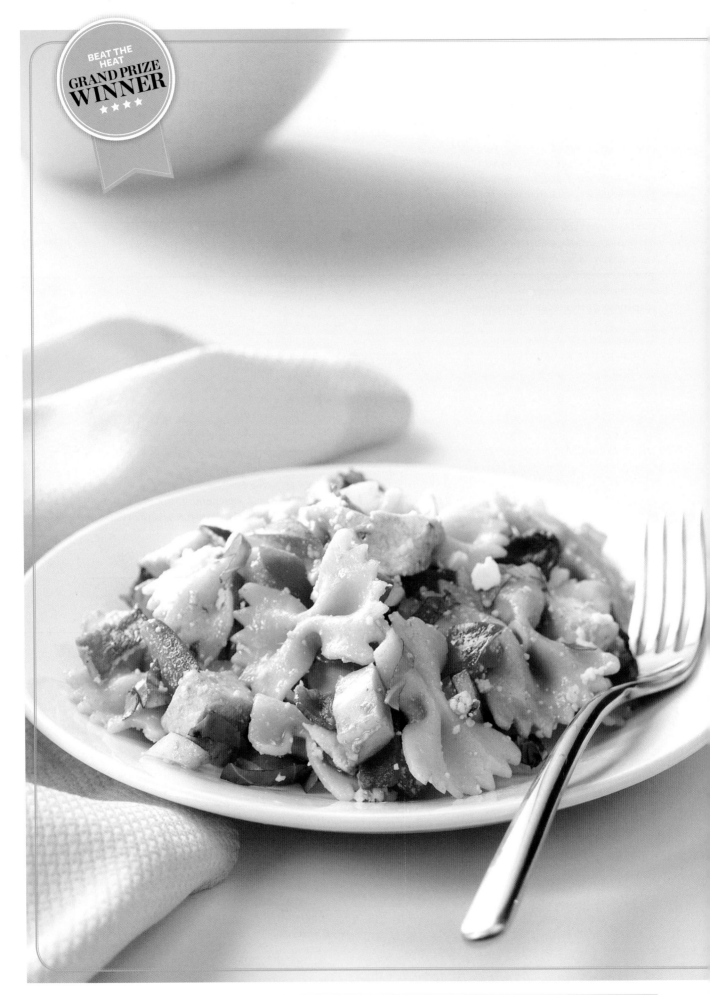

BEAT THE
HEAT
GRAND PRIZE
WINNER
★ ★ ★

Balsamic Chicken Pasta Salad

I love all the colors and flavors of this quick and easy dish and I serve it often in summer. The flavors are also great with grilled shrimp instead of chicken.
—**TERRI MCCARTY** ORO GRANDE, CA

START TO FINISH: 25 MIN. • **MAKES:** 8 SERVINGS

- 3 cups uncooked bow tie pasta
- 4 cups cubed cooked chicken breast
- 2 cups chopped tomatoes
- ½ cup chopped red onion
- 4 bacon strips, cooked and crumbled
- ¼ cup crumbled Gorgonzola cheese
- ½ cup olive oil
- ¼ cup minced fresh basil
- ¼ cup balsamic vinegar
- 2 tablespoons brown sugar
- 1 teaspoon minced garlic
- ¼ teaspoon salt
- ¼ teaspoon pepper
- ½ cup grated Parmesan cheese

1. Cook pasta according to package directions. Drain and rinse in cold water; transfer to a large bowl. Add the chicken, tomatoes, onion, bacon and Gorgonzola cheese.
2. In a small bowl, whisk the oil, basil, vinegar, brown sugar, garlic, salt and pepper. Drizzle over salad and toss to coat; sprinkle with Parmesan cheese.

Texas Confetti Rice Salad

A spicy way to dress up rice, this Southwestern salad is always popular at potlucks. It's also a welcome dish during the holidays.
—**LINDA MORTEN** SOMERVILLE, TX

PREP: 30 MIN. + COOLING • **MAKES:** 12 SERVINGS (1⅓ CUPS EACH)

- 2 cans (14½ ounces each) chicken broth
- 2 cups uncooked long grain rice
- ½ cup water
- 4 cups cubed cooked turkey
- 4 medium tomatoes, seeded and chopped
- 2 cups fresh or frozen corn, thawed
- 1 large green pepper, chopped
- 1 medium red onion, chopped
- 1 cup olive oil
- ½ cup minced fresh cilantro
- 1 can (4 ounces) chopped green chilies
- 3 tablespoons white wine vinegar
- 3 tablespoons lime juice
- 2 tablespoons Dijon mustard
- 2½ teaspoons ground cumin
- 1 teaspoon garlic salt
- ½ teaspoon crushed red pepper flakes
- 1 medium ripe avocado, peeled and cubed

1. In a large saucepan, bring the broth, rice and water to a boil. Reduce heat; cover and simmer for 15-18 minutes or until liquid is absorbed and rice is tender. Transfer to a large bowl; cool completely.
2. Stir in the turkey, tomatoes, corn, green pepper and onion. In a small bowl, whisk the oil, cilantro, chilies, vinegar, lime juice, mustard, cumin, garlic salt and pepper flakes. Pour over salad; toss to coat. Chill until serving. Just before serving, stir in the avocado..

Safely pit and peel an avocado
with these easy steps.

1 Cut avocado in half. Slip a spoon under the pit to loosen it from the flesh.

2 Slip the spoon between the flesh and peel to remove the peel.

Corn and Spinach Salad

As a child, I loved the combination of fresh spinach, crunchy nuts, red onions and a good tangy cheese. I would search different restaurants to discover how chefs prepared such a special salad. Here is my own creation.
—**ROBIN HAAS** CRANSTON, RI

START TO FINISH: 30 MIN.
MAKES: 8 SERVINGS (½ CUP DRESSING)

- ½ cup chopped walnuts
- 1 tablespoon sugar
- 1½ teaspoons cider vinegar
- 1 package (6 ounces) fresh baby spinach
- 1 medium sweet red pepper, diced
- 1 medium red onion, diced
- 1 cup fresh or frozen corn, thawed
- 1 cup crumbled goat cheese
- ¼ cup dried cranberries

DRESSING
- 3 tablespoons cider vinegar
- 2 tablespoons orange marmalade
- 2 tablespoons mayonnaise
- ½ teaspoon salt
- ½ teaspoon pepper
- ¼ teaspoon Worcestershire sauce

1. In a small heavy skillet, cook walnuts over medium heat until toasted, about 3 minutes. Sprinkle with sugar and vinegar. Cook and stir for 2-4 minutes or until sugar is melted. Spread on foil to cool.
2. In a large bowl, combine the spinach, red pepper, onion, corn, cheese and cranberries; sprinkle with walnuts. In a small bowl, whisk the dressing ingredients. Serve with salad.

Italian Basil Pasta Salad

You can use any kind of bell pepper in this Italian salad, but I'm a big fan of the yellow ones. I like the color they add.
—**CHARLOTTE GEHLE** BROWNSTOWN, MI

PREP: 30 MIN. + CHILLING • **MAKES:** 18 SERVINGS (¾ CUP EACH)

- 1 package (16 ounces) bow tie pasta
- 2 cups grape tomatoes
- 7 ounces fresh mozzarella cheese, cubed
- 1 medium sweet yellow pepper, chopped
- 1 small red onion, chopped
- ½ cup pickled banana pepper rings
- 1 can (2¼ ounces) sliced ripe olives, drained
- 4 thin slices hard salami, diced
- ½ cup fresh basil leaves, thinly sliced

DRESSING
- ¾ cup olive oil
- ¾ cup red wine vinegar
- 1 garlic clove, minced
- 1 teaspoon salt
- ½ teaspoon pepper
- ¼ teaspoon dried basil

1. Cook pasta according to package directions; drain and rinse in cold water. In a large bowl, combine the pasta, tomatoes, cheese, yellow pepper, onion, pepper rings, olives, salami and basil.
2. In a small bowl, whisk the dressing ingredients. Pour over salad and toss to coat. Cover and refrigerate for at least 1 hour before serving..

Macaroni Coleslaw

My friend Peggy brought this coleslaw to one of our picnics, and everyone liked it so much, we all had to have the recipe. The water chestnuts are a fun touch and give this creamy salad a nice crunch.
—**SANDRA MATTESON** WESTHOPE, ND

PREP: 25 MIN. + CHILLING • **MAKES:** 16 SERVINGS (¾ CUP EACH)

- 1 **package (7 ounces) ring macaroni or ditalini**
- 1 **package (14 ounces) coleslaw mix**
- 2 **medium onions, finely chopped**
- 2 **celery ribs, finely chopped**
- 1 **medium cucumber, finely chopped**
- 1 **medium green pepper, finely chopped**
- 1 **can (8 ounces) whole water chestnuts, drained and chopped**

DRESSING

- 1½ **cups Miracle Whip Light**
- ⅓ **cup sugar**
- ¼ **cup cider vinegar**
- ½ **teaspoon salt**
- ¼ **teaspoon pepper**

1. Cook macaroni according to package directions; drain and rinse in cold water. Transfer to a large bowl; add the coleslaw mix, onions, celery, cucumber, green pepper and water chestnuts.
2. In a small bowl, whisk the dressing ingredients. Pour over salad; toss to coat. Cover and refrigerate for at least 1 hour.
PER SERVING *150 cal., 5 g fat (1 g sat. fat), 6 mg chol., 286 mg sodium, 24 g carb., 2 g fiber, 3 g pro.* **Diabetic Exchanges:** *1 starch, 1 vegetable, 1 fat.*

Cucumber & Spinach Tortellini Salad

An easy way to bulk up a fresh salad is to add tortellini. Sometimes I use bow tie pasta and add cooked chicken instead.
—**EMILY HANSON** LOGAN, UT

START TO FINISH: 25 MIN. • **MAKES:** 6 SERVINGS

- 1 **package (9 ounces) refrigerated cheese tortellini**
- ½ **cup sugar**
- ¼ **cup red wine vinegar**
- ¼ **cup olive oil**
- 1 **tablespoon sesame seeds, toasted**
- 1 **tablespoon grated onion**
- ½ **teaspoon salt**
- ¼ **teaspoon paprika**
- 1 **package (6 ounces) fresh baby spinach**
- 2 **cups sliced cucumbers**
- 1 **can (11 ounces) mandarin oranges, drained**
- ¼ **cup honey-roasted sliced almonds**
- ¼ **cup real bacon bits**

1. Cook tortellini according to package directions. Meanwhile, for dressing, in a small heavy saucepan, combine the sugar, vinegar and oil. Cook and stir over low heat just until sugar is dissolved. Remove from the heat. Stir in the sesame seeds, onion, salt and paprika; set aside.
2. Drain tortellini and rinse in cold water. In a large bowl, combine the tortellini, spinach, cucumbers, oranges, almonds and bacon. Pour dressing over salad; toss to coat. Serve immediately.

Radish Asparagus Salad

Lemon zest and mustard in the dressing add the perfect punch to crisp asparagus and spicy radishes in this fun spring salad. My family loves it!

—NANCY LATULIPPE SIMCOE, ON

START TO FINISH: 25 MIN. • **MAKES:** 6 SERVINGS

- 1 **pound fresh asparagus, trimmed and cut into 2-inch pieces**
- 7 **radishes, thinly sliced**
- 2 **tablespoons sesame seeds**

DRESSING

- 2 **tablespoons olive oil**
- 2 **tablespoons thinly sliced green onion**
- 1 **tablespoon white wine vinegar**
- 1 **tablespoon lemon juice**
- 2 **teaspoons honey**
- 1 **teaspoon Dijon mustard**
- ¼ **teaspoon garlic powder**
- ¼ **teaspoon grated lemon peel**
- ¼ **teaspoon pepper**

1. In a large saucepan, bring 6 cups water to a boil. Add asparagus; cover and boil for 3 minutes. Drain and immediately place asparagus in ice water. Drain and pat dry.
2. Transfer to a large bowl; add radishes and sesame seeds. Place dressing ingredients in a jar with a tight-fitting lid; shake well. Pour over salad; toss to coat.
PER SERVING *73 cal., 6 g fat (1 g sat. fat), 0 chol., 28 mg sodium, 5 g carb., 1 g fiber, 2 g pro.* ***Diabetic Exchanges:** 1 vegetable, 1 fat.*

Hazelnut and Pear Salad

My husband, daughter and I raise hazelnuts in the Willamette Valley, so this salad is a family favorite. Since pears and cherries are in an abundance in our area, too, I included them in this recipe I dreamed up.

—KAREN KIRSCH SAINT PAUL, OR

START TO FINISH: 25 MIN. • **MAKES:** 6 SERVINGS

- ⅓ **cup plus ½ cup chopped hazelnuts, toasted, divided**
- 2 **tablespoons plus ½ cup chopped red onion, divided**
- 2 **tablespoons water**
- 4½ **teaspoons balsamic vinegar**
- 4½ **teaspoons sugar**
- ½ **teaspoon salt**
- 1 **garlic clove, halved**
- ⅛ **teaspoon paprika**
- ¼ **cup olive oil**
- 1 **package (5 ounces) spring mix salad greens**
- 1 **medium pear, thinly sliced**
- ½ **cup crumbled Gorgonzola cheese**
- ¼ **cup dried cherries**

1. For dressing, place ⅓ cup hazelnuts, 2 tablespoons onion, water, vinegar, sugar, salt, garlic and paprika in a food processor; cover and process until blended. While processing, gradually add oil in a steady stream.
2. In a large bowl, combine salad greens and remaining onion; add ½ cup dressing and toss to coat. Divide among six salad plates.
3. Top each salad with pear, cheese, cherries and remaining hazelnuts; drizzle with the remaining dressing..

Fruit Salad with Lemon Dressing

The vibrant colors make this dish a pretty first course or light dessert. You'll simply love the citrusy dressing. It's wonderful draped over fruit.

—PATRICIA HARMON BADEN, PA

START TO FINISH: 20 MIN.
MAKES: 2 SERVINGS

- 1 can (8 ounces) unsweetened pineapple chunks, drained
- 1 medium nectarine, chopped
- 1 medium kiwifruit, peeled and chopped
- ½ cup halved fresh strawberries
- 2 tablespoons fresh blueberries
- 1 tablespoon lime juice
- 2 teaspoons honey
- ⅛ teaspoon ground nutmeg

DRESSING
- 2 tablespoons mayonnaise
- 2 tablespoons lemon yogurt
- 1 tablespoon honey
- 1 teaspoon lemon juice
- 1 teaspoon orange juice
- ½ teaspoon grated lemon peel
- ½ teaspoon grated orange peel

1. In a small bowl, combine the first five ingredients. Whisk the lime juice, honey and nutmeg; pour over fruit. Toss to coat.

2. In another bowl, whisk the dressing ingredients; drizzle over salad.

FRUIT SALAD

When making a fruit salad, I toss the juice from a small can of pineapple with my sliced apples and bananas. The juice keeps the fruit from browning. And bits of pineapple in the salad give it a tropical zing.

—FRAN A. ROHNERT PARK, CA

Thai Beef Pasta Salad

START TO FINISH: 30 MIN. • **MAKES:** 6 SERVINGS

    8 ounces uncooked spaghetti

THAI SALAD DRESSING

    ½ cup rice vinegar
    ⅓ cup peanut oil or canola oil
    2 tablespoons lime or lemon juice
    1 tablespoon sugar
    1½ teaspoons minced fresh gingerroot
    1½ teaspoons hot pepper sauce
    1½ teaspoons soy sauce
    1 teaspoon salt
    1 garlic clove, minced
    ½ teaspoon crushed red pepper flakes

SALAD

    1 package (5 ounces) spring mix salad greens
    1 small sweet red pepper, thinly sliced
    4 green onions, chopped
    1 pound deli roast beef, cut into strips
    2 tablespoons chopped salted peanuts, optional

1. Cook spaghetti according to package directions. Meanwhile, in a small bowl, whisk the dressing ingredients.
2. Drain spaghetti and rinse in cold water; toss with ½ cup dressing. Place in a large serving dish.
3. In a large bowl, combine the salad greens, red pepper and onions. Drizzle with remaining dressing; toss to coat. Arrange lettuce mixture over spaghetti. Top with roast beef; sprinkle with peanuts if desired.

> "A local restaurant served this unique salad, and we loved it so much that we created our own version. It's a great way to use up leftover beef." —ALMA WINBERRY GREAT FALLS, MT

Grilled Sweet Potato and Red Pepper Salad

Grilled sweet potatoes make this salad perfect for cookouts. It's unlike most potato salads, but it's always a hit with the crowd.
—**IRENE EAGER** CLAREMONT, NH

PREP: 30 MIN. • **GRILL:** 20 MIN. • **MAKES:** 8 SERVINGS

    ¼ cup olive oil
    2 tablespoons lime juice
    1 garlic clove, minced
    1 teaspoon chopped seeded jalapeno pepper, optional
    1 teaspoon salt
    ½ teaspoon ground cumin
    ¼ teaspoon pepper
    2 large sweet red peppers
    1½ pounds medium sweet potatoes, peeled and cut into
        ½-inch slices
    2 celery ribs, thinly sliced
    3 green onions, thinly sliced
    ⅓ cup minced fresh cilantro

1. For dressing, in a small bowl, whisk the first seven ingredients; set aside.
2. Moisten a paper towel with cooking oil; using long-handled tongs, lightly coat the grill rack. Grill red peppers over medium heat for 10-15 minutes or until the skins blister, turning frequently. Immediately place peppers in a large bowl; cover and let stand for 15 minutes.
3. Meanwhile, in a shallow bowl, drizzle sweet potato slices with 2 tablespoons dressing; toss to coat. Set remaining dressing aside. Arrange potato slices on a grilling grid; place on a grill rack. Grill, covered, over medium heat for 5-6 minutes on each side or until tender. Cut potatoes into bite-size pieces.
4. Peel off and discard charred skin from peppers; seed and coarsely chop peppers. In a large bowl, combine the potatoes, peppers, celery, onions and cilantro. Whisk the reserved dressing; pour over salad and toss to coat. Serve at room temperature.

EDITOR'S NOTE *We recommend wearing disposable gloves when cutting hot peppers. Avoid touching your face. If you do not have a grilling grid, use a disposable foil pan. Poke holes in the bottom of the pan with a meat fork to allow liquid to drain.*

PER SERVING *130 cal., 7 g fat (1 g sat. fat), 0 chol., 312 mg sodium, 16 g carb., 3 g fiber, 2 g pro.* **Diabetic Exchanges:** *1 starch, 1 fat.*

Fresh Mozzarella & Tomato Salad

A splash of lemon and hint of refreshing mint brighten up the medley of red tomatoes, creamy mozzarella and ripe avocados in this sensational salad.

—**LYNN SCULLY** RANCHO SANTA FE, CA

PREP: 25 MIN. + CHILLING. • **MAKES:** 8 SERVINGS

- 6 plum tomatoes, chopped
- 2 cartons (8 ounces each) fresh mozzarella cheese pearls, drained
- ⅓ cup minced fresh basil
- 1 tablespoon minced fresh parsley
- 2 teaspoons minced fresh mint
- ¼ cup lemon juice
- ¼ cup olive oil
- ¾ teaspoon salt
- ¼ teaspoon pepper
- 2 medium ripe avocados, peeled and chopped

1. In a large bowl, combine the tomatoes, cheese, basil, parsley and mint; set aside.
2. In a small bowl, whisk the lemon juice, oil, salt and pepper. Pour over tomato mixture; toss to coat. Cover and refrigerate for at least 1 hour before serving.
3. Just before serving, stir in avocados. Serve salad with a slotted spoon.

Mediterranean Green Salad

On days when it's too hot to cook, I buy a rotisserie chicken from the grocery store and serve it alongside this salad to make a light, easy meal.

—**ANGELA LARSON** TOMAHAWK, WI

START TO FINISH: 15 MIN. • **MAKES:** 10 SERVINGS

- 1 package (16 ounces) ready-to-serve salad greens
- 2 cups grape tomatoes
- 6 green onions, thinly sliced
- 1 jar (7½ ounces) marinated quartered artichoke hearts, drained and coarsely chopped
- 1 cup (4 ounces) crumbled feta cheese
- 1 medium sweet yellow pepper, cut into thin strips
- ¾ cup pitted Greek olives, halved
- ½ cup sunflower kernels
- ½ cup Italian salad dressing

In a large salad bowl, combine the first eight ingredients. Just before serving, drizzle with salad dressing; toss to coat.

QUICK DINNER IDEAS

Serve the Mediterranean Green Salad with rotisserie chicken, take-and-bake pizza, grilled steaks, or Greek or Italian chicken sausages.

Fruited Turkey Salads

What a perfectly lovely salad! This one is bursting with juicy peaches, sun-kissed blueberries, cold turkey and crunchy toasted walnuts. Best of all, it's a cinch to make.

—**DEBORAH WILLIAMS** PEORIA, AZ

START TO FINISH: 15 MIN. • **MAKES:** 4 SERVINGS

- 3 tablespoons plain yogurt
- 3 tablespoons orange marmalade
- 4½ teaspoons mayonnaise
- 2 teaspoons lemon juice
  Dash pepper
- 2 cups cubed cooked turkey breast
- 2 medium peaches, sliced
- 1¼ cups fresh blueberries
- 4 large lettuce leaves
- ¼ cup chopped walnuts, toasted

In a large bowl, combine the first five ingredients. Stir in the turkey, peaches and blueberries. Serve on lettuce leaves; sprinkle with walnuts.

PER SERVING *274 cal., 10 g fat (1 g sat. fat), 64 mg chol., 84 mg sodium, 23 g carb., 2 g fiber, 24 g pro.* **Diabetic Exchanges:** *3 lean meat, 2 fat, 1 fruit, ½ starch.*

South-of-the-Border Caprese Salad

Plump heirloom tomatoes are the stars of this garden-fresh medley, topped with a sweet-tart dressing and freshly crumbled cheese.

—**KATHLEEN MERKLEY** LAYTON, UT

START TO FINISH: 30 MIN.
MAKES: 6 SERVINGS (1 CUP DRESSING)

CILANTRO VINAIGRETTE
- ⅓ cup white wine vinegar
- ½ cup fresh cilantro leaves
- 3 tablespoons sugar
- 1 jalapeno pepper, seeded and chopped
- 1 garlic clove, peeled and quartered
- ¾ teaspoon salt
- ⅔ cup olive oil

SALAD
- 4 cups torn mixed salad greens
- 3 large heirloom or other tomatoes, sliced
- ½ cup crumbled queso fresco or diced part-skim mozzarella cheese
- ¼ teaspoon salt
- ⅛ teaspoon pepper
- 1½ teaspoons fresh cilantro leaves

1. In a blender, combine the first six ingredients. While processing, gradually add oil in a steady stream.
2. Arrange greens on a serving platter; top with tomatoes. Sprinkle with cheese, salt and pepper.
3. Just before serving, drizzle salad with ½ cup dressing; garnish with cilantro leaves. Refrigerate leftover dressing.

NOTE *Wear disposable gloves when cutting hot peppers; the oils can burn skin. Avoid touching your face.*

KEEP HERB BUNCHES FRESH

You can keep herbs like parsley and cilantro fresh for up to a month with the following technique.

Trim the stems with sharp kitchen scissors and place the herb bunch in a short tumbler containing an inch or two of water. Remove any loose leaves so only the stems (and no greenery) are in the water. Loosely tie a produce bag around the tumbler to trap humidity around the leaves and pop the tumbler in the fridge. Each time you use the herbs, change the water. Turn the produce bag inside out before placing it over the herbs so any excess moisture that has built up inside of the bag can evaporate.

YOU SAY
TOMATO
GRAND PRIZE
WINNER
★ ★ ★ ★

Vanilla-Lime Fruit Salad

Feel free to be creative with the fruits you use in this recipe. The dressing is also amazing tossed with fresh strawberries or even drizzled over pound cake.
—**KATE DAMPIER** QUAIL VALLEY, CA

PREP: 40 MIN. + CHILLING
MAKES: 16 SERVINGS (⅔ CUP EACH)

- ½ **cup sugar**
- ½ **cup water**
- 1½ **teaspoons light corn syrup**
- ½ **vanilla bean**
- 2 **tablespoons lime juice**
- 1½ **teaspoons grated lime peel**
- 3 **cups cubed fresh pineapple**
- 2 **large navel oranges, peeled and sectioned**
- 1 **large grapefruit, peeled and sectioned**
- 4 **cups fresh blueberries**

1. In a small saucepan, combine the sugar, water and corn syrup. With a sharp knife, scrape the vanilla bean to remove the seeds; add bean and seeds to pan.

2. Bring to a boil. Reduce heat; simmer for 20 minutes or until reduced by half. Remove from the heat; cool mixture for 10 minutes. Discard vanilla bean. Stir in lime juice and lime peel.

3. In a large bowl, combine the pineapple, oranges, grapefruit and blueberries. Drizzle with vanilla-lime sauce and toss to coat. Refrigerate until chilled.

PER SERVING *79 cal., trace fat (trace sat. fat), 0 chol., 1 mg sodium, 20 g carb., 2 g fiber, 1 g pro.* **Diabetic Exchanges:** *1 fruit, ½ starch.*

FROM THE WEB

A very big hit at a recent dinner party. I used 2 packages each of fresh raspberries and blackberries rather than blueberries. Next day I served the scant leftovers over a Sara Lee pound cake and added a dollop of real whipped cream. Another knockout delicious idea. YUM!!! —**PATRICIA KENNEDY**
TASTEOFHOME.COM

Fresh & Fruity Spinach Salad

Fruit and spinach make a delicious combination, especially when drizzled with a lovely strawberry vinaigrette and topped with toasted walnuts.

—AMY BLOM MARIETTA, GA

START TO FINISH: 20 MIN. • **MAKES:** 8 SERVINGS

- 1 package (6 ounces) fresh baby spinach
- 1 medium nectarine, chopped
- ½ cup chopped fresh strawberries
- 2 medium kiwifruit, peeled and sliced
- ½ cup chopped walnuts, toasted

STRAWBERRY VINAIGRETTE

- ½ cup halved fresh strawberries
- 1 tablespoon balsamic vinegar
- 1 tablespoon sugar
- ¼ teaspoon salt
- ⅛ teaspoon dried tarragon
- ⅛ teaspoon pepper
- ⅓ cup plus 2 tablespoons olive oil

1. In a large bowl, combine the spinach, nectarine, strawberries, kiwi and walnuts.

2. Place the first six vinaigrette ingredients in a blender; cover and process for 15 seconds. While processing, gradually add oil in a steady stream. Drizzle over salad and toss to coat. Serve immediately.

Southwest Crunch Chicken Salad

The blend of bright citrus, cumin and smoky bacon makes this chicken salad stand out from the rest. If you don't have cumin, chili powder is a great substitution.

—SALLY SIBTHORPE SHELBY TOWNSHIP, MI

START TO FINISH: 30 MIN. • **MAKES:** 13 SERVINGS (1 CUP EACH)

- 1⅓ cups fat-free mayonnaise
- ½ cup minced fresh cilantro
- ¼ cup lime juice
- ¼ cup orange juice
- 2 garlic cloves, minced
- 1¾ teaspoons ground cumin
- ¾ teaspoon grated orange peel
- ½ teaspoon salt
- 9 cups cubed cooked chicken breast
- 1¾ cups julienned peeled jicama
- 1¾ cups chopped celery
- 1¾ cups chopped sweet red peppers
- 1 cup chopped cashews
- ½ pound turkey bacon strips, diced and cooked

In a small bowl, combine the first eight ingredients. In a large bowl, combine the remaining ingredients. Add mayonnaise mixture; toss to coat. Chill until serving.
PER SERVING *286 cal., 12 g fat (3 g sat. fat), 95 mg chol., 653 mg sodium, 11 g carb., 3 g fiber, 33 g pro.* ***Diabetic Exchanges:*** *4 lean meat, 1½ fat, 1 starch.*

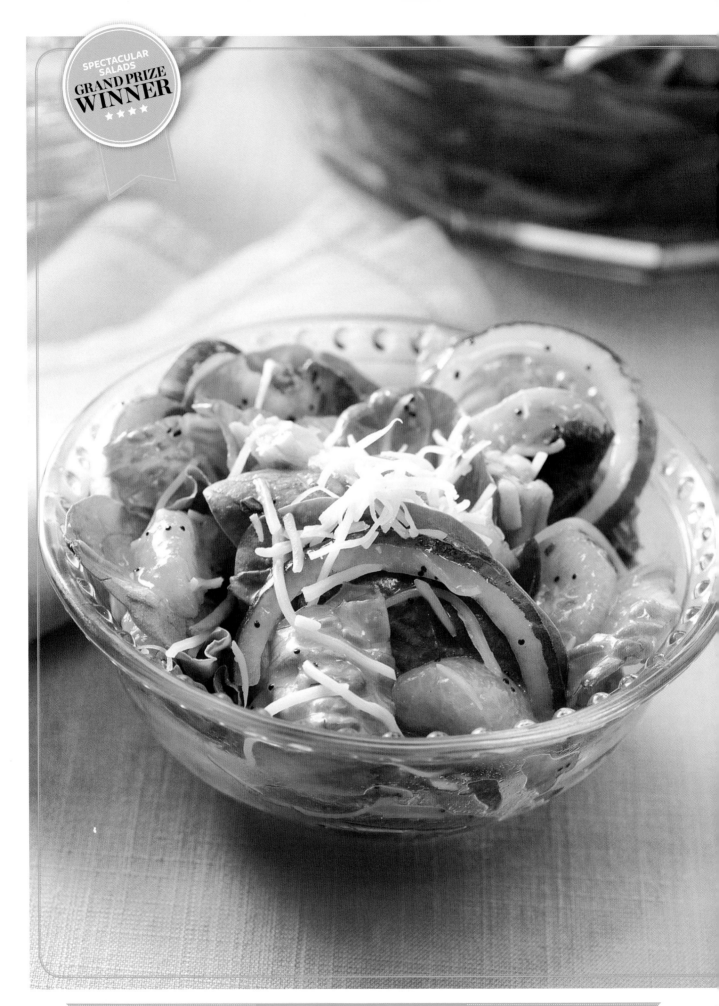

Orange Spinach Salad

The combination of mustard-onion dressing with juicy oranges, cheese and crunchy sweet almonds is a joy for every taste bud! We eat this salad several times a week.

—**JENNIFER RYTTING** WEST JORDAN, UT

START TO FINISH: 30 MIN. • **MAKES:** 16 SERVINGS (1 CUP EACH)

- ¼ cup sugar
- ½ cup slivered almonds
- 1 bunch romaine, torn
- 1 package (6 ounces) fresh baby spinach
- ½ pound sliced fresh mushrooms
- 3 cups (12 ounces) shredded Swiss cheese
- 1 medium red onion, sliced
- ½ pound sliced bacon, cooked and crumbled
- 1 can (15 ounces) mandarin oranges, drained

POPPY SEED DRESSING

- ⅓ cup white vinegar
- ⅓ cup sugar
- ¼ cup finely chopped onion
- 2 tablespoons Dijon mustard
- ¾ teaspoon salt
- ¾ cup canola oil
- 2 teaspoons poppy seeds

1. In a small heavy skillet, melt sugar over low heat. Add the almonds; cook and stir for 3-5 minutes or until golden brown. Spread onto a greased sheet of foil; break apart if necessary.

2. In a large bowl, combine the romaine, spinach, mushrooms, cheese, red onion, bacon and oranges.

3. For dressing, in a blender, combine the vinegar, sugar, onion, mustard and salt; cover and process until blended. While processing, gradually add oil in a steady stream. Stir in poppy seeds.

4. Pour dressing over salad and toss to coat. Sprinkle with sugared almonds. Serve immediately..

BACON AT THE READY

I buy several pounds of bacon when it's on sale. Then I put the strips in a single layer on jelly roll pans and pop them in the oven to bake at 350° until crisp. I place the strips on paper towels to drain before storing them in single layers in a freezer container. It's easy to remove only the number of strips I need for a quick breakfast, sandwich or salad. A short time in the microwave reheats the bacon.

—**DALE H.** HOLLAND, MI

Ambrosia Fruit Salad

This fresh and creamy salad is a favorite around my house. I make it with plenty of fruit, yogurt for dressing, then mix in just enough goodies (marshmallows and coconut) so it tastes like the rich version I grew up with.·

—**TRISHA KRUSE** EAGLE, ID

START TO FINISH: 10 MIN. • **MAKES:** 6 SERVINGS

- 1 can (8¼ ounces) fruit cocktail, drained
- 1 can (8 ounces) unsweetened pineapple chunks, drained
- 1 cup green grapes
- 1 cup seedless red grapes
- 1 cup miniature marshmallows
- 1 medium banana, sliced
- ¾ cup vanilla yogurt
- ½ cup flaked coconut

In a large bowl, combine all ingredients. Chill until serving.

Spinach Bean Salad with Maple Dressing

Warm maple dressing slightly wilts the spinach, giving it a delightful texture and flavor. If you want to be wowed by a salad, you've got to try this one!

—**SALLY MALONEY** DALLAS, GA

START TO FINISH: 15 MIN. • **MAKES:** 11 SERVINGS

- ¼ cup maple syrup
- 3 tablespoons cider vinegar
- 1 tablespoon olive oil
- 1 tablespoon Dijon mustard
- ¼ teaspoon salt
- ¼ teaspoon coarsely ground pepper
- 1 can (15½ ounces) great northern beans, rinsed and drained
- 2 packages (6 ounces each) fresh baby spinach
- 4 green onions, thinly sliced
- 1 small sweet red pepper, chopped
- 5 bacon strips, cooked and crumbled

1. For dressing, in a small microwave-safe bowl, combine the first six ingredients; set aside. Place beans in another microwave-safe bowl. Microwave, uncovered, for 1-2 minutes or until heated through.

2. In a large salad bowl, combine the spinach, onions, red pepper, bacon and beans. Microwave the dressing, uncovered, for 30-60 seconds or until heated through. Whisk until smooth; drizzle over salad and toss to coat.

PER SERVING *90 cal., 3 g fat (1 g sat. fat), 3 mg chol., 272 mg sodium, 13 g carb., 3 g fiber, 4 g pro.* **Diabetic Exchanges:** *1 starch, 1 vegetable.*

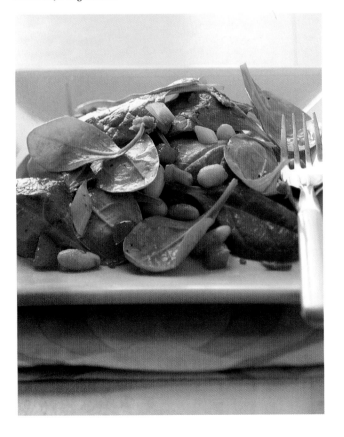

Greek-Inspired Quinoa Salad

I like to serve this salad with toasted pita bread. You can also turn it into a main dish simply by tossing in cut-up chicken breast.

—**JULIE STOCKEL** FARMINGTON HILLS, MI

PREP: 30 MIN. + CHILLING • **MAKES:** 10 SERVINGS

- 2 cups water
- 1 cup quinoa, rinsed
- 1 package (10 ounces) frozen chopped spinach, thawed and squeezed dry
- 1½ cups (6 ounces) crumbled feta cheese
- 1 cup grape tomatoes
- ¾ cup canned black beans, rinsed and drained
- ½ cup chopped seeded peeled cucumber
- ½ cup sliced pepperoncini
- ½ cup Greek olives, pitted and halved
- ¾ cup reduced-fat Greek or Italian salad dressing, divided

1. In a small saucepan, bring water to a boil. Add quinoa. Reduce heat; cover and simmer for 12-15 minutes or until water is absorbed. Remove from the heat.

2. In a large bowl, combine the quinoa, spinach, cheese, tomatoes, beans, cucumber, pepperoncini and olives. Pour ½ cup dressing over quinoa mixture and toss to coat. Cover and refrigerate for at least 1 hour.

3. Just before serving, drizzle remaining dressing over salad; toss to coat.

NOTE *Look for quinoa in the cereal, rice or organic food aisle.*
PER SERVING *184 cal., 8 g fat (2 g sat. fat), 9 mg chol., 472 mg sodium, 19 g carb., 4 g fiber, 7 g pro.* **Diabetic Exchanges:** *1½ fat, 1 starch, 1 lean meat.*

Salads with Pistachio-Crusted Goat Cheese

Walnuts, juicy oranges and tomatoes with warm pistachio-crusted goat cheese medallions make up this vegetarian entree salad. I serve it with a crusty loaf of French bread.

—GLORIA BRADLEY NAPERVILLE, IL

START TO FINISH: 30 MIN.
MAKES: 4 SERVINGS

- 6 **cups torn mixed salad greens**
- 2 **medium oranges, peeled and segmented**
- 1 **cup cherry tomatoes**
- ½ **cup chopped walnuts, toasted**
- ¼ **medium red onion, thinly sliced**
- 2 **tablespoons orange juice**
- 1 **tablespoon white wine vinegar**
- 1 **teaspoon grated orange peel**
- 1 **teaspoon honey**
- ½ **teaspoon salt**
- ¼ **teaspoon ground cumin**
- 6 **tablespoons walnut or olive oil, divided**
- ⅓ **cup pistachios**
- 4½ **teaspoons seasoned bread crumbs**
- 1 **log (4 ounces) fresh goat cheese**

1. In a large bowl, combine the first five ingredients. In a small bowl, whisk orange juice, vinegar, orange peel, honey, salt, cumin and 5 tablespoons of walnut oil. Pour over the salad; toss to coat. Divide among four serving plates.

2. Place pistachios in a food processor; cover and process until ground. Transfer to a small bowl; stir in bread crumbs. Cut goat cheese into four slices; brush slices with the remaining oil. Coat in crumb mixture.

3. In a small nonstick skillet coated with cooking spray, cook cheese slices over medium heat for 1-2 minutes on each side or until golden brown. Place on salads.

Chili Verde, page 52

54

59

68

Soups & Sandwiches

Turn here for dozens of fresh takes on **classic comfort food** for lunchtime and beyond. **Piping hot** soups, crowd-size **submarines**, **bacony** burgers, good-for-you chili and...**the sassiest sliders**? We've got 'em!

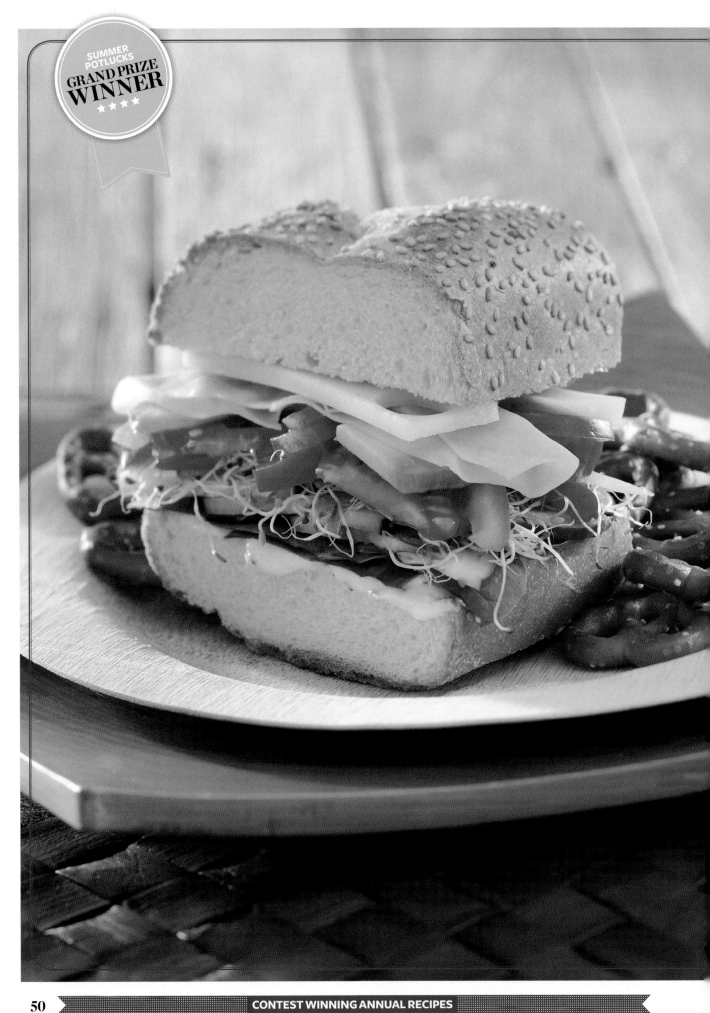

Summer Veggie Subs

Every Sunday night during the summer, a local park near our house holds free outdoor concerts. We've been going for years. These subs are perfect for picnics, and I've taken them to the park several times.
—**JENNIE TODD** LANCASTER, PA

PREP: 30 MIN. + STANDING • **MAKES:** 12 SERVINGS

- 4 **medium sweet red peppers**
- ½ **cup fat-free mayonnaise**
- 2 **tablespoons minced fresh basil**
- 1 **tablespoon minced fresh parsley**
- 1 **tablespoon minced fresh tarragon**
- 2 **loaves French bread (1 pound each), halved lengthwise**
- 2 **cups fresh baby spinach**
- 2 **cups thinly sliced cucumbers**
- 2 **cups alfalfa sprouts**
- 4 **medium tomatoes, sliced**
- 2 **medium ripe avocados, peeled and sliced**
- ¾ **pound thinly sliced deli turkey**
- 6 **slices reduced-fat Swiss cheese, halved**

1. Broil peppers 4 in. from the heat until skins blister, about 5 minutes. With tongs, rotate peppers a quarter turn. Broil and rotate until all sides are blistered and blackened. Immediately place peppers in a large bowl; cover and let stand for 15-20 minutes.
2. Peel off and discard charred skin. Remove stems and seeds. Julienne peppers.
3. Combine the mayonnaise, basil, parsley and tarragon; spread over bread bottoms. Top with spinach, cucumbers, sprouts, roasted peppers, tomatoes, avocados, turkey and cheese. Replace tops. Cut each loaf into six slices.

Roasted Red Pepper Soup

I love oven-roasted peppers, especially when I transform them into this silky soup seasoned with garlic and thyme. Dip a grilled cheese sandwich into it and enjoy!
—**KATHY RAIRIGH** MILFORD, IN

PREP: 45 MIN. • **COOK:** 30 MIN. • **MAKES:** 12 SERVINGS (3 QUARTS)

- 2 **pounds sweet red peppers, cut into 1-inch pieces (about 6 medium)**
- 1 **large onion, sliced**
- 2 **medium carrots, sliced**
- 1 **jalapeno pepper, quartered and seeded**
- 2 **tablespoons olive oil**
- 5 **garlic cloves, minced**
- 2 **tablespoons whole fresh thyme leaves plus 1 teaspoon minced fresh thyme, divided**
- 4 **cups vegetable broth or water**
- 4 **cups chicken broth**
- 2 **cups cubed peeled potatoes**
- 2 **cups cubed peeled sweet potato**
- 2 **cups cubed peeled butternut squash**
- 1 **teaspoon salt**
- ⅛ **teaspoon pepper**

1. Place the red peppers, onion, carrots and jalapeno in two greased 15-in. x 10-in. x 1-in. baking pans; drizzle with oil and toss to coat. Bake at 425° for 25-30 minutes or until tender, stirring occasionally. Add garlic and whole thyme leaves; bake 5 minutes longer.
2. Meanwhile, in a Dutch oven, combine the vegetable broth, chicken broth, potatoes, sweet potato, squash, salt, pepper and minced thyme. Bring to a boil. Reduce heat; cover and simmer for 15 minutes or until the vegetables are tender.
3. Add roasted pepper mixture; cook 5 minutes longer. Cool slightly. In a blender, process soup in batches until smooth. Return all to the pan and heat through.
NOTE *Wear disposable gloves when cutting hot peppers; the oils can burn skin. Avoid touching your face.*

Peel garlic like a pro with this simple tip.

Using the flat side of a chef's knife's blade, crush the garlic clove. Peel away the skin. Chop or mince the garlic as directed in the recipe.

Chili Verde

This is one of my family's most-requested recipes. We enjoy it any time of year, but it's especially good on a cool and rainy day.

—**SHERRIE SCETTRINI** SALINAS, CA

PREP: 15 MIN. • **COOK:** 1½ HOURS • **MAKES:** 8 SERVINGS

- 4 tablespoons canola oil, divided
- 4 pound boneless pork, cut into ¾-inch cubes
- ¼ cup all-purpose flour
- 1 can (4 ounces) chopped green chilies
- ½ teaspoon ground cumin
- ¼ teaspoon salt
- ¼ teaspoon pepper
- 3 garlic cloves, minced
- ½ cup minced fresh cilantro
- ½ to 1 cup salsa
- 1 can (14½ ounces) chicken broth
  Flour tortillas, warmed

1. In a Dutch oven, heat 1 tablespoon oil over medium-high. Add 1 pound of pork; cook and stir until lightly browned. Remove and set aside. Repeat with remaining meat, adding more oil as needed. Return all of the meat to Dutch oven.
2. Sprinkle flour over meat; mix well. Add the chilies, cumin, salt, pepper, garlic, cilantro, salsa and broth. Cover and simmer until pork is tender and chili reaches desired consistency, about 1½ hours. Serve with warmed tortillas.

Cheeseburger French Loaf

My husband and kids have always been big on burgers. After having something similar at a friend's house—but without the meat—I knew I had to try it out at home. This version of the ever-popular cheeseburger is sure to become a favorite.

—**NANCY DAUGHERTY** CORTLAND, OH

PREP: 25 MIN. • **BAKE:** 25 MIN. • **MAKES:** 6 SERVINGS

- ¾ pound lean ground beef (90% lean)
- ½ cup chopped sweet onion
- 1 small green pepper, chopped
- 2 garlic cloves, minced
- 2 tablespoons all-purpose flour
- 2 tablespoons Dijon mustard
- 1 tablespoon ketchup
- 1 tube (11 ounces) refrigerated crusty French loaf
- 4 slices reduced-fat process American cheese product
- 1 egg white, lightly beaten
- 3 tablespoons shredded Parmesan cheese

1. In a large skillet, cook the beef, onion and pepper over medium heat until meat is no longer pink. Add garlic; cook 1 minute longer. Stir in the flour, mustard and ketchup; set aside.
2. Unroll dough starting at the seam. Pat into a 14-in. x 12-in. rectangle. Spoon meat mixture lengthwise down the center of the dough; top with cheese slices. Bring long sides of dough to the center over filling; pinch seam to seal.
3. Place seam side down on a baking sheet coated with cooking spray. Brush with egg white. Sprinkle with Parmesan cheese.
4. With a sharp knife, cut diagonal slits in top of loaf. Bake at 350° for 25-30 minutes or until golden brown. Serve warm.
PER SERVING *277 cal., 7 g fat (3 g sat. fat), 33 mg chol., 697 mg sodium, 30 g carb., 1 g fiber, 21 g pro.* **Diabetic Exchanges:** *2 starch, 2 lean meat.*

Pepper & Jack Smothered Burgers

To add a little Southwestern bite to your chicken burgers, just add peppers. The cheesy pepper-onion topping and chipotle glaze give these chicken patties a nice kick.

—DEBORAH BIGGS OMAHA, NE

PREP: 30 MIN. • **BAKE:** 20 MIN. • **MAKES:** 4 SERVINGS

- ½ cup honey mustard salad dressing
- 1 tablespoon lime juice
- 1 tablespoon minced chipotle pepper in adobo sauce

BURGERS
- 1 egg white, beaten
- ¼ cup crushed tortilla chips
- 3 tablespoons minced seeded jalapeno peppers
- ½ teaspoon salt
- 1 pound ground chicken

TOPPINGS
- 2 poblano peppers, julienned
- 2 Anaheim peppers, julienned
- 1 medium sweet red pepper, julienned
- 1 small onion, halved and sliced
- 2 tablespoons canola oil
- 3 tablespoons minced fresh cilantro
- ¼ teaspoon salt
- 4 slices pepper Jack cheese
- 4 hamburger buns, split

1. For glaze, combine the salad dressing, lime juice and chipotle pepper in a blender; cover and process until blended. Set aside.

2. In a large bowl, combine the egg white, tortilla chips, jalapenos and salt. Crumble chicken over mixture and mix well. Shape into four patties. Place in a greased 15-in. x 10-in. x 1-in. baking pan.

3. Bake at 375° for 9-11 minutes on each side or until a thermometer reads 165° and juices run clear, basting occasionally with glaze.

4. Meanwhile, in a large skillet, saute peppers and onion in oil until crisp-tender. Remove from the heat; stir in cilantro and salt.

5. Top burgers with pepper mixture and cheese. Broil 4 in. from the heat for 2-3 minutes or until cheese is melted. Serve on buns.

NOTE *Wear disposable gloves when cutting hot peppers; the oils can burn skin. Avoid touching your face.*

Chicken Pesto Clubs

START TO FINISH: 10 MIN. • **MAKES:** 2 SERVINGS

- 4 slices ready-to-serve fully cooked bacon
- 4 slices sourdough bread
- 2 tablespoons prepared pesto
- 1 cup ready-to-use grilled chicken breast strips
- 2 slices cheddar cheese
- 1 medium tomato, sliced
- 1 cup fresh arugula or baby spinach
- 1 tablespoon olive oil

1. Heat bacon according to package directions. Meanwhile, spread bread slices with pesto. Layer two slices with chicken, cheese, tomato, arugula and bacon; top with remaining bread slice.

2. Brush outsides of sandwiches with oil. Cook on an indoor grill for 3-4 minutes or until bread is browned and cheese is melted.

"This sandwich is crispy and golden brown on the outside, and with a filling the whole family will love. It's supper in 10 minutes flat!"

—TERRI CRANDALL GARDNERVILLE, NV

Italian BLTs

Toasting BLTs in a coating of crispy bread crumbs takes these sandwiches from satisfying to spectacular. You will love this brilliant method.

—**JOYCE MOUL** YORK HAVEN, PA

START TO FINISH: 20 MIN. • **MAKES:** 2 SERVINGS

- 2 turkey bacon strips, diced
- 4 slices Italian bread (½ inch thick)
- 2 slices reduced-fat provolone cheese
- 2 lettuce leaves
- 1 small tomato, sliced
- 4 teaspoons fat-free Italian salad dressing
- ⅓ cup panko (Japanese) bread crumbs
  Butter-flavored cooking spray
- ½ teaspoon olive oil

1. In a small skillet, cook bacon over medium heat until crisp. Layer two bread slices with cheese, bacon, lettuce and tomato; top with remaining bread.
2. Brush outsides of sandwiches with salad dressing. Place bread crumbs in a shallow bowl. Coat sandwiches with bread crumbs; spray with butter-flavored cooking spray.
3. In a large skillet over medium heat, toast sandwiches in oil for 2-3 minutes on each side or until the bread is lightly browned.
PER SERVING *272 cal., 11 g fat (4 g sat. fat), 25 mg chol., 761 mg sodium, 30 g carb., 2 g fiber, 13 g pro.* ***Diabetic Exchanges:*** *2 starch, 2 lean meat.*

Cranberry Chicken Focaccia

With goat cheese, cranberries and pecans, this recipe puts a whole new slant on the chicken sandwich. The bistro-inspired meal is a hit every time I serve it.

—**CHARLENE CHAMBERS** ORMOND BEACH, FL

PREP: 25 MIN. • **BAKE:** 40 MIN. + COOLING • **MAKES:** 6 SERVINGS

- 1¾ pounds bone-in chicken breast halves
- 6 fresh thyme sprigs
- ½ teaspoon salt
- ¼ teaspoon pepper
- 1 cup fresh or frozen cranberries, thawed
- ½ cup orange segments
- 2 tablespoons sugar
- 1 loaf (12 ounces) focaccia bread, split
- ⅓ cup crumbled goat cheese
- 3 large lettuce leaves
- ¼ cup chopped pecans, toasted

1. With fingers, carefully loosen skin from each chicken breast to form a pocket. Place thyme sprigs under the skin and sprinkle with salt and pepper. Place in an 11-in. x 7-in. baking dish coated with cooking spray. Bake, uncovered, at 350° for 40-45 minutes or until a thermometer reads 170°.
2. Set chicken aside until cool enough to handle. Remove meat from bones; discard bones and slice chicken. Place the cranberries, orange segments and sugar in a small food processor; cover and process until blended.
3. Layer bread bottom with cheese, lettuce, cranberry mixture, chicken and pecans. Replace bread top. Cut into six wedges.

Golden Squash Soup

This special recipe from my mother-in-law is one that I enjoy making every fall. The soup is so pretty that it dresses up the table. We enjoy it on crisp evenings.

—MARY ANN KLEIN
WASHINGTON TOWNSHIP, NJ

PREP: 35 MIN. • **COOK:** 30 MIN. + COOLING
MAKES: 12-14 SERVINGS (3½ QUARTS)

- 3 leeks (white portion only), sliced
- 4 medium carrots, chopped
- 5 tablespoons butter
- 3 pounds butternut squash, peeled and cubed
- 6 cups chicken broth
- 3 medium zucchini, peeled and sliced
- 2 teaspoons salt
- ½ teaspoon dried thyme
- ¼ teaspoon white pepper
- 1 cup half-and-half cream
- ½ cup 2% milk
  Grated Parmesan cheese and chives, optional

1. In a Dutch oven, saute leeks and carrots in butter for 5 minutes, stirring occasionally. Add the squash, broth, zucchini, salt, thyme and pepper; bring to a boil. Reduce heat; cover and simmer for 30-35 minutes or until vegetables are tender. Cool until lukewarm.

2. In a blender, puree soup in small batches until smooth; return to pan. Stir in cream and milk; heat through (do not boil). Sprinkle with cheese and chives if desired.

NO-STICK TRICK

I have found that shredding cheese is much easier (and so is the cleanup!) when I spritz the cheese grater with cooking spray before I begin.

—SHERRY B. WHITTER, CA

Buttery Onion Soup

I developed this recipe when I once had an abundance of sweet onions. I like making it for guests. Sometimes I'll halve the recipe and make some just for me!

—**SHARON BERTHELOTE** SUNBURST, MT

PREP: 5 MIN. • **COOK:** 30 MIN. • **MAKES:** 6 SERVINGS

  2 **cups thinly sliced onions**
  ½ **cup butter, cubed**
  ¼ **cup all-purpose flour**
  2 **cups chicken broth**
  2 **cups milk**
  1½ **to 2 cups (6 to 8 ounces) shredded part-skim mozzarella**
      cheese
      Salt and pepper to taste
      Croutons, optional

1. In a large saucepan, cook onions in butter over low heat until tender and transparent, about 20 minutes.
2. Stir in flour. Gradually add broth and milk; cook and stir over medium heat until bubbly. Cook and stir for 1 minute longer; reduce heat to low. Add mozzarella cheese and stir constantly until melted (do not boil). Season to taste with salt and pepper. Serve with croutons if desired.

Roast Pork Sandwiches with Peach Chutney

This combination of roast pork with peach chutney used to be a favorite Sunday dinner. Since most of my family's on their own now, I cut the recipe down for sandwiches.

—**LILY JULOW** LAWRENCEVILLE, GA

PREP: 15 MIN. • **BAKE:** 35 MIN. • **MAKES:** 4 SERVINGS

  1 **pork tenderloin (1 pound)**
  2 **tablespoons spicy brown mustard**
PEACH CHUTNEY
  ¼ **cup peach preserves**
  3 **tablespoons finely chopped onion**
  2 **tablespoons red wine vinegar**
  1 **small garlic clove, minced**
  ¼ **teaspoon mustard seed**
  ⅛ **teaspoon salt**
  ⅛ **teaspoon ground ginger**
  ⅛ **teaspoon ground cinnamon**
      Dash cayenne pepper
      Dash ground cloves
SANDWICHES
  ¼ **cup fat-free mayonnaise**
  4 **onion rolls, split and toasted**
  4 **lettuce leaves**

1. Brush pork with mustard; place on a rack in a shallow roasting pan. Bake at 425° for 35-40 minutes or until a thermometer reads 160°. Let stand for 5 minutes before slicing.
2. Meanwhile, for chutney, in a small saucepan, combine the preserves, onion, vinegar, garlic and seasonings. Bring to a boil. Reduce heat; simmer, uncovered, for 7-8 minutes or until thickened. Set aside to cool.
3. Spread mayonnaise over roll bottoms. Layer with lettuce, pork slices and chutney. Replace tops.
PER SERVING *357 cal., 7 g fat (2 g sat. fat), 65 mg chol., 589 mg sodium, 42 g carb., 2 g fiber, 29 g pro.* **Diabetic Exchanges:** *3 lean meat, 2½ starch.*

GET TO KNOW CHUTNEY

Originating in India but increasingly popular in the West, this versatile condiment has sweet, sour, spicy and savory flavors. Western chutney is typically fruit-flavored, with mango being the most popular. Chutney's flavor profile enhances savory dishes. Try mixing a little chutney into your favorite deviled egg recipe, serving it alongside curried dishes, or spooning it over cream cheese and sprinkling with green onions for an impromptu appetizer.

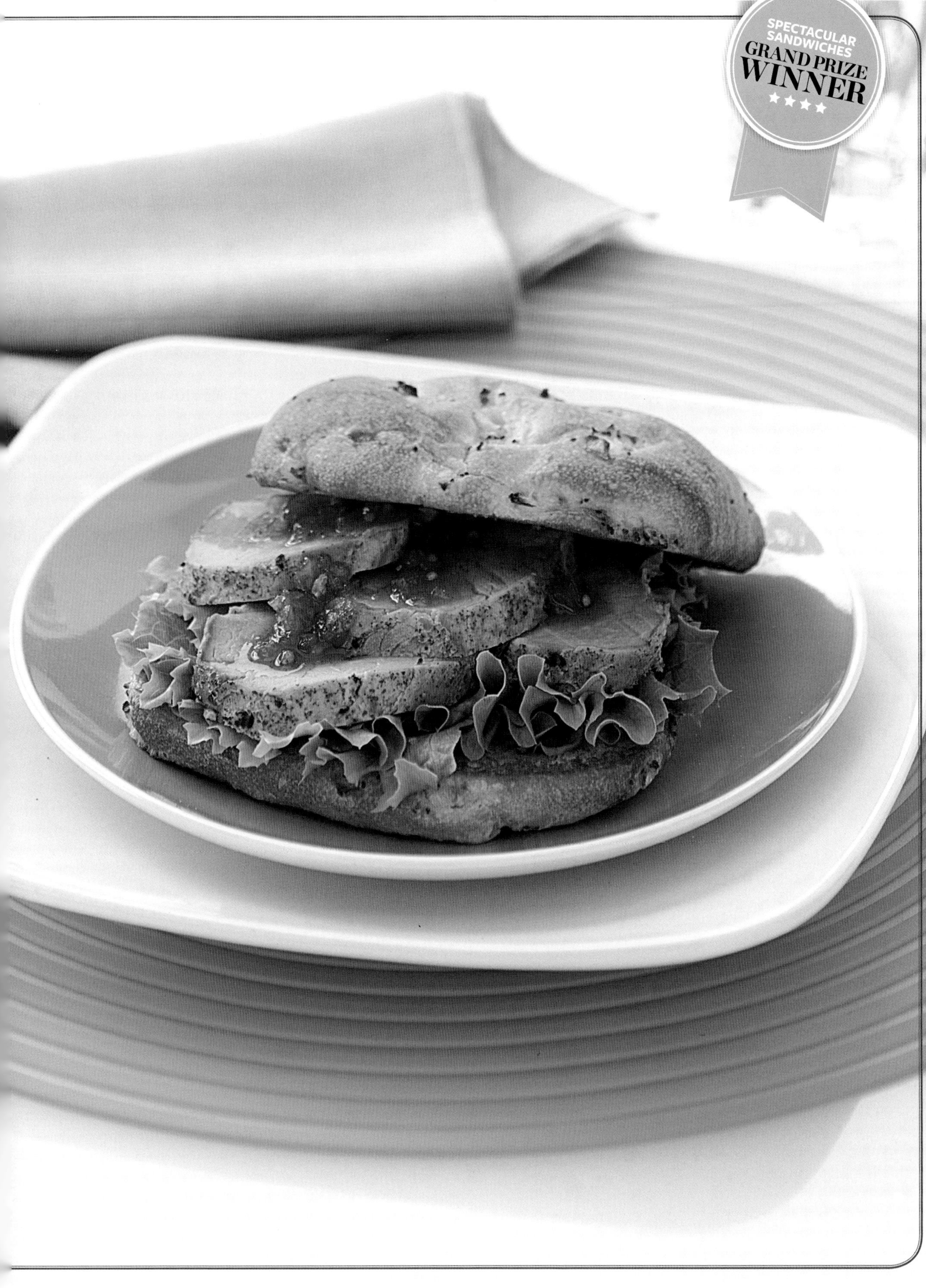
SPECTACULAR SANDWICHES
GRAND PRIZE
WINNER

Asian Burgers

The East-meets-West flavor of these burgers has made them a family staple for over 20 years. They're equally delicious cooked on the grill.

—CHARLOTTE GILTNER MESA, AZ

START TO FINISH: 30 MIN. • **MAKES:** 8 SERVINGS

- 2 **tablespoons soy sauce**
- 1 **tablespoon sesame oil**
- 1 **can (8 ounces) sliced water chestnuts, drained and chopped**
- 1 **cup bean sprouts**
- ½ **cup finely chopped fresh mushrooms**
- 1 **celery rib, finely chopped**
- 4 **green onions, finely chopped**
- 1 **teaspoon pepper**
- ½ **teaspoon salt**
- 2 **pounds ground beef**
- 4 **teaspoons canola oil**
- ½ **cup mayonnaise**
- 1 **tablespoon prepared wasabi**
- 8 **sesame seed hamburger buns, split**
- 3 **cups shredded Chinese or napa cabbage**

1. In a large bowl, combine the first nine ingredients. Crumble beef over mixture and mix well. Shape into eight patties.

2. In two large skillets, cook burgers in oil over medium heat for 5-6 minutes on each side or until a thermometer reads 160°.

3. Meanwhile, combine mayonnaise and wasabi; spread over buns. Serve burgers on buns with cabbage.

Sausage Tortellini Soup

I'm always searching for new and different soup recipes. I came across this one in an old church cookbook and changed a few ingredients to suit my family's tastes. Now it's one of our favorites. I always get requests for the recipe.

—HEATHER PERSCH HUDSONVILLE, MI

PREP: 10 MIN. • **COOK:** 30 MIN.
MAKES: 10 SERVINGS (2½ QUARTS)

- 1 **pound bulk Italian sausage**
- 2 **cups water**
- 2 **cups chopped cabbage**
- 1 **can (14½ ounces) Italian stewed tomatoes, undrained and cut up**
- 1 **can (14½ ounces) beef broth**
- 1 **can (10½ ounces) condensed French onion soup**
- 1 **package (9 ounces) refrigerated cheese tortellini**
- ½ **cup grated Parmesan cheese**

In a large saucepan, cook sausage over medium heat until no longer pink; drain. Stir in the water, cabbage, tomatoes, broth and soup. Bring to a boil. Reduce heat; simmer, uncovered, for 8 minutes. Stir in the tortellini; cook for 7-9 minutes longer or until the pasta is tender. Sprinkle with cheese.

FREEZE OPTION *Before adding cheese, freeze cooled soup in freezer containers. To use, partially thaw in refrigerator overnight. Heat through in a saucepan, stirring occasionally and adding a little broth, water or milk if necessary. Serve with cheese.*

Chili con Carne

At chili suppers, this one always disappears first! It's nice at home, too, since the longer it sits in the refrigerator, the better this wonderful chili seems to taste.

—**JANIE TURNER** TUTTLE, OK

PREP: 20 MIN. • **COOK:** 1½ HOURS
MAKES: 8-10 SERVINGS (ABOUT 2½ QUARTS)

- 2 **pounds ground beef**
- 2 **tablespoons olive oil**
- 2 **medium onions, chopped**
- 2 **garlic cloves, minced**
- 1 **medium green pepper, chopped**
- 1½ **teaspoons salt**
- 2 **tablespoons chili powder**
- ⅛ **teaspoon cayenne pepper**
- ¼ **teaspoon ground cinnamon**
- 1 **teaspoon ground cumin**
- 1 **teaspoon dried oregano**
- 2 **cans (14½ ounces each) diced tomatoes, undrained**
- 3 **teaspoons beef bouillon granules**
- 1 **cup boiling water**
- 1 **can (16 ounces) kidney beans, rinsed and drained**

1. In a Dutch oven, cook beef over medium heat until no longer pink; drain and set aside.
2. In the same pot, heat oil; saute onions until tender. Add garlic; cook 1 minute longer. Stir in the green pepper, salt, chili powder, cayenne, cinnamon, cumin and oregano. Cook for 2 minutes, stirring until combined.
3. Add tomatoes and reserved beef. Stir in bouillon and water. Bring to a boil. Reduce heat; cover and simmer for about 1 hour. Add beans and heat through.

Southwestern Burgers

We love burgers and have them every Saturday in summer. We also have a favorite burrito recipe. One day, we got the bright idea to combine these two meals. Voila! Our Southwestern Burgers were born.

—**TAMMY FORTNEY** DEER PARK, WA

START TO FINISH: 30 MIN. • **MAKES:** 8 SERVINGS

- 1 **can (4 ounces) chopped green chilies**
- 4 **teaspoons ground cumin**
- 1 **teaspoon chili powder**
- ¾ **teaspoon garlic powder**
- ¾ **teaspoon salt**
- ½ **teaspoon pepper**
- 2 **pounds lean ground beef**
- ¾ **pound bulk pork sausage**
- 8 **slices Monterey Jack cheese**
- 8 **hamburger buns, split, toasted**
- 8 **lettuce leaves**
- 1 **large tomato, sliced**
- 1 **to 2 ripe avocados, peeled and sliced**
  Mayonnaise or mustard, optional

1. In a large bowl, combine the first six ingredients. Crumble beef and sausage over mixture; mix well. Shape into eight patties.
2. Grill, covered, over medium heat for 5 minutes on each side or until a thermometer reads 160° and juices run clear. Top each burger with a cheese slice.
3. Grill 1-2 minutes longer or until cheese begins to melt. Serve on buns with the lettuce, tomato, avocado and, if desired, mayonnaise or mustard.

Pork Tenderloin Panini with Fig Port Jam

I serve these rather sophisticated yet simple sandwiches for dinner or cut them into smaller servings for appetizers. They're great hot or cold, but if serving cold, I like to add some watercress for a bit of crunch and color.
—**CASEY GALLOWAY** COLUMBIA, MO

PREP: 1 HOUR • **COOK:** 5 MIN. • **MAKES:** 4 SERVINGS

- ⅓ cup port wine or grape juice
- 2 tablespoons water
- 2 dried figs, chopped
- 1 fresh rosemary sprig
- 1 tablespoon honey
- ⅛ teaspoon salt
  Dash pepper

SANDWICHES
- 1 pork tenderloin (¾ pound)
- ¼ teaspoon salt
- ¼ teaspoon pepper
- 8 slices sourdough bread
- ¼ cup crumbled goat cheese
- 1 cup watercress, optional
  Cooking spray

1. For jam, in small saucepan, combine the first seven ingredients. Bring to a boil. Reduce heat; simmer, uncovered, until liquid is reduced to about ¼ cup, about 15 minutes.

2. Remove from the heat. Cool slightly; discard rosemary. Transfer mixture to blender; cover and process until blended. Cover and chill until serving.

3. Meanwhile, sprinkle tenderloin with salt and pepper; place on a rack in a shallow roasting pan. Bake, uncovered, at 350° for 40-50 minutes or until a thermometer reads 160°. Let stand for 10 minutes before slicing. Cut pork into ⅛-in. slices.

4. On four bread slices, layer the pork, jam, cheese and, if desired, watercress; top with remaining bread. Coat outsides of sandwiches with cooking spray.

5. Cook on a panini maker or indoor grill for 3-4 minutes or until bread is lightly browned.

Vegetarian Polka Dot Stew

Here's a speedy and satisfying version of traditional minestrone. The fun polka-dot shapes of the couscous, black beans and sliced baby carrots give this stew its name.
—**TEAGAN O'TOOLE** BOSTON, MA

START TO FINISH: 30 MIN. • **MAKES:** 5 SERVINGS

- 2 cups water
- 1 cup uncooked Israeli couscous
- 2 medium carrots, sliced
- 1 plum tomato, chopped
- ¼ cup chopped onion
- 1 garlic clove, minced
- 2 cans (19 ounces each) ready-to-serve tomato soup
- 1 can (15 ounces) black beans, rinsed and drained
- 1 package (10 ounces) frozen chopped spinach, thawed and squeezed dry
- 1 tablespoon minced fresh basil or 1 teaspoon dried basil
- ½ teaspoon salt
- ½ teaspoon dried oregano
- ½ teaspoon dried marjoram
- ¼ teaspoon pepper
  Shredded Parmesan cheese

In a large saucepan, bring water to a boil. Stir in the couscous, carrots, tomato, onion and garlic. Bring to a boil. Reduce heat; simmer, uncovered, for 10-15 minutes or until tender and water is absorbed. Stir in the remaining ingredients; heat through. Sprinkle with cheese.

EDITOR'S NOTE *You may substitute 1 cup quick-cooking barley for the couscous if desired.*

FROM THE WEB

This recipe is good. I cooked it in a slow cooker by putting all the ingredients in except the couscous and water. I doubled the beans, added two 14½-ounce cans of diced tomatoes, and stirred in the cooked couscous at the end.
—**RKJ620** TASTEOFHOME.COM

Asian Meatless Wraps

START TO FINISH: 10 MIN. • **MAKES:** 4 SERVINGS

- 4   frozen vegetarian chicken patties
- 1   cup coleslaw mix
- ⅓   cup Asian toasted sesame salad dressing
- 4   flour tortillas (10 inches), warmed
- ½   cup chow mein noodles
- ¼   cup sliced almonds

1. Microwave patties according to package directions. Meanwhile, combine coleslaw mix and dressing; set aside.
2. Cut patties in half; place two halves off center on each tortilla. Top with 3 tablespoon coleslaw mixture, 2 tablespoons chow mein noodles and 1 tablespoon almonds. Fold sides and ends over filling and roll up.
NOTE *This recipe was tested in a 1,100-watt microwave.*

> "I had purchased some vegetarian chicken patties but had no idea how to serve them. This recipe, an impromptu creation on a busy weeknight, turned out so well that my husband never knew it wasn't real chicken!"

—**HEIDI HEIMGARTNER** BLOOMING PRAIRIE, MN

Mango Shrimp Pitas

Mango, ginger and curry combine with a splash of lime juice to coat this juicy grilled shrimp. Stuffed in pitas, the shrimp combo makes for a fun and fabulous entree! You could also serve it on a bed of rice for a less casual presentation.

—**BEVERLY OFERRALL** LINKWOOD, MD

PREP: 15 MIN. + MARINATING • **GRILL:** 10 MIN. • **MAKES:** 4 SERVINGS

- ½   cup mango chutney
- 3   tablespoons lime juice
- 1   teaspoon grated fresh gingerroot
- ½   teaspoon curry powder
- 1   pound uncooked large shrimp, peeled and deveined
- 2   pita breads (6 inches), halved
- 8   Bibb or Boston lettuce leaves
- 1   large tomato, thinly sliced

1. In a small bowl, combine the chutney, lime juice, ginger and curry. Pour ½ cup marinade into a large resealable plastic bag; add the shrimp. Seal bag and turn to coat; refrigerate for at least 15 minutes. Cover and refrigerate remaining marinade.
2. Drain shrimp and discard marinade. Thread shrimp onto four metal or soaked wooden skewers. Moisten a paper towel with cooking oil; using long-handled tongs, lightly coat the grill rack.
3. Grill shrimp, covered, over medium heat or broil 4 in. from the heat for 6-8 minutes or until shrimp turn pink, turning frequently.
4. Fill pita halves with lettuce, tomato and shrimp; spoon reserved chutney mixture over filling.
PER SERVING *230 cal., 2 g fat (trace sat. fat), 138 mg chol., 410 mg sodium, 29 g carb., 1 g fiber, 22 g pro.* **Diabetic Exchanges:** *3 lean meat, 2 starch.*

Shaker Bean Soup

My family loves soup, especially this hearty one. We often enjoyed it during the winters when we were living in Michigan. It chases away the cold.

—DEBORAH AMRINE FORT MYERS, FL

PREP: 15 MIN. + SOAKING • **COOK:** 2¼ HOURS
MAKES: 5 QUARTS

- 1 pound dried great northern beans
- 1 meaty ham bone or 2 smoked ham hocks
- 8 cups water
- 1 large onion, chopped
- 3 celery ribs, diced
- 2 medium carrots, shredded
   Salt to taste
- ½ teaspoon pepper
- ½ teaspoon dried thyme
- 1 can (28 ounces) crushed tomatoes in puree
- 2 tablespoons brown sugar
- 1½ cups finely shredded fresh spinach

1. Soak beans according to package directions. In a Dutch oven, bring the beans, ham bone and water to a boil. Reduce heat; cover and simmer for 1½ hours or until meat easily falls off the bone.
2. Remove bone from broth; cool. Trim meat from the bone. Discard bone. Add the meat, onion, celery, carrots, salt, pepper and thyme to broth. Cover and cook for 30-60 minutes or until beans and vegetables are tender.
3. Add tomatoes and brown sugar. Cook 10 minutes longer. Just before serving, add spinach.

Stuffed Burgers on Portobellos

Here's a low-carb treat that allows my husband and me to still enjoy burgers without extra calories. It's actually a combination of several recipes pulled together into one…and nobody ever asks for a bun!

—DEBBIE DRIGGERS GREENVILLE, TX

START TO FINISH: 30 MIN. • **MAKES:** 4 SERVINGS

- 1 teaspoon Worcestershire sauce
- ½ teaspoon salt
- ½ teaspoon pepper
- 1⅓ pounds ground beef
- ½ cup shredded cheddar cheese
- 5 bacon strips, cooked and crumbled
- 4 large portobello mushrooms (about 4 inches), stems removed
- 1 tablespoon olive oil
- 4 tomato slices
- 4 lettuce leaves

1. In a large bowl, combine the Worcestershire sauce, salt and pepper. Crumble beef over mixture; mix well. Shape into eight thin patties. Combine cheese and bacon. Spoon into center of four patties. Top with remaining patties; press edges firmly to seal.
2. Grill, covered, over medium heat for 6 minutes on each side or until a thermometer reads 160° and juices run clear.
3. Meanwhile, brush the mushroom caps with oil. Grill, covered, over medium heat for 3-4 minutes on each side or until tender. Place mushrooms, rounded side down, on serving plates. Top with tomato, lettuce and burgers.

Stuffed burgers are a cinch to prepare this way.

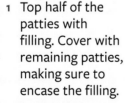

1 Top half of the patties with filling. Cover with remaining patties, making sure to encase the filling.

2 Seal the edges with a fork. Grill burgers to desired doneness.

Ginger Chicken Burgers with Sesame Slaw

Ginger and garlic give this chicken burger an Asian twist. The creamy sesame-flavored coleslaw would also go great with fish or pork.

—**DEBORAH BIGGS** OMAHA, NE

START TO FINISH: 25 MIN.
MAKES: 2 SERVINGS

- 1 teaspoon minced fresh gingerroot
- ¾ teaspoon minced garlic
- ½ teaspoon kosher salt
- ½ pound ground chicken
- 1¼ cups coleslaw mix
- 2 tablespoons thinly sliced green onion
- 2 tablespoons Asian toasted sesame salad dressing
- 1 tablespoon mayonnaise
- 1¼ teaspoons black sesame seeds or sesame seeds
- 2 sesame seed hamburger buns, split

1. In a small bowl, combine the ginger, garlic and salt. Crumble chicken over mixture and mix well. Shape into two patties. Broil 4-6 in. from the heat for 4-6 minutes on each side or until a thermometer reads 165° and juices run clear.

2. In a large bowl, combine the coleslaw mix, onion, salad dressing, mayonnaise and sesame seeds. Serve burgers on buns with coleslaw.

FROM THE WEB

The second time I made these burgers, I added a tablespoon of olive oil mayo to the mixture before grilling to keep them moist. Also brushed them with a low-sodium teriyaki sauce and added grilled pineapple for more pizazz. My guest loved the changes. This slaw is wonderful. I added toasted almond slices.

—**MSPATTYINLOVELAND**
TASTEOFHOME.COM

Cucumber-Egg Salad Sandwiches

Cool, crisp cucumber adds a refreshing crunch to these tasty egg sandwiches. I sometimes substitute rye bread for sourdough and add chopped celery to the salad mixture.

—**KELLY MCCUNE** WESTERVILLE, OH

START TO FINISH: 15 MIN. • **MAKES:** 6 SERVINGS

- ½ **cup chopped red onion**
- ½ **cup mayonnaise**
- ¼ **cup sour cream**
- 2 **tablespoons Dijon mustard**
- ½ **teaspoon pepper**
- ¼ **teaspoon salt**
- 8 **hard-cooked eggs, chopped**
- 1 **large cucumber, sliced**
- 1 **tablespoon dill weed**
- 12 **slices sourdough bread, toasted**

In a small bowl, combine the first six ingredients. Add eggs; stir gently to combine. In another bowl, toss cucumber and dill. Spread egg salad over six slices of toast; top with cucumbers and remaining toast.

Apricot Turkey Sandwiches

Apricot jam and Dijon mustard come together for a wonderful spread on this sandwich stacked with Swiss cheese, turkey bacon and peppered turkey slices.

—**CHARLOTTE GEHLE** BROWNSTOWN, MI

START TO FINISH: 15 MIN. • **MAKES:** 2 SERVINGS

- 2 **turkey bacon strips**
- 4 **pieces multigrain bread, toasted**
- 2 **tablespoons apricot jam**
- 3 **ounces thinly sliced deli peppered turkey**
- 2 **slices tomato**
- 2 **slices red onion**
- 2 **pieces leaf lettuce**
- 2 **slices reduced-fat Swiss cheese**
- 4 **teaspoons Dijon mustard**

1. In a small skillet, cook bacon over medium heat until crisp. Remove to paper towels to drain.
2. Spread two toast slices with jam. Layer with turkey, bacon, tomato, onion, lettuce and cheese. Spread remaining toast with mustard; place on top.

Portobello Burgers with Pear-Walnut Mayonnaise

Looking for a gourmet-style veggie burger? Go with portobellos, the filet mignon of mushrooms. A dollop of nutty pear mayonnaise adds subtle sweetness.

—**LINDSAY SPRUNK** NOBLESVILLE, IN

PREP: 30 MIN. + MARINATING • **GRILL:** 10 MIN.
MAKES: 4 SERVINGS

- ¼ cup olive oil
- ¼ cup balsamic vinegar
- 3 garlic cloves, minced
- 1 tablespoon minced fresh thyme or 1 teaspoon dried thyme
- 4 large portobello mushrooms, stems removed
- 1 medium pear, peeled and chopped
- 1 tablespoon olive oil
- 1 tablespoon lemon juice
- 2 tablespoons mayonnaise
- 4½ teaspoons chopped walnuts
- 4 slices onion
- 6 ounces Gorgonzola cheese, thinly sliced
- 4 whole wheat hamburger buns, split
- 2 cups fresh arugula

1. In a large resealable plastic bag, combine the oil, vinegar, garlic and thyme. Add mushrooms; seal bag and turn to coat. Refrigerate for up to 2 hours.
2. In a small skillet over medium heat, cook pear in oil and lemon juice until tender. Transfer to a small food processor; cover and process until blended. Stir in mayonnaise and walnuts. Refrigerate until serving.
3. Drain mushrooms and discard marinade. Grill mushrooms, covered, over medium heat or broil 4 in. from the heat for 3-4 minutes on each side or until tender. Top with onion and cheese.
4. Grill 2-3 minutes longer or until cheese is melted. Serve on buns with mayonnaise mixture and arugula.

PORTOBELLOS SATISFY

With their rich taste and meaty texture, portobello mushrooms make vegetarian meals feel wonderfully satisfying. They are fully grown cremini mushrooms, a cousin of the familiar button mushrooms found in most stores. The portobellos' stems are tough and woody; either discard them, or use well-rinsed and coarsely chopped stems in soups or broth.

Italian Sausage with Peppers

Local fairs in these parts are famous for sausage-and-pepper sandwiches. I came up with my own recipe so our friends and family can savor the tasty treats year-round.

—**BECKI CLEMETSON** SHARPSVILLE, PA

PREP: 40 MIN. • **BAKE:** 35 MIN. • **MAKES:** 8 SERVINGS

- 5 Hungarian wax peppers
- 1 large sweet yellow pepper
- 1 large sweet red pepper
- 2 medium sweet onions, chopped
- 2 tablespoons olive oil
- 1 can (14½ ounces) Italian diced tomatoes, undrained
- 1 can (6 ounces) tomato paste
- ½ cup water
- 4 garlic cloves, minced
- 2 bay leaves
- 1 tablespoon dried parsley flakes
- ½ teaspoon dried basil
- ½ teaspoon dried oregano
- ½ teaspoon salt
- ⅛ teaspoon white pepper
- 8 Italian sausage links (4 ounces each)
- 8 hoagie buns, split

1. Seed wax peppers if desired; cut wax and bell peppers into 2-in. pieces. In a large skillet, saute peppers and onions in oil until tender. Stir in the tomatoes, tomato paste, water, garlic, bay leaves and seasonings; heat through.
2. Meanwhile, in another large skillet, brown sausages. Transfer to an ungreased 13-in. x 9-in. baking dish. Top with pepper mixture.
3. Cover and bake at 350° for 35-40 minutes or until a thermometer reads 160°. Discard bay leaves. Serve on buns.
NOTE *Wear disposable gloves when cutting hot peppers; the oils can burn skin. Avoid touching your face.*

Creamy Reuben Soup

I had a professor in college who loved Reuben sandwiches. When he got the flu, I came up with this creamy stick-to-your-ribs soup. He really enjoyed it!

—**JAY DAVIS** KNOXVILLE, TN

START TO FINISH: 30 MIN. • **MAKES:** 5 CUPS

- ½ cup chopped onion
- ¼ cup chopped celery
- ¼ cup chopped green pepper
- ¼ cup butter, cubed
- 2 tablespoons all-purpose flour
- 1 cup beef broth
- 2 cups half-and-half cream
- ¼ pound sliced deli corned beef, coarsely chopped
- ¾ cup sauerkraut, rinsed and well drained
- ¼ teaspoon salt
- ¼ teaspoon pepper
- 1 cup (4 ounces) shredded Swiss cheese

1. In a large saucepan, saute the onion, celery and green pepper in butter until tender. Stir in flour until blended; gradually add broth. Bring to a boil; cook and stir for 2 minutes or until thickened.

2. Reduce heat to low. Add the cream, corned beef, sauerkraut, salt and pepper; heat through (do not boil). Stir in cheese until melted.

Breaded Eggplant Sandwiches

Eggplant Parmesan is one of my family's favorite comfort foods. We love this sandwich rendition, especially served alongside a healthful green salad.

—**HOLLY GOMEZ** SEABROOK, NH

PREP: 30 MIN. • **BAKE:** 25 MIN. • **MAKES:** 6 SERVINGS

- ¼ cup minced fresh basil
- 2 teaspoons olive oil
- ¼ teaspoon dried oregano
- ¼ teaspoon pepper
- ⅛ teaspoon salt
- 2 egg whites, lightly beaten
- 1 cup seasoned bread crumbs
- 1 medium eggplant
- 2 large tomatoes
- 1½ cups (6 ounces) shredded part-skim mozzarella cheese
- 2 tablespoons grated Parmesan cheese
- 1 garlic clove, peeled
- 12 slices Italian bread (½ inch thick), toasted

1. Combine the basil, oil, oregano, pepper and salt; set aside. Place egg whites and bread crumbs in separate shallow bowls. Cut eggplant lengthwise into six slices. Dip slices in egg whites, then coat in crumbs.

2. Place on a baking sheet coated with cooking spray. Bake at 375° for 20-25 minutes or until tender and golden brown, turning once.

3. Cut each tomato into six slices; place two slices on each eggplant slice. Spoon reserved basil mixture over tomatoes and sprinkle with cheeses. Bake for 3-5 minutes or until cheese is melted.

4. Meanwhile, rub garlic over one side of each bread slice; discard garlic or save for another use. Place each eggplant stack on a slice of bread; top with remaining bread.

PER SERVING *288 cal., 9 g fat (4 g sat. fat), 18 mg chol., 628 mg sodium, 38 g carb., 5 g fiber, 15 g pro.* **Diabetic Exchanges:** *2 starch, 1 lean meat, 1 vegetable, 1 fat.*

Yellow Tomato Soup with Goat Cheese Croutons

Get your next dinner party off to an impressive start with this creamy soup. Guests will love the roasted tomato flavor and crispy bread slices. If you make it in summer, try grilling the tomatoes instead.
—**PATTERSON WATKINS** PHILADELPHIA, PA

PREP: 45 MIN. • **COOK:** 30 MIN. • **MAKES:** 6 SERVINGS

- 3 pounds yellow tomatoes, halved (about 9 medium)
- 2 tablespoons olive oil, divided
- 4 garlic cloves, minced, divided
- 1 teaspoon salt
- 1 teaspoon pepper
- 1 teaspoon minced fresh rosemary
- 1 teaspoon minced fresh thyme
- 1 large onion, chopped
- 1 cup vegetable broth
- ½ cup milk
- ½ cup heavy whipping cream

CROUTONS
- 12 slices French bread baguette (½ inch thick)
- 1 tablespoon olive oil
- 2 tablespoons prepared pesto
- ½ cup crumbled goat cheese
- 1 teaspoon pepper

1. Place tomatoes, cut side down, in a greased 15-in. x 10-in. x 1-in. baking pan; brush with 1 tablespoon oil. Sprinkle with 2 teaspoons garlic and the salt, pepper, rosemary and thyme.
2. Bake at 400° for 25-30 minutes or until tomatoes are tender and skins are charred. Cool slightly. Discard tomato skins. In a blender, process tomatoes until blended.
3. In a large saucepan, saute onion in remaining oil until tender. Add remaining garlic; saute 1 minute longer. Add broth and milk; bring to a boil. Carefully stir in tomato puree. Simmer, uncovered, for 15 minutes to allow flavors to blend. Stir in cream; heat through (do not boil).
4. Meanwhile, for croutons, place bread on a baking sheet and brush with oil. Bake for 5-6 minutes or until golden brown. Spread with pesto and sprinkle with goat cheese and pepper. Bake 2 minutes longer. Ladle soup into bowls and top with croutons.

Crab Toast

When you're in the mood for casual dining, try this toasty open-faced sandwich that's crunchy, creamy and delightfully rich. You can also serve it as an appetizer by cutting thinner slices.
—**TERI LEE RASEY** CADILLAC, MI

PREP: 20 MIN. • **BAKE:** 20 MIN. • **MAKES:** 6 SERVINGS

- 1 loaf (16 ounces) French bread
- ¼ cup butter, cubed
- 4 plum tomatoes, peeled and finely chopped, divided
- 1 jalapeno pepper, seeded and chopped
- 2 garlic cloves, minced
- 2 teaspoons minced fresh cilantro
- 2 packages (8 ounces each) imitation crabmeat
- ¾ cup ricotta cheese
- ½ cup sour cream
- 2 cups (8 ounces) shredded Italian cheese blend, divided

1. Cut bread in half horizontally; hollow out top and bottom, leaving 1-in. shells. Crumble removed bread; set aside.
2. In a large skillet, melt butter over medium heat; add half of the tomatoes. Add the jalapeno, garlic and cilantro; cook and stir for 4 minutes. Remove from the heat.
3. In a large bowl, combine the crab, ricotta and sour cream. Stir in the tomato mixture, reserved bread crumbs and 1 cup cheese blend. Spoon into bread shells. Place on an ungreased baking sheet. Bake at 375° for 15 minutes. Top with remaining cheese blend and tomatoes. Bake 5-7 minutes longer or until cheese is melted.
NOTE *Wear disposable gloves when cutting hot peppers; the oils can burn skin. Avoid touching your face.*

Spicy Chicken Chili

My recipe was inspired by the low-calorie, low-fat, high-fiber diet I was on at the time. I entered it in a chili cook-off and had several people say that it was the best chili they'd ever had!

—NATALIE HUGHES JOPLIN, MO

PREP: 30 MIN. • **COOK:** 30 MIN. • **MAKES:** 12 SERVINGS (4 QUARTS)

- 1 small onion, chopped
- 1 small green pepper, chopped
- 1 small sweet red pepper, chopped
- 2 jalapeno peppers, seeded and chopped
- 1 serrano pepper, seeded and chopped
- 1 tablespoon olive oil
- 3 garlic cloves, minced
- 1 can (28 ounces) crushed tomatoes
- 1 can (14½ ounces) stewed tomatoes, cut up
- 1 can (14½ ounces) diced tomatoes with mild green chilies
- 1 can (16 ounces) kidney beans, rinsed and drained
- 1 can (15 ounces) black beans, rinsed and drained
- 1 carton (32 ounces) reduced-sodium chicken broth
- 3 tablespoons chili powder
- 1 tablespoon ground cumin
- 1 to 2 teaspoons crushed red pepper flakes
- 2 to 4 tablespoons Louisiana-style hot sauce
- 2½ cups cubed cooked chicken breast
- 2 cups frozen corn
- ¾ cup reduced-fat sour cream
- ¾ cup shredded reduced-fat cheddar cheese

1. In a Dutch oven, saute the first five ingredients in oil until tender. Add garlic; cook 1 minute longer. Add the tomatoes, beans, broth, seasonings and hot sauce. Bring to a boil. Reduce heat; simmer, uncovered, for 15 minutes.

2. Stir in chicken and corn; heat through. Garnish each serving with 1 tablespoon each of sour cream and cheese.

NOTE *Wear disposable gloves when cutting hot peppers; the oils can burn skin. Avoid touching your face.*

PER SERVING *242 cal., 6 g fat (2 g sat. fat), 32 mg chol., 694 mg sodium, 31 g carb., 7 g fiber, 19 g pro.* **Diabetic Exchanges:** *2 lean meat, 2 vegetable, 1 starch, 1 fat.*

Turkey Sliders with Chili Cheese Mayo

Serve these juicy sliders with an assortment of toppings as a fun family dinner or a scrumptious appetizer. The chili cheese mayo adds a kick!

—LISA HUNDLEY ABERDEEN, NC

PREP: 25 MIN. • **COOK:** 10 MIN. • **MAKES:** 1 DOZEN

- 4 bacon strips
- 1 medium onion, finely chopped
- 2 garlic cloves, minced
- 2 tablespoons Worcestershire sauce
- ½ teaspoon salt
- ¼ teaspoon pepper
- 1 pound ground turkey
- 2 tablespoons olive oil
- 12 heat-and-serve rolls

MAYO
- 1 cup mayonnaise
- 1 jar (5 ounces) sharp American cheese spread
- 1 teaspoon onion powder
- 1 teaspoon garlic powder
- 1 teaspoon chili powder

TOPPINGS
- 12 small lettuce leaves
- 2 plum tomatoes, thinly sliced

1. In a large skillet, cook bacon over medium heat until crisp. Remove to paper towels; drain. Crumble bacon and set aside. In the same skillet, saute onion in the drippings until tender. Add garlic; cook 1 minute longer.

2. Transfer to a large bowl. Add the bacon, Worcestershire sauce, salt and pepper. Crumble turkey over mixture and mix well. Shape into 12 patties.

3. Cook in a large skillet in oil over medium heat for 3-4 minutes on each side or until a thermometer reads 165° and juices run clear. Meanwhile, bake rolls according to package directions.

4. For mayo, in a small bowl, combine the mayonnaise, cheese spread, onion powder, garlic powder and chili powder. Split rolls; spread with mayo. Top each burger with lettuce and tomato.

SHORTCUT TO SMOKY BURGERS

We like the smoky flavor of bacon in our burgers and meat loaf. To save time, I sometimes mix packaged bacon bits into the meat instead of cooking the bacon beforehand. Use 2 tablespoons of bacon bits for each bacon strip that your recipe may call for.

—CHARLENE F. COALDALE, AB

Portobello Waffles with Balsamic Syrup, page 82

88

77

74

Breakfast & Brunch

Glorious mornings are guaranteed with these start-the-day standouts. **Light up their faces** with citrusy **sun-kissed** doughnuts, colossal cinnamon rolls, **savory** egg dishes and **whimsical** treats!

Hot Buttered Rum Rolls

I've had this recipe for about 30 years and consider it one of my top choices. If you enjoy something sweet with breakfast, you'll love these melt-in-your-mouth rum rolls.

—ROSALIE PETERS CALDWELL, TX

PREP: 35 MIN. + RISING • **BAKE:** 15 MIN. • **MAKES:** 8 ROLLS

- 1¼ teaspoons active dry yeast
- ¼ cup plus 2 tablespoons warm water (110° to 115°)
- 2 tablespoons sugar
- 2 tablespoons beaten egg
- 1 tablespoon plus 1 teaspoon canola oil
- ⅛ teaspoon salt
- 1 to 1¼ cups all-purpose flour

TOPPING
- 2 tablespoons butter
- ¼ cup packed brown sugar
- 1½ teaspoons 2% milk
- 1 teaspoon all-purpose flour
- ¼ to ½ teaspoon rum extract

FILLING
- ¼ cup chopped pecans
- ¼ cup packed brown sugar
- 2 tablespoons butter, melted
- ¼ teaspoon rum extract

1. In a large bowl, dissolve yeast in warm water. Add the sugar, egg, oil, salt and ½ cup flour. Beat on medium speed for 3 minutes or until smooth. Stir in enough remaining flour to form a soft dough (dough will be sticky).

2. Turn onto a lightly floured surface; knead until smooth and elastic, about 6-8 minutes. Place in a bowl coated with cooking spray, turning once to coat the top. Cover and let rise in a warm place until doubled, about 1 hour.

3. For topping, in a small saucepan, melt butter over medium heat. Stir in brown sugar, milk, flour and extract. Bring to a boil; cook and stir until smooth. Pour into a 9-in. round baking pan coated with cooking spray; set aside.

4. Punch dough down. Turn onto a lightly floured surface; roll into an 8-in. square. Combine filling ingredients; spread over dough to within ½ in. of edges. Roll up jelly-roll style; pinch seam to seal. Cut into eight slices. Place rolls,

cut side down, in prepared pan. Cover and let rise until doubled, about 30 minutes.

5. Bake at 350° for 12-15 minutes or until golden brown. Immediately invert onto serving platter. Serve warm.

Ginger Currant Scones

I like to add loads of currants to these flaky scones. Served warm with a drizzle of honey, they make breakfast or brunch something to look forward to.

—SHEILA PARKER RENO, NV

PREP: 15 MIN. • **BAKE:** 20 MIN. • **MAKES:** 4 SCONES

- 1½ cups all-purpose flour
- ⅓ cup sugar
- 1 teaspoon baking powder
- ½ teaspoon baking soda
- 6 tablespoons cold butter, cubed
- ½ cup buttermilk
- ¾ cup dried currants
- ½ teaspoon minced fresh gingerroot
- 2 teaspoons honey

1. In a small bowl, combine the flour, sugar, baking powder and baking soda. Cut in butter until mixture resembles coarse crumbs. Add buttermilk just until moistened. Stir in currants and ginger. Turn onto a floured surface; knead 10 times.

2. Pat or roll out to 1-in. thickness; cut with a floured 2½-in. biscuit cutter. Place 2 in. apart on a baking sheet coated with cooking spray.

3. Bake at 375° for 20-25 minutes or until golden brown. Drizzle with honey. Serve warm.

Bear's Breakfast Burritos

Everyone loves these hearty burritos. It's so convenient to freeze some and bake them for a lazy Saturday breakfast.

—LARRY & SANDY KELLEY GRANGEVILLE, ID

PREP: 45 MIN. • **COOK:** 15 MIN. • **MAKES:** 12 SERVINGS

- 2 **packages (22½ ounces each) frozen hash brown patties**
- 15 **eggs, lightly beaten**
- 2 **tablespoons chili powder**
- 2 **tablespoons garlic salt**
- 1 **tablespoon ground cumin**
- ½ **pound uncooked chorizo or bulk spicy pork sausage**
- 6 **jalapeno peppers, seeded and minced**
- 1 **large green pepper, chopped**
- 1 **large sweet red pepper, chopped**
- 1 **large onion, chopped**
- 1 **bunch green onions, chopped**
- 3 **cups salsa**
- 12 **flour tortillas (12 inches), warmed**
- 4 **cups (16 ounces) shredded Monterey Jack cheese**
  Sour cream, optional

1. Cook hash browns according to package directions; crumble and keep warm. Meanwhile, in a large bowl, whisk the eggs, chili powder, garlic salt and cumin. Set aside.

2. Crumble chorizo into a large skillet; add the jalapenos, peppers and onions. Cook and stir over medium heat until chorizo is fully cooked; drain. Add egg mixture; cook and stir until eggs are set. Stir in salsa.

3. Spoon ½ cup hash browns and ½ cup egg mixture off center on each tortilla; sprinkle with ⅓ cup cheese. Fold sides and ends over filling and roll up. Wrap each burrito in waxed paper and foil. Serve warm with sour cream if desired. Cool remaining burritos to room temperature; freeze for up to 1 month.

TO USE FROZEN BURRITOS *Remove foil and waxed paper. Place burritos 2 in. apart on an ungreased baking sheet. Bake, uncovered, at 350° for 50-55 minutes or until heated through.*

NOTE *Wear disposable gloves when cutting hot peppers; the oils can burn skin. Avoid touching your face.*

Monkey Muffins

These bite-sized mini muffins will be a favorite with your family and friends—or anyone who loves bananas, peanut butter and chocolate! A nice way to use up overripe bananas.

—**AMIE LONGSTAFF** PAINESVILLE TOWNSHIP, OH

PREP: 20 MIN. • **BAKE:** 15 MIN./BATCH • **MAKES:** 6 DOZEN

- ½ cup butter, softened
- 1 cup plus 1 tablespoon sugar, divided
- 2 eggs
- 1 cup mashed ripe bananas
- ⅔ cup peanut butter
- 1 tablespoon milk
- 1 teaspoon vanilla extract
- 2 cups all-purpose flour
- 1 teaspoon baking soda
- ½ teaspoon salt
- ¾ cup miniature semisweet chocolate chips

1. In a large bowl, cream butter and 1 cup sugar until light and fluffy. Add eggs, one at a time, beating well after each addition. Beat in the bananas, peanut butter, milk and vanilla. Combine the flour, baking soda and salt; add to creamed mixture just until moistened. Fold in chips.
2. Fill greased or paper-lined miniature muffin cups three-fourths full. Sprinkle with remaining sugar. Bake at 350° for 14-16 minutes or until a toothpick inserted near the center comes out clean. Cool for 5 minutes before removing from pans to wire racks. Serve warm.
TO FREEZE *Wrap muffins in foil and freeze for up to 3 months.*
TO USE FROZEN MUFFINS *Thaw at room temperature. Warm if desired.*
PER (2-MUFFIN) SERVING *126 cal., 6 g fat (3 g sat. fat), 18 mg chol., 112 mg sodium, 16 g carb., 1 g fiber, 3 g pro.*
Diabetic Exchanges: *1 starch, 1 fat.*

Peanut Butter & Jelly Waffles

Crisp and full of peanut butter flavor, these fun waffles are a sure way to get the kids to eat breakfast. No syrup is required, just add their favorite flavor of jelly.

—**HELENA GEORGETTE MANN** SACRAMENTO, CA

START TO FINISH: 25 MIN. • **MAKES:** 10 WAFFLES

- 1¼ cups all-purpose flour
- 3 tablespoons sugar
- 1 tablespoon baking powder
- ¼ teaspoon baking soda
- ¼ teaspoon ground cinnamon
- 2 eggs, separated
- 1¼ cups milk
- ⅓ cup peanut butter
- 3 tablespoons butter, melted
  Jelly of your choice

1. In a large bowl, combine the flour, sugar, baking powder, baking soda and cinnamon. In another bowl, whisk the egg yolks, milk, peanut butter and butter; stir mixture into dry ingredients just until moistened.
2. In a small bowl, beat egg whites until stiff peaks form; fold into batter. Bake in a preheated waffle iron according to manufacturer's directions until golden brown. Serve with jelly.
TO FREEZE *Arrange waffles in a single layer on pans. Freeze overnight or until frozen. Transfer to a resealable plastic freezer bag. Waffles may be frozen for up to 2 months.*
TO USE FROZEN WAFFLES *Reheat waffles in a toaster. Serve with jelly.*

Blueberry Oat Pancakes

I use ground oats in this recipe, which boosts the health value. But oats aren't the only power food in these fluffy pancakes: You get plenty of bursting-with-flavor blueberries in every bite, too!

—**CANDY SUMMERHILL** ALEXANDER, AR

PREP: 20 MIN. • **COOK:** 5 MIN./BATCH • **MAKES:** 10 PANCAKES

- ¾ cup quick-cooking oats, divided
- 3 tablespoons orange juice
- 1 egg, lightly beaten
- ⅔ cup fat-free evaporated milk
- ¼ cup reduced-fat sour cream
- 2 tablespoons unsweetened applesauce
- ½ teaspoon vanilla extract
- ½ cup whole wheat flour
- ¼ cup all-purpose flour
- 3 tablespoons brown sugar
- 1 teaspoon baking powder
- ½ teaspoon ground cinnamon
- ¼ teaspoon salt
- ¼ teaspoon baking soda
- 1 cup fresh or frozen blueberries

1. In a small bowl, combine ¼ cup oats and orange juice; let stand for 5 minutes. Stir in the egg, milk, sour cream, applesauce and vanilla; set aside.

2. Place remaining oats in a small food processor; cover and process until ground. Transfer to a large bowl; add the flours, brown sugar, baking powder, cinnamon, salt and baking soda. Stir in the wet ingredients just until moistened.

3. Pour batter by ¼ cupfuls onto a hot griddle coated with cooking spray; sprinkle with blueberries. Turn when bubbles form on top; cook until second side is golden brown.

PER (2-PANCAKE) SERVING *221 cal., 3 g fat (1 g sat. fat), 48 mg chol., 327 mg sodium, 41 g carb., 4 g fiber, 9 g pro. Diabetic Exchanges: 2 starch, ½ fruit, ½ fat.*

Fruit Salad with O.J. Reduction

PREP: 15 MIN. • **COOK:** 25 MIN.
MAKES: 12 SERVINGS (¾ CUP EACH)

- 2 medium red apples, cubed
- 1 medium green apple, cubed
- 2 medium peaches, cubed
- 2 tablespoons lemon juice
- 1 cup orange juice
- ⅓ cup sugar
- 2 medium navel oranges, peeled, sectioned and chopped
- 2 cups fresh blueberries

1. Place the apples, peaches and lemon juice in a large bowl. Cover with water; set aside.

2. In a small saucepan, combine orange juice and sugar. Bring to a boil; cook until liquid is reduced to about ½ cup. Drain apple mixture. Add the oranges, blueberries and orange juice mixture; toss to coat.

PER SERVING *75 cal., trace fat (trace sat. fat), 0 chol., 1 mg sodium, 19 g carb., 2 g fiber, 1 g pro. Diabetic Exchange: 1 fruit.*

❝This fruit fusion is best prepared an hour or two before you are ready to serve. Its brilliant colors and beautiful arrangement bring on the wows.❞

—**ROGER EBERLIN** BALTIMORE, MD

Chocolate Peppermint Scones

I deck out these scones in peppermint candy for the holidays and serve them with afternoon coffee and mint tea. They also make an extra-special breakfast or brunch treat.

—**SHELLY PLATTEN** AMHERST, WI

PREP: 25 MIN. • **BAKE:** 20 MIN.
MAKES: 1 DOZEN

- 2 **cups all-purpose flour**
- ½ **cup whole wheat pastry flour**
- ½ **cup baking cocoa**
- ½ **cup packed brown sugar**
- 2 **teaspoons baking powder**
- 1 **teaspoon baking soda**
- ½ **cup cold butter, cubed**
- ¾ **cup (6 ounces) vanilla yogurt**
- ½ **cup buttermilk**
- 1 **egg**
- 1 **teaspoon peppermint extract**
- 1 **cup 60% cacao bittersweet chocolate baking chips**
- 1 **tablespoon coarse sugar**
- 2 **ounces bittersweet chocolate, melted**
- ¼ **cup crushed peppermint candies**

1. In a large bowl, combine the first six ingredients. Cut in butter until mixture resembles coarse crumbs. In a small bowl, whisk the yogurt, buttermilk, egg and extract; add to crumb mixture just until moistened. Stir in chocolate chips.

2. Turn onto a floured surface; knead 10 times. Divide dough in half; transfer each portion to a greased baking sheet. Pat into a 6-in. circle. Cut into six wedges, but do not separate. Sprinkle with coarse sugar.

3. Bake at 400° for 18-20 minutes or until puffed and tops are cracked. Remove to wire racks; cool slightly. Drizzle with melted chocolate and sprinkle with peppermint candies. Serve warm.

Spiral Omelet Supreme

You can substitute 2 cups of any combination of your favorite omelet fillings for the vegetables in this recipe. A serrated knife works well for slicing it.

—**DEBBIE MORRIS** HAMILTON, OH

PREP: 20 MIN. • **BAKE:** 20 MIN. • **MAKES:** 8 SERVINGS

- 4 ounces cream cheese, softened
- ¾ cup 2% milk
- ¼ cup plus 2 tablespoons grated Parmesan cheese, divided
- 2 tablespoons all-purpose flour
- 12 eggs
- 1 large green pepper, chopped
- 1 cup sliced fresh mushrooms
- 1 small onion, chopped
- 2 teaspoons canola oil
- 1½ cups (6 ounces) shredded part-skim mozzarella cheese
- 1 plum tomato, seeded and chopped
- 1¼ teaspoons Italian seasoning, divided

1. Line the bottom and sides of a greased 15-in. x 10-in. x 1-in. baking pan with parchment paper; grease the paper and set aside.

2. In a small bowl, beat cream cheese and milk until smooth. Beat in ¼ cup Parmesan cheese and flour until blended. In a large bowl, beat eggs; add cream cheese mixture and mix well. Pour into prepared pan.

3. Bake at 375° for 20-25 minutes or until set. Meanwhile, in a large skillet, saute the pepper, mushrooms and onion in oil until crisp-tender. Keep warm.

4. Turn omelet onto a work surface; peel off parchment paper. Sprinkle with the vegetable mixture, mozzarella cheese, tomato and 1 teaspoon Italian seasoning. Roll up jelly-roll style, starting with a short side. Place on a serving platter. Sprinkle with remaining Parmesan cheese and Italian seasoning.

Benedict Eggs in Pastry

Here's a new twist on an old favorite. Inside these puffy golden bundles is an omelet-like filling of eggs, ham, cheese and rich, lemony hollandaise sauce.

—**CATHY SLUSSLER** MAGNOLIA, TX

PREP: 30 MIN. • **BAKE:** 20 MIN. • **MAKES:** 4 SERVINGS

- 2 egg yolks
- 2 tablespoons lemon juice
- 1 teaspoon Dijon mustard
- ½ cup butter, melted
  Dash cayenne pepper
- 2 cups cubed fully cooked ham
- 2 green onions, chopped
- 1 tablespoon butter
- 6 eggs
- 2 tablespoons 2% milk
- 1 package (17.3 ounces) frozen puff pastry, thawed
- 1 cup (4 ounces) shredded cheddar cheese

EGG WASH
- 1 egg
- 1 tablespoon water
  Minced fresh tarragon, optional

1. In a double boiler over simmering water or a small heavy saucepan, constantly whisk the egg yolks, lemon juice and mustard until mixture begins to thicken and reaches 160°. Reduce heat to low. Slowly drizzle in warm melted butter, whisking constantly. Whisk in cayenne. Keep warm, stirring occasionally, until ready to use.

2. In a large skillet over medium heat, cook and stir ham and onions in butter until onions are tender. In a large bowl, whisk eggs and milk. Add egg mixture to the pan; cook and stir until set. Remove from the heat; stir in ⅓ cup reserved hollandaise sauce. Set aside.

3. On a lightly floured surface, unfold puff pastry. Roll each sheet into a 12-in. x 9½-in. rectangle; cut each in half widthwise. Place 1 cup egg mixture on half of each rectangle; sprinkle with cheese.

4. Beat egg and water; brush over pastry edges. Bring an opposite corner of pastry over the egg mixture; pinch seams to seal. With a small sharp knife, cut several slits in the top.

5. Transfer to a greased baking sheet; brush with remaining egg mixture. Bake at 400° for 18-22 minutes or until golden brown. Serve with remaining hollandaise sauce. Sprinkle with tarragon if desired.

Banana Chip Pancakes

Birthday-morning special, these fluffy pancakes can be customized to your heart's content! One of my kids eats the plain banana pancakes, another likes just chocolate chips added, and a third one goes for the works.
—**CHRISTEEN PRZEPIOSKI** NEWARK, CA

START TO FINISH: 30 MIN. • **MAKES:** 12 PANCAKES

- 2 cups biscuit/baking mix
- 1 egg
- 1 cup milk
- 1 cup mashed ripe bananas
- ¾ cup swirled milk chocolate and peanut butter chips
  Maple syrup and additional swirled milk chocolate and peanut butter chips, optional

1. Place biscuit mix in a large bowl. Combine the egg, milk and bananas; stir into biscuit mix just until moistened. Stir in chips.

2. Pour batter by ¼ cupfuls onto a greased hot griddle; turn when bubbles form on top. Cook until the second side is golden brown. Serve with syrup and additional chips if desired.

Baked Blueberry & Peach Oatmeal

This oatmeal bake is a staple in our home. It's very easy to prepare the night before—just keep the dry and wet ingredients separate until ready to bake. I've tried a variety of fruits, but the blueberry and peach is our favorite.
—**ROSEMARIE WELESKI** NATRONA HEIGHTS, PA

PREP: 20 MIN. • **BAKE:** 35 MIN. • **MAKES:** 9 SERVINGS

- 3 cups old-fashioned oats
- ½ cup packed brown sugar
- 2 teaspoons baking powder
- ½ teaspoon salt
- 2 egg whites
- 1 egg
- 1¼ cups fat-free milk
- ¼ cup canola oil
- 1 teaspoon vanilla extract
- 1 can (15 ounces) sliced peaches in juice, drained and chopped
- 1 cup fresh or frozen blueberries
- ⅓ cup chopped walnuts
  Additional fat-free milk, optional

1. In a large bowl, combine the oats, brown sugar, baking powder and salt. Whisk the egg whites, egg, milk, oil and vanilla; add to dry ingredients and stir until blended. Let stand for 5 minutes. Stir in peaches and blueberries.

2. Transfer to an 11-in. x 7-in. baking dish coated with cooking spray. Sprinkle with walnuts. Bake, uncovered, at 350° for 35-40 minutes or until top is lightly browned and a thermometer reads 160°. Serve with additional milk if desired.

PER SERVING *277 cal., 11 g fat (1 g sat. fat), 24 mg chol., 263 mg sodium, 38 g carb., 3 g fiber, 8 g pro. **Diabetic Exchanges:** 2 starch, 2 fat, ½ fruit.*

Cook up perfect pancakes with these pointers.

Allow several inches between pancakes on the griddle. Flip them when the edges become dry and the bubbles that appear on top begin to pop.

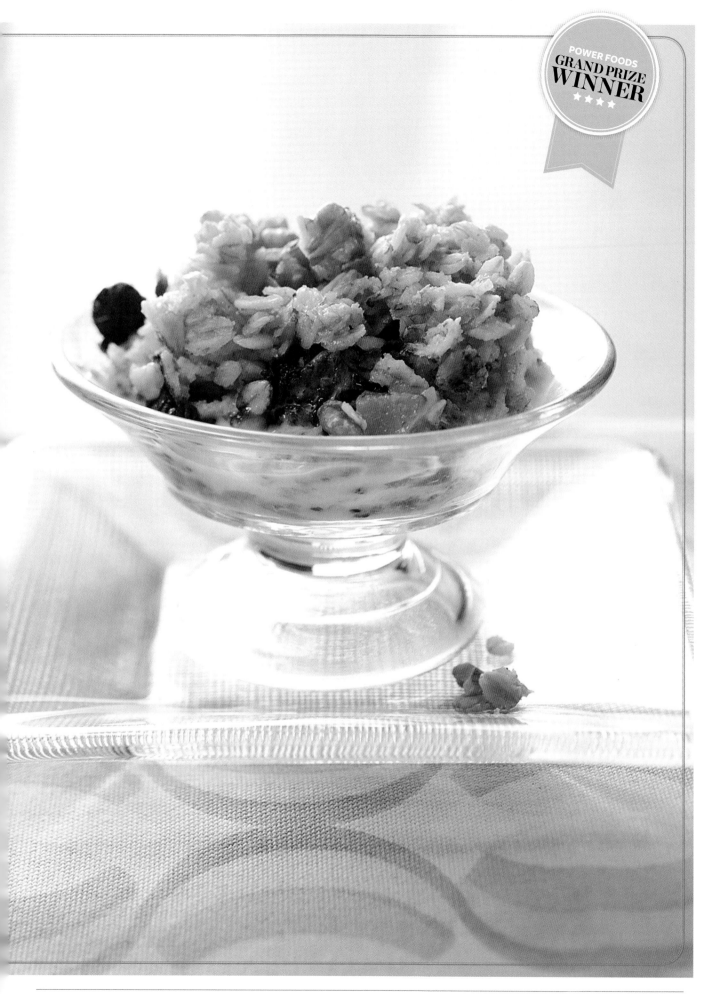

Raspberry Cheese Blintz Bake

For a special breakfast, try this twist on traditional blintzes. It puffs during baking and will fall a bit while standing. It makes a beautiful presentation.

—KRISTI TWOHIG WATERLOO, WI

PREP: 25 MIN. • **BAKE:** 40 MIN. + STANDING • **MAKES:** 12 SERVINGS

- ½ cup orange juice
- 6 eggs
- 2 egg whites
- 1½ cups (12 ounces) sour cream
- 1 cup all-purpose flour
- ½ cup sugar
- ¼ cup butter, softened
- 2 teaspoons baking powder
- 1 teaspoon grated orange peel
- 1 teaspoon vanilla extract
  - Dash salt

FILLING
- 2 egg yolks
- 1 teaspoon vanilla extract
- 2 cups (16 ounces) 4% cottage cheese
- 1 package (8 ounces) cream cheese, softened
- ¼ cup sugar

TOPPING
- 1 package (12 ounces) frozen unsweetened raspberries, thawed
- 2 tablespoons cornstarch
- ¾ cup orange juice
  - Mandarin oranges, optional

1. Combine the first 11 ingredients in a blender. Cover and process until smooth. Set aside 2 cups of batter; pour remaining batter into a greased 13-in. x 9-in. baking dish.
2. For filling, combine the egg yolks, vanilla, cottage cheese, cream cheese and sugar in a blender. Cover and process until smooth. Spoon filling over batter; cut through with a knife to swirl. Top with reserved batter. Bake, uncovered, at 350° for 40-45 minutes or until center is just set (mixture will jiggle). Let stand for 10 minutes before cutting.
3. For topping, press raspberries through a strainer; discard seeds and pulp. In a small saucepan, combine cornstarch and orange juice until smooth; stir in raspberry puree. Bring to a boil. Cook and stir for 2 minutes or until thickened. Serve with blintz bake. Top with mandarin oranges if desired.

Portobello Waffles with Balsamic Syrup

For a delightful breakfast or brunch surprise, serve crisp golden waffles that feature portobello mushrooms and bacon in the batter. They're topped with tangy goat cheese butter and a drizzle of sweet balsamic reduction.

—DAVID BRIDGES SHREVEPORT, LA

PREP: 40 MIN. • **COOK:** 5 MIN./BATCH
MAKES: 16 WAFFLES (1 CUP BUTTER AND ⅓ CUP SYRUP)

- 1 cup balsamic vinegar
- 2 tablespoons brown sugar
- 2 bacon strips, chopped
- ½ cup butter, softened
- ⅓ cup crumbled goat cheese
- ½ pound portobello mushrooms, stems removed, cubed
- 2 tablespoons olive oil
- 1¾ cups all-purpose flour
- 1 teaspoon baking powder
- ½ teaspoon baking soda
- ½ teaspoon dried thyme
- ½ teaspoon pepper
- ¼ teaspoon salt
- 2 eggs
- 1½ cups plus 2 tablespoons milk
- ½ cup canola oil

1. In a small saucepan, combine vinegar and brown sugar. Bring to a boil; cook until liquid is reduced to ⅓ cup. In a small skillet, cook bacon over medium heat until crisp. Transfer bacon and drippings to a small bowl; cool slightly. Add butter and goat cheese; beat until blended.
2. In a large skillet, saute mushrooms in oil until tender; cool slightly. Place ¼ cup mushrooms in a food processor. Cover and process until very finely chopped. In a large bowl, combine the flour, baking powder, baking soda, thyme, pepper and salt. In another bowl, combine the eggs, milk, oil and chopped mushrooms; add to dry ingredients just until moistened. Fold in the cubed mushrooms.
3. Bake in a preheated waffle iron according to manufacturer's directions until golden brown. Serve with goat cheese butter and balsamic syrup.

Double-Chip Pumpkin Cinnamon Muffins

I lightened up an old-fashioned recipe I found and this is the result. These delicious muffins taste just as good a day or two later, if they last that long!

—VERA DECKER WINDSOR, NY

PREP: 20 MIN. • **BAKE:** 15 MIN. + COOLING • **MAKES:** 2 DOZEN

- 1 can (15 ounces) solid-pack pumpkin
- 1 cup sugar
- ½ cup buttermilk
- ⅓ cup canola oil
- 2 eggs
- 2 egg whites
- 1 teaspoon vanilla extract
- 2 cups all-purpose flour
- ½ cup oat flour
- 2 teaspoons baking powder
- 1 teaspoon baking soda
- 1 teaspoon ground cinnamon
- ½ teaspoon salt
- ¼ teaspoon ground nutmeg
- ½ cup cinnamon baking chips, chopped
- ½ cup miniature semisweet chocolate chips

TOPPING

- ¼ cup sugar
- 3 teaspoons ground cinnamon

1. In a large bowl, beat the first seven ingredients until well blended. Combine the flours, baking powder, baking soda, cinnamon, salt and nutmeg; gradually beat into pumpkin mixture until blended. Stir in chips.

2. Coat muffin cups with cooking spray or use foil liners; fill two-thirds full with batter. Combine topping ingredients; sprinkle over batter.

3. Bake at 400° for 12-15 minutes or until a toothpick comes out clean. Cool for 5 minutes before removing from pans to wire racks.

NOTE *As a substitute for 1 cup oat flour, process 1¼ cups quick-cooking or old-fashioned oats until finely ground.*

PER SERVING *174 cal., 6 g fat (2 g sat. fat), 18 mg chol., 164 mg sodium, 27 g carb., 2 g fiber, 3 g pro.* **Diabetic Exchanges:** *2 starch, 1 fat.*

Bistro Breakfast Panini

After trying an omelet that contained Brie, bacon and apples, I thought it might be tasty as a breakfast panini—and it is!

—KATHY HARDING RICHMOND, MO

START TO FINISH: 25 MIN. • **MAKES:** 2 SERVINGS

- 6 bacon strips
- 1 teaspoon butter
- 4 eggs, beaten
- 4 slices sourdough bread (¾ inch thick)
- ⅛ teaspoon salt
- ⅛ teaspoon pepper
- 3 ounces Brie cheese, thinly sliced
- 8 thin slices apple
- ½ cup fresh baby spinach
- 2 tablespoons butter, softened

1. In a large skillet, cook bacon over medium heat until crisp. Remove to paper towels to drain.

2. Meanwhile, heat butter in a large skillet over medium heat. Add eggs; cook and stir until set.

3. Place eggs on two slices of bread; sprinkle with salt and pepper. Layer with cheese, apple, bacon, spinach and remaining bread. Butter outsides of sandwiches.

4. Cook on a panini maker or indoor grill for 3-4 minutes or until bread is browned and cheese is melted.

SIMPLE SKILLET PANINI

If you don't have a panini maker or indoor grill, simply cook the sandwiches in a large skillet with a bit of melted butter, as you would a grilled cheese. If desired, weigh down the panini as they cook with a clean cast-iron skillet that is free of rust.

Chocolate Ribbon Banana Loaf

This bread is a combination of three of my best-loved foods: bananas, chocolate and peanut butter. I try to make other quick breads but this one is always requested the most.

—SHARON GILJUM ARLINGTON, VA

PREP: 20 MIN. • **BAKE:** 40 MIN. + COOLING
MAKES: 1 LOAF (12 SLICES)

- ¼ cup butter, softened
- 1 cup sugar
- 2 eggs
- 1 cup mashed ripe bananas (about 2 medium)
- ⅓ cup fat-free plain yogurt
- 1 teaspoon vanilla extract
- 1½ cups all-purpose flour
- ½ cup whole wheat pastry flour
- ¾ teaspoon baking soda
- ½ teaspoon salt
- ½ teaspoon ground cinnamon
- ½ cup peanut butter chips
- ½ cup semisweet chocolate chips, melted

1. In a large bowl, beat butter and sugar until crumbly. Add eggs, one at a time, beating well after each addition. Beat in the bananas, yogurt and vanilla. Combine the flours, baking soda, salt and cinnamon; gradually add to butter mixture just until moistened. Fold in peanut butter chips.

2. Remove 1 cup of batter to a small bowl; stir in chocolate until well blended. Pour half of the remaining plain batter into a 9-in. x 5-in. loaf pan coated with cooking spray; top with half of the chocolate batter. Repeat layers. Cut through batter with a knife to swirl.

3. Bake at 350° for 40-50 minutes or until a toothpick inserted near the center comes out clean. Cool 10 minutes before removing from pan to a wire rack.

PBJ-Stuffed French Toast

START TO FINISH: 10 MIN. • **MAKES:** 2 SERVINGS

- 3 tablespoons cream cheese, softened
- 2 tablespoons creamy peanut butter
- 4 slices Italian bread (¾ inch thick)
- 2 tablespoons red raspberry preserves
- 2 eggs
- 1 tablespoon evaporated milk
    Maple syrup, optional

1. In a small bowl, combine cream cheese and peanut butter. Spread on two slices of bread; top with preserves and remaining bread. In a shallow bowl, whisk eggs and milk. Dip sandwiches into egg mixture.

2. In a greased large nonstick skillet, toast sandwiches for 2-3 minutes on each side or until golden brown. Serve with syrup if desired.

❝I combined some of my favorite foods to create this delightfully different French toast. Now, it's one of my go-to recipes when I have morning guests.❞

—RUTH ANN BOTT LAKE WALES, FL

Butter Pecan French Toast

Flavored coffee creamer is the secret ingredient in this fast and easy breakfast treat the whole family will go for. I sometimes use French vanilla or caramel-flavored creamer and add a little nutmeg and cinnamon to the eggs.
—**CATHY HALL** LYNDHURST, VA

START TO FINISH: 25 MIN.
MAKES: 3 SERVINGS

- 1 teaspoon plus 1 tablespoon butter, divided
- ½ cup chopped pecans
- 2 eggs
- ½ cup refrigerated Southern butter pecan nondairy creamer
- 6 slices French bread (1 inch thick)
- ¼ cup confectioners' sugar
- ¼ teaspoon ground cinnamon
  Maple syrup, optional

1. In a small skillet, melt 1 teaspoon butter over medium heat. Add the pecans; cook and stir for 3 minutes or until toasted.

2. In a shallow bowl, whisk the eggs and creamer. Dip bread slices in the egg mixture.

3. In a large skillet, melt remaining butter over medium heat. Cook bread for 2-3 minutes on each side or until golden brown.

4. Sprinkle the French toast with pecans, confectioners' sugar and cinnamon. Serve with maple syrup if desired.

FROM THE WEB

This is just WONDERFUL! It's an all-time family favorite. I was skeptical of using the creamer since I don't like those nondairy creamers. But in this recipe, it's great. A must-try if you like French toast.

—**MINNIE** TASTEOFHOME.COM

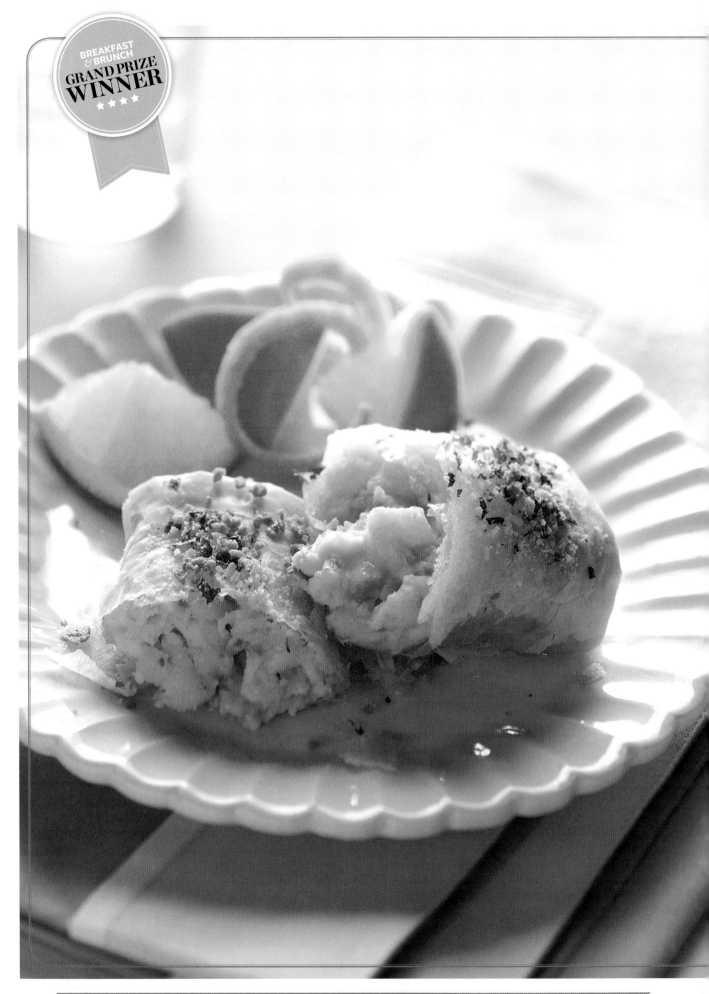

Ham & Cheese Breakfast Strudels

Golden breakfast strudels are guaranteed to get the morning off to a great start. Sometimes I assemble them ahead and freeze them individually before baking.

—JO GROTH PLAINFIELD, IA

PREP: 25 MIN. • **BAKE:** 15 MIN. • **MAKES:** 6 SERVINGS

- 3 tablespoons butter, divided
- 2 tablespoons all-purpose flour
- 1 cup milk
- ⅓ cup shredded Swiss cheese
- 2 tablespoons grated Parmesan cheese
- ¼ teaspoon salt
- 5 eggs, lightly beaten
- ¼ pound ground fully cooked ham (about ¾ cup)
- 6 sheets phyllo dough (14x9-inch size)
- ½ cup butter, melted
- ¼ cup dry bread crumbs

TOPPING
- 2 tablespoons grated Parmesan cheese
- 2 tablespoons minced fresh parsley

1. In a small saucepan, melt 2 tablespoons butter. Stir in flour until smooth; gradually add milk. Bring to a boil; cook and stir for 2 minutes or until thickened. Stir in cheeses and salt. Set aside.

2. In a large nonstick skillet, melt remaining butter over medium heat. Add eggs to the pan; cook and stir until almost set. Stir in ham and reserved cheese sauce; heat through. Remove from the heat.

3. Place one sheet of phyllo dough on a work surface. (Keep remaining phyllo covered with plastic wrap and a damp towel to prevent it from drying out.) Brush with melted butter. Sprinkle with 2 teaspoons bread crumbs. Fold in half lengthwise; brush again with butter. Spoon ½ cup filling onto phyllo about 2 in. from a short side. Fold side and edges over filling and roll up.

4. Brush with butter. Repeat. Place on a greased baking sheet; sprinkle each with 1 teaspoon of cheese and 1 teaspoon parsley. Bake at 375° for 10-15 minutes or until golden brown. Serve immediately.

FREEZE OPTION *After topping strudels with cheese and parsley, freeze unbaked on a waxed paper-lined baking sheet until firm. Transfer to a freezer container; return to freezer. To use, bake strudels as directed, increasing time to 30-35 minutes or until heated through and exteriors are golden brown.*

Rhubarb Coffee Cake with Caramel Sauce

When I was growing up, I couldn't wait for the rhubarb to ripen so Mom could bake this luscious coffee cake. Now, the recipe is part of my own collection.

—ANGIE FEHR OTTOSEN, IA

PREP: 20 MIN. • **BAKE:** 35 MIN. + COOLING
MAKES: 18 SERVINGS (1⅔ CUPS SAUCE)

- ½ cup shortening
- 1½ cups sugar
- 1 egg
- 2 cups all-purpose flour
- 1 teaspoon baking soda
- 1 cup buttermilk
- 1½ cups finely chopped fresh or frozen rhubarb

TOPPING
- ½ cup packed brown sugar
- ¼ cup all-purpose flour
- 1 teaspoon ground cinnamon
- 3 tablespoons cold butter

SAUCE
- ½ cup butter, cubed
- 1 cup packed brown sugar
- ½ cup heavy whipping cream

1. In a large bowl, cream shortening and sugar until light and fluffy. Add egg; beat well. Combine flour and baking soda; add to creamed mixture alternately with buttermilk. Fold in the rhubarb. Transfer to a greased 13-in. x 9-in. baking pan.

2. For topping, in a small bowl, combine the brown sugar, flour and cinnamon; cut in butter until crumbly. Sprinkle over batter.

3. Bake at 350° for 35-40 minutes or until a toothpick inserted near the center comes out clean. Cool 10 minutes before serving.

4. For sauce, in a small saucepan, melt butter. Stir in brown sugar and cream; bring to a boil. Reduce heat; simmer for 3 to 4 minutes or until slightly thickened. Serve with warm coffee cake.

Cappuccino Cinnamon Rolls

Rich coffee flavor accents the cinnamon filling of these giant cinnamon rolls. And the icing practically melts over the top for a touch of extra sweetness.

—SHERRI COX LUCASVILLE, OH

PREP: 45 MIN. + RISING • **BAKE:** 25 MIN. • **MAKES:** 1 DOZEN

- 1 package (¼ ounce) active dry yeast
- 1 cup warm water (110° to 115°)
- ¾ cup warm milk (110° to 115°)
- ½ cup warm buttermilk (110° to 115°)
- 3 tablespoons sugar
- 2 tablespoons butter, softened
- 1¼ teaspoons salt
- 5½ to 6 cups all-purpose flour

FILLING
- ¼ cup butter, melted
- 1 cup packed brown sugar
- 4 teaspoons instant coffee granules
- 2 teaspoons ground cinnamon

ICING
- 1½ cups confectioners' sugar
- 2 tablespoons butter, softened
- 1 to 2 tablespoons milk
- 2 teaspoons cappuccino mix
- ½ teaspoon vanilla extract

1. In a large bowl, dissolve yeast in warm water. Add the warm milk, buttermilk, sugar, butter, salt and 4 cups flour. Beat on medium speed until smooth. Stir in enough remaining flour to form a soft dough (dough will be sticky).

2. Turn onto a floured surface; knead until smooth and elastic, about 6-8 minutes. Place in a greased bowl, turning once to grease the top. Cover and let rise in a warm place until doubled, about 1 hour.

3. Punch dough down; turn onto a floured surface. Roll into an 18-in. x 12-in. rectangle; brush with butter. Combine the brown sugar, coffee granules and cinnamon; sprinkle over dough to within ½ in. of edges.

4. Roll up jelly-roll style, starting with a long side; pinch seam to seal. Cut into 12 slices. Place rolls, cut side down, in a greased 13-in. x 9-in. baking pan. Cover and let rise until doubled, about 30 minutes.

5. Bake at 350° for 22-28 minutes or until golden brown. Place pan on a wire rack. In a small bowl, beat the icing ingredients until smooth. Spread over rolls. Serve warm.

Bacon Vegetable Quiche

The best part about this recipe is that you can tailor it to the season and use whatever veggies and cheese you have on hand. I especially love this in spring with fresh greens and asparagus.

—SHANNON KOENE BLACKSBURG, VA

PREP: 25 MIN. • **BAKE:** 35 MIN. • **MAKES:** 6 SERVINGS

- 1 unbaked pastry shell (9 inches)
- 1 cup sliced fresh mushrooms
- 1 cup chopped fresh broccoli
- ¾ cup chopped sweet onion
- 2½ teaspoons olive oil
- 2 cups fresh baby spinach
- 3 eggs, lightly beaten
- 1 can (5 ounces) evaporated milk
- 1 tablespoon minced fresh rosemary or 1 teaspoon dried rosemary, crushed
- ¼ teaspoon salt
- ¼ teaspoon pepper
- 1 cup (4 ounces) shredded cheddar cheese
- 6 bacon strips, cooked and crumbled
- ½ cup crumbled tomato and basil feta cheese

1. Line unpricked pastry shell with a double thickness of heavy-duty foil. Bake at 450° for 8 minutes. Remove foil; bake 5 minutes longer.

2. Meanwhile, in a large skillet, saute the mushrooms, broccoli and onion in oil until tender. Add spinach; cook until wilted.

3. In a large bowl, whisk the eggs, milk, rosemary, salt and pepper. Stir in the vegetables, cheddar cheese and bacon. Pour into crust. Sprinkle with feta cheese.

4. Cover edges loosely with foil. Bake at 375° for 30-35 minutes or until a knife inserted near the center comes out clean. Let stand for 5 minutes before cutting.

FREEZE OPTION *Cover and freeze unbaked quiche. To use, remove from freezer 30 minutes before baking (do not thaw). Preheat oven to 375°. Place quiche on a baking sheet; cover edges loosely with foil. Bake as directed, increasing time as necessary for a knife inserted near the center to come out clean.*

Oatmeal Brulee with Ginger Cream

Here is an awesome dish for a chilly morning. I love the crispy caramelized top and raspberry surprise at the bottom.

—YVONNE STARLIN HERMITAGE, TN

PREP: 30 MIN. • **BROIL:** 10 MIN.
MAKES: 4 SERVINGS

GINGER CREAM

- ½ cup heavy whipping cream
- 2 slices fresh gingerroot (about ¾-inch diameter)
- 1 cinnamon stick (3 inches)
- 1 tablespoon grated orange peel
- 3 tablespoons maple syrup
- ⅛ teaspoon ground nutmeg

OATMEAL

- 4 cups water
- 2 cups old-fashioned oats
- ¼ cup chopped dried apricots
- ¼ cup dried cherries, chopped
- ½ teaspoon salt
- 3 tablespoons brown sugar
- 2 tablespoons butter, softened
- 1 cup fresh or frozen unsweetened raspberries, thawed
- ¼ cup sugar

1. In a small saucepan, combine the cream, ginger, cinnamon stick and orange peel; bring to a boil. Reduce heat; simmer, covered, for 10 minutes. Remove from heat; strain and discard solids. Stir in syrup and nutmeg.

2. In a large saucepan, bring water to a boil; stir in the oats, apricots, cherries and salt. Reduce heat to medium; cook for 5 minutes, stirring occasionally. Remove from the heat; stir in brown sugar and ¼ cup ginger cream. Let stand, covered, for 2 minutes.

3. Grease four 10-oz. broiler-safe ramekins with butter; place on a baking sheet. Divide raspberries among ramekins. Spoon oatmeal over raspberries; sprinkle evenly with sugar. Broil 4-6 in. from the heat for 7-9 minutes or until the sugar is caramelized. Serve with remaining ginger cream.

Sunny Morning Doughnuts

I love, love, love doughnuts, but buying them can get expensive. This recipe is economical and so delicious! It beats any store-bought doughnut.

—SHERRY FLAQUEL CUTLER BAY, FL

PREP: 30 MIN. + CHILLING
COOK: 5 MIN./BATCH
MAKES: 20 DOUGHNUTS

4½ to 5 cups all-purpose flour
1¼ cups sugar
4 teaspoons baking powder
1 teaspoon salt
3 eggs, lightly beaten
1 cup 2% milk
¼ cup canola oil
2 tablespoons orange juice
4 teaspoons grated orange peel
Oil for deep-fat frying
Confectioners' sugar

1. In a large bowl, combine 4½ cups flour, sugar, baking powder and salt.
2. Combine the eggs, milk, oil, orange juice and peel; stir into dry ingredients just until moistened. Stir in enough remaining flour to form a soft dough. Cover and refrigerate for at least 1 hour.
3. Turn onto a floured surface; roll to ½-in. thickness. Cut with a floured 2½-in. doughnut cutter.
4. In an electric skillet or deep-fat fryer, heat oil to 375°. Fry doughnuts, a few at a time, until golden brown on both sides. Drain on paper towels. Dust warm doughnuts with confectioners' sugar.
5. To freeze, wrap doughnuts in foil; transfer to a resealable plastic freezer bag. May be frozen for up to 3 months.
TO USE FROZEN DOUGHNUTS
Remove foil. Thaw at room temperature. Warm if desired. Dust warm doughnuts with confectioners' sugar.

FAMILY FUN

Kids love to help make (and eat) doughnuts. Place some regular and confectioners' sugar in small paper bags and let the kids shake away. Older children can also help with rolling out the dough and cutting the shapes.

Petite Sticky Buns

No kneading is required to bake these muffin-tin sticky buns. Once inverted on a platter, each one has a gooey topping and soft, sweet middle. But be careful not to overbake, or they're difficult to get out of the pan.

—LISA NAUGLE FAYETTEVILLE, PA

PREP: 30 MIN. + RISING • **BAKE:** 15 MIN. • **MAKES:** 2 DOZEN

- 3 to 3¼ cups all-purpose flour
- ¼ cup sugar
- 1 package (¼ ounce) active dry yeast
- 1 teaspoon salt
- 1¼ cups milk
- ¼ cup butter, cubed
- 1 egg

TOPPING
- 1 cup packed brown sugar
- ¾ cup butter, cubed
- ¾ cup chopped pecans, toasted
- 2 tablespoons honey
- 1 teaspoon ground cinnamon
- ½ teaspoon maple flavoring

1. In a large bowl, combine 2 cups flour, sugar, yeast and salt. In a small saucepan, heat the milk and butter to 120°-130°. Add to dry ingredients; beat just until moistened. Add egg; beat until smooth. Stir in enough remaining flour to form a soft dough (dough will be sticky). Do not knead. Cover and let rise in a warm place until doubled, about an hour.
2. In a small saucepan over low heat, cook topping ingredients until butter is melted. Drop by rounded teaspoonfuls into 24 well-greased muffin cups.
3. Stir dough down. Fill prepared muffin cups half-full. Cover and let rise until doubled, about 30 minutes.
4. Place muffin cups on foil-lined baking sheets. Bake at 375° for 12-15 minutes or until golden brown. Cool for 2 minutes before inverting onto baking sheets. Transfer to serving platters. Serve warm.

Blueberry Cheesecake Flapjacks

This stunning stack of flapjacks is pretty as a picture. It's tempting to just sit and stare at them—but not for long. Pair them with your favorite breakfast meat and dig in!

—DONNA CLINE PENSACOLA, FL

PREP: 30 MIN. • **COOK:** 5 MIN./BATCH
MAKES: 12 PANCAKES (¾ CUP TOPPING)

- 1 package (3 ounces) cream cheese, softened
- ¾ cup whipped topping
- 1 cup all-purpose flour
- ½ cup graham cracker crumbs
- 1 tablespoon sugar
- 1 teaspoon baking powder
- ½ teaspoon baking soda
- ¼ teaspoon salt
- 2 eggs, lightly beaten
- 1¼ cups buttermilk
- ¼ cup butter, melted
- 1 cup fresh or frozen blueberries
- ¾ cup maple syrup, warmed
  Additional blueberries, optional

1. For topping, in a small bowl, beat cream cheese and whipped topping until smooth. Chill until serving.
2. In a large bowl, combine the flour, cracker crumbs, sugar, baking powder, baking soda and salt. Combine the eggs, buttermilk and butter; add to dry ingredients just until moistened. Fold in blueberries.
3. Pour batter by ¼ cupfuls onto a greased hot griddle; turn when bubbles form on top. Cook until the second side is golden brown. Spread topping over pancakes. Top with warm syrup; sprinkle with additional blueberries if desired.
EDITOR'S NOTE *If using frozen blueberries, do not thaw them before adding to the pancake batter. But be sure to thaw any berries used in the optional garnish.*

Italian Strip Steaks with Focaccia, page 95

96

98

102

Beef Entrees

From **fork-tender** pot roast to **magnificent** lasagna, sizzling **grilled steak** and kid-favorite **pasta**, these winning beef recipes will **earn you accolades**.

Six-Cheese Lasagna

No one will ever guess how easy this hearty lasagna is to make. No-boil noodles and jarred spaghetti sauce save time, and you'll have fewer pots and pans to wash. If your family is like mine, they'll love this!

—**JODI ANDERSON** OVERBROOK, KS

PREP: 25 MIN. • **BAKE:** 1 HOUR + STANDING • **MAKES:** 12 SERVINGS

- 1 **pound ground beef**
- 1 **pound bulk Italian sausage**
- 1 **jar (24 ounces) meatless spaghetti sauce**
- 2 **eggs, beaten**
- 1 **carton (15 ounces) ricotta cheese**
- 1½ **cups (12 ounces) 4% cottage cheese**
- ¼ **cup grated Parmesan cheese**
- ¼ **cup grated Romano or Asiago cheese**
- 8 **no-cook lasagna noodles**
- 4 **cups (16 ounces) shredded part-skim mozzarella cheese**
- 6 **slices provolone cheese, quartered**

1. In a large skillet, cook beef and sausage over medium heat until no longer pink; drain. Stir in spaghetti sauce. In a large bowl, combine the eggs, ricotta, cottage, Parmesan and Romano cheeses.

2. Spread 1½ cups sauce mixture in a greased 13-in. x 9-in. baking dish. Top with four noodles. Spread 1½ cups sauce to edges of noodles. Sprinkle with 2 cups mozzarella cheese. Top with ricotta mixture, provolone cheese and remaining noodles, sauce and mozzarella cheese.

3. Cover and bake at 350° for 50 minutes or until a thermometer reads 160°. Uncover; bake 10 minutes longer or until cheese is lightly browned. Let stand for 15 minutes before cutting.

Pepperoni Pizza Skillet

START TO FINISH: 30 MIN. • **MAKES:** 8 SERVINGS

- 5 **cups uncooked wide egg noodles**
- 1½ **pounds ground beef**
- ½ **cup chopped onion**
- ½ **cup chopped green pepper**
- 1½ **cups chopped pepperoni**
- 1 **jar (14 ounces) pizza sauce**
- 1 **can (10¾ ounces) condensed cream of mushroom soup, undiluted**
- 1 **can (4½ ounces) sliced mushrooms, drained**
- ½ **cup grated Parmesan cheese**
- ¼ **teaspoon garlic powder**
- ¼ **teaspoon dried oregano**
- ½ **cup shredded part-skim mozzarella cheese**

1. Cook noodles according to package directions.

2. Meanwhile, in a large skillet, cook the beef, onion and pepper over medium heat until meat is no longer pink; drain. Stir in the pepperoni, pizza sauce, soup, mushrooms, Parmesan cheese, garlic powder and oregano.

3. Drain noodles; stir into skillet and heat through. Sprinkle with mozzarella cheese.

❝On hectic school nights, no household should be without a 30-minute supper the whole family loves. This flavor-packed skillet is one recipe you'll reach for time and again.❞ —**ANNA MILLER** QUAKER CITY, OH

Italian Strip Steaks with Focaccia

I'm a grandmother who loves to cook and bake for others, but my husband is my chief taste tester. We both love Italian, so I created this easy-to-prepare dish with our favorite flavors.
—**PATRICIA HARMON** BADEN, PA

PREP: 15 MIN. • **COOK:** 25 MIN. • **MAKES:** 4 SERVINGS

- 4 boneless beef top loin steaks (8 ounces each)
- 3 tablespoons olive oil, divided
- ½ pound sliced baby portobello mushrooms
- 1 shallot, finely chopped
- 3 tablespoons chopped red onion
- 2 garlic cloves, minced
- 2 teaspoons minced fresh rosemary
- ½ cup roasted sweet red peppers, cut into strips
- ¼ cup dry red wine or beef broth
- ¼ teaspoon salt
- ¼ teaspoon coarsely ground pepper
- 1 focaccia bread (12 ounces), cut into quarters
- ⅔ cup shredded Asiago cheese
- ¼ cup sliced pimiento-stuffed olives

1. In a large skillet, cook steaks in 2 tablespoons oil over medium heat for 5-6 minutes on each side or until meat reaches desired doneness (for medium-rare, a thermometer should read 145°; medium, 160°; well-done, 170°). Remove and keep warm.

2. In the same skillet, saute the mushrooms, shallot and onion in remaining oil. Add garlic and rosemary; saute 1-2 minutes longer. Stir in the red peppers, wine, salt and pepper; heat through.

3. Place focaccia on serving plates; top each with a steak and ½ cup mushroom mixture. Sprinkle with cheese and olives.

NOTE *Top loin steak may be labeled as strip steak, Kansas City steak, New York strip steak, ambassador steak or boneless club steak in your region.*

Tuscan Steak Flatbreads

Wrap tender grilled flatbreads around steak and top with cheese and homemade sun-dried tomato pesto for an instant party! People love the fun presentation and the mouthwatering taste.
—**MICHAEL COHEN** LOS ANGELES, CA

PREP: 25 MIN. • **GRILL:** 15 MIN. • **MAKES:** 4 SERVINGS

SUN-DRIED TOMATO PESTO
- ⅓ cup packed fresh parsley sprigs
- 2 tablespoons fresh basil leaves
- 1 garlic clove, quartered
- 2 tablespoons grated Parmesan cheese
- 2 tablespoons oil-packed sun-dried tomatoes, patted dry
- 2 tablespoons sherry
- ¼ teaspoon salt
  Dash pepper
- ¼ cup olive oil

STEAK FLATBREADS
- 1 beef top sirloin steak (¾ inch thick and 1¼ pounds)
- ¼ teaspoon salt
- ¼ teaspoon pepper
- 4 flatbreads or whole pita breads
- 2 tablespoons olive oil
- 1 cup (4 ounces) shredded fontina cheese
- ¼ cup fresh basil leaves, thinly sliced

1. For pesto, place the parsley, basil and garlic in a food processor; cover and pulse until chopped. Add the Parmesan cheese, tomatoes, sherry, salt and pepper; cover and process until blended. While processing, gradually add oil in a steady stream. Set aside.

2. Sprinkle steak with salt and pepper. Grill, covered, over medium heat for 6-10 minutes on each side or until meat reaches desired doneness (for medium-rare, a meat thermometer should read 145°; medium, 160°; well-done, 170°). Remove and keep warm.

3. Brush one side of each flatbread with oil; place oiled side down on grill rack. Grill, covered, over medium heat for 1-2 minutes or until heated through.

4. Spread the grilled side of each flatbread with pesto. Cut steak into thin strips; place over pesto. Top with fontina cheese and basil.

Hearty Beef and Noodles

Beef and Noodles is a longtime family favorite. Growing up, my kids always asked to bring home friends on nights we served it. When my oldest son was in the army, he and his wife asked for the recipe so they could make it while he was on leave.

—SYLVIA STREU NORMAN, OK

PREP: 15 MIN. • **COOK:** 30 MIN. • **MAKES:** 6 SERVINGS

- 1½ pounds beef top sirloin steak, cut into ½-inch strips
- 2 teaspoons olive oil
- ½ cup chopped onion
- 1½ teaspoons minced garlic
- 1 can (10¾ ounces) condensed cream of mushroom soup, undiluted
- 1 cup water
- 1 cup half-and-half cream
- ⅓ cup brewed coffee
- 2 envelopes brown gravy mix
- 5 cups uncooked egg noodles
- 1 cup (8 ounces) sour cream
- ½ teaspoon paprika
- ¼ teaspoon pepper

1. In a large skillet, brown beef in oil on all sides; remove and keep warm. In the same skillet, saute onion until tender. Add garlic; cook 1 minute longer. Return beef to the pan; stir in the soup, water, cream, coffee and gravy mix. Bring to a boil. Reduce heat; cover and simmer for 20-25 minutes or until meat is tender, stirring occasionally.
2. Meanwhile, cook noodles according to package directions. Add the sour cream, paprika and pepper to skillet; heat through. Drain noodles. Serve with beef.

Bacon Cheeseburger Spaghetti

I run a day care center and it's always hard to find different foods that the kids will actually eat. I spruced up a variation of this simple and quick recipe to my tastes, and now the kids (and my husband) request it all the time!

—NICHELLE NELL ISLE, MN

START TO FINISH: 30 MIN. • **MAKES:** 6 SERVINGS

- 10 ounces uncooked spaghetti
- 1 pound lean ground beef (90% lean)
- ⅔ cup chopped onion
- 6 slices ready-to-serve fully cooked bacon, chopped
- 1½ cups ketchup
- 1 cup chopped dill pickles
- 1 cup barbecue sauce
- ½ cup prepared mustard
- 2 cups (8 ounces) shredded cheddar cheese

1. Cook spaghetti according to package directions. Meanwhile, in a large skillet, cook beef and onion over medium heat until meat is no longer pink; drain.
2. Stir in the bacon, ketchup, pickles, barbecue sauce and mustard. Bring to a boil. Reduce heat; simmer, uncovered, for 5 minutes. Drain spaghetti; stir into meat mixture.
3. Sprinkle with cheese. Remove from the heat; cover and let stand until cheese is melted.

Special Pot Roast

Served with cooked carrots and potatoes, it doesn't get much more homey than this. What a perfect Sunday dinner for the family.

—**VERA CARROLL** MEDFORD, MA

PREP: 10 MIN. • **COOK:** 6½ HOURS
MAKES: 6 SERVINGS

- 1 large sweet onion, chopped
- 1 cup sliced baby portobello mushrooms
- 1 beef rump roast or bottom round roast (3 pounds)
- ½ teaspoon salt
- ¼ teaspoon pepper
- 1 cup dry red wine or beef broth
- 1 tablespoon brown sugar
- 1 tablespoon Dijon mustard
- 1 teaspoon Worcestershire sauce
- 2 tablespoons cornstarch
- 2 tablespoons cold water

1. Place onion and mushrooms in a 5-qt. slow cooker. Rub roast with salt and pepper; cut in half and place over onion mixture. In a small bowl, combine wine, brown sugar, mustard and Worcestershire sauce; pour over roast. Cover and cook on low for 6-8 hours or until meat is tender.

2. Mix cornstarch and water until smooth; stir into cooking juices. Cover and cook on high for 30 minutes or until gravy is thickened.

PER SERVING *356 cal., 11 g fat (4 g sat. fat), 136 mg chol., 342 mg sodium, 9 g carb., 1 g fiber, 45 g pro.* **Diabetic Exchanges:** *6 lean meat, 1 fat, ½ starch.*

FROM THE WEB

I actually made this with a chunk of venison and it was wonderful! I added baby carrots and chunks of potatoes (didn't put in mushrooms because I didn't have any.) I used the beef broth instead of wine. I also tripled the seasonings and liquids (since after adding the carrots and potatoes there wasn't enough juice to cover the meat). Wonderful!

—**NDREAMER** TASTEOFHOME.COM

Italian Meatball Tortes

With classic Italian flavor, these hearty dinner pies filled with tomatoes, mozzarella and savory homemade meatballs will be a hit with your family. Preparation takes some time, but the results are well worth it.

—SANDY BLESSING OCEAN SHORES, WA

PREP: 1¼ HOURS + RISING • **BAKE:** 30 MIN.
MAKES: 2 TORTES (6 SERVINGS EACH)

- 1 package (¼ ounce) active dry yeast
- ¼ cup warm water (110° to 115°)
- ¾ cup warm milk (110° to 115°)
- ¼ cup sugar
- ¼ cup shortening
- 1 egg
- 1 teaspoon salt
- 3½ to 3¾ cups all-purpose flour

MEATBALLS
- 1 can (5 ounces) evaporated milk
- 2 eggs, lightly beaten
- 1 cup quick-cooking oats
- 1 cup crushed saltines
- ½ cup chopped onion
- ½ cup chopped celery
- 2 teaspoons salt
- 2 teaspoons chili powder
- ½ teaspoon garlic powder
- ½ teaspoon pepper
- 3 pounds ground beef

FILLING
- 1 can (15 ounces) crushed tomatoes
- ½ cup chopped onion
- ⅓ cup grated Parmesan cheese
- 1½ teaspoons dried basil

- 1½ teaspoons dried oregano
- 1 teaspoon minced fresh parsley
- 1 teaspoon salt
- 1½ cups (6 ounces) shredded part-skim mozzarella cheese

1. In a large bowl, dissolve yeast in warm water. Add the milk, sugar, shortening, egg, salt and 2 cups flour. Beat until smooth. Stir in enough remaining flour to form a soft dough.

2. Turn onto a floured surface; knead until smooth and elastic, about 6-8 minutes. Place in a greased bowl, turning once to grease the top. Cover and let rise in a warm place until doubled, 1 to 1½ hours.

3. In a large bowl, combine the milk, eggs, oats, saltines, onion, celery and seasonings. Crumble beef over mixture and mix well. Shape into 1½-in. balls. In a large skillet over medium heat, cook meatballs in batches until no longer pink.

4. Meanwhile, place tomatoes and onion in a small saucepan. Bring to a boil. Reduce heat; simmer, uncovered, for 10 minutes or until slightly thickened. Stir in the Parmesan cheese, herbs and salt.

5. Punch dough down. Divide into three portions. Roll two portions into 11-in. circles; line the bottoms and press partially up the sides of two greased 9-in. springform pans. Roll third portion into a 12x10-in. rectangle; cut into twelve 10x1-in. strips.

6. Place meatballs in prepared crusts; top with tomato mixture and mozzarella cheese. Make lattice crusts with strips of dough; trim and seal edges. Cover and let rise for 30 minutes.

7. Preheat oven to 350°. Bake 30-35 minutes or until golden brown. Cut into wedges.

Nacho Pizza

I love Mexican food and I love pizza, so I combined the best of both in this hearty recipe. People seem to just love it...especially my brothers!

—LAURA STONESIFER LUCK, WI

PREP: 30 MIN. • **BAKE:** 15 MIN. • **MAKES:** 8 SLICES

- 1 package (6½ ounces) pizza crust mix
- 1 teaspoon cornmeal
- ¾ pound ground beef
- ⅓ cup chopped onion
- 1 teaspoon chili powder
- ¼ teaspoon salt
- ⅛ teaspoon pepper
- 1 cup salsa
- ½ cup sour cream
- 1 medium tomato, chopped
- 2 tablespoons chopped ripe olives
- 2 cups (8 ounces) shredded cheddar cheese
- ½ cup crushed tortilla chips

1. Prepare pizza dough according to package directions. Coat a 12-in. pizza pan with cooking spray; sprinkle with cornmeal. With floured hands, press dough onto pan. Bake at 425° for 6-8 minutes or until lightly browned.

2. Meanwhile, in a small skillet, cook beef and onion over medium heat until meat is no longer pink; drain. Stir in the chili powder, salt and pepper.

3. Combine salsa and sour cream; spread over crust to within 1 in. of edges. Top with beef mixture, tomatoes, olives and cheese. Bake for 10 minutes.

4. Sprinkle with crushed chips; bake 5-6 minutes longer or until cheese is melted and crust is golden brown.

Moroccan Beef Kabobs

My grandmother's homemade marinade adds tang and tenderness to these beefy kabobs. Her blend of herbs and spices punches up the flavor without adding lots of calories.

—JENNIFER SHAW DORCHESTER, MA

PREP: 25 MIN. + MARINATING • **GRILL:** 10 MIN. • **MAKES:** 8 SERVINGS

- 1 cup chopped fresh parsley
- 1 cup chopped fresh cilantro
- ¼ cup grated onion
- 3 tablespoons lemon juice
- 2 tablespoons olive oil
- 1 tablespoon ground cumin
- 1 tablespoon ground coriander
- 1 tablespoon paprika
- 1 tablespoon cider vinegar
- 1 tablespoon ketchup
- 2 garlic cloves, minced
- 1 teaspoon minced fresh gingerroot
- 1 teaspoon Thai red chili paste
    Dash salt and pepper
- 2 pounds beef top sirloin steak, cut into 1-inch pieces

1. In a large resealable plastic bag, combine the parsley, cilantro, onion, lemon juice, oil, cumin, coriander, paprika, vinegar, ketchup, garlic, ginger, chili paste, salt and pepper; add beef. Seal bag and turn to coat; refrigerate for 8 hours or overnight.

2. Drain and discard marinade. On eight metal or soaked wooden skewers, thread beef cubes. Moisten a paper towel with cooking oil; using long-handled tongs, lightly coat the grill rack.

3. Grill beef, covered, over medium-hot heat or broil 4 in. from the heat for 8-12 minutes or until meat reaches desired doneness, turning occasionally.

PER SERVING *185 cal., 9 g fat (3 g sat. fat), 63 mg chol., 91 mg sodium, 3 g carb., 1 g fiber, 22 g pro.* **Diabetic Exchanges:** *3 lean meat, ½ fat.*

Mushroom Beef Tips With Rice

Here's a quick and simple version of my husband's favorite dish. Even though the recipe calls for premade beef tips, the finished dish tastes delightfully homemade. Think: savory Stroganoff flavor with only five ingredients!

—PAMELA SHANK PARKERSBURG, WV

START TO FINISH: 10 MIN. • **MAKES:** 3 SERVINGS

- 1 cup sliced fresh mushrooms
- 2 tablespoons butter
- 1 package (17 ounces) refrigerated beef tips with gravy
- 1 package (8.8 ounces) ready-to-serve long grain rice
- ½ cup sour cream

1. In a large skillet, saute mushrooms in butter for 2 minutes. Add beef to pan; cook for 4-6 minutes or until heated through, stirring occasionally.
2. Meanwhile, cook rice according to package directions. Remove beef mixture from the heat; stir in sour cream. Serve with rice.

Savory Grilled T-Bones

No one flavor overpowers the others in this perfectly balanced marinade. It's the ultimate combination of savory, tart and sweet.

—ANNA DAVIS HALF WAY, MO

PREP: 15 MIN. + MARINATING • **GRILL:** 15 MIN. • **MAKES:** 6 SERVINGS

- ¼ cup chopped onion
- ¼ cup olive oil
- 2 tablespoons lemon juice
- 2 tablespoons soy sauce
- 1 tablespoon sugar
- 1 tablespoon cider vinegar
- 1 tablespoon honey
- 2 teaspoons minced garlic
- 2 teaspoons Worcestershire sauce
- 1 teaspoon salt
- ½ teaspoon pepper
- 6 beef T-bone steaks (16 ounces each)

1. In a large resealable plastic bag, combine the first 11 ingredients; add steaks. Seal bag and turn to coat; refrigerate for 2-4 hours.
2. Drain and discard marinade. Grill steaks, covered, over medium heat for 6-10 minutes on each side or until the meat reaches desired doneness (for medium-rare, a thermometer should read 145°; medium, 160°; well-done, 170°).

Macaroni Taco Bake

Comforting mac and cheese with a touch of taco flavoring and tortilla-chip crunch...no wonder everyone loves this! It's a fun change of pace from regular macaroni.

—**BETSY KING** DULUTH, MN

PREP: 30 MIN. • **BAKE:** 15 MIN. • **MAKES:** 8 SERVINGS

- 2 **packages (7¼ ounces each) macaroni and cheese dinner mix**
- 1 **pound ground beef**
- 1 **cup chunky salsa**
- 2 **cups crushed tortilla chips**
- 1 **can (2¼ ounces) sliced ripe olives, drained**
- 2 **cups (8 ounces) shredded Mexican cheese blend**
   Sour cream, optional

1. Prepare macaroni and cheese according to package directions. Meanwhile, in a large skillet, cook beef until no longer pink; drain. Stir in salsa; set aside.
2. Spread macaroni into a greased 13-in. x 9-in. baking dish. Layer with beef mixture, chips and olives; sprinkle with cheese.
3. Bake, uncovered, at 350° for 15-20 minutes or until heated through. Serve with sour cream if desired.

Cider Mushroom Brisket

Whoever would have thought to add gingersnap cookies to slow-cooked brisket? Along with the cider, they add a sweet autumn flavor to this homey dish.

—**COLLEEN WESTON** DENVER, CO

PREP: 10 MIN. • **COOK:** 6 HOURS • **MAKES:** 12 SERVINGS

- 1 **fresh beef brisket (6 pounds)**
- 2 **jars (12 ounces each) mushroom gravy**
- 1 **cup apple cider or juice**
- 1 **envelope onion mushroom soup mix**
- ⅓ **cup crushed gingersnap cookies**

1. Cut brisket into thirds; place in a 5- or 6-qt. slow cooker. In a large bowl, combine the gravy, cider, soup mix and cookie crumbs; pour over beef. Cover and cook on low for 6-8 hours or until meat is tender.
2. Thinly slice meat across the grain. Skim fat from cooking juices; thicken if desired.
NOTE *This is a fresh beef brisket, not corned beef.*
PER SERVING *336 cal., 11 g fat (4 g sat. fat), 101 mg chol., 566 mg sodium, 9 g carb., trace fiber, 47 g pro.* **Diabetic Exchanges:** *6 lean meat, ½ starch, ½ fat.*

Peppered Filets with Tomato-Mushroom Salsa

The secret to these filets is in the salsa. It's full of fresh veggies and seasonings that bring a true taste of summer to any time of the year.

—ANN HILLMEYER SANDIA PARK, NM

PREP: 30 MIN. • **COOK:** 15 MIN. • **MAKES:** 6 SERVINGS

- 6 plum tomatoes, seeded and chopped
- 1 cup chopped fresh mushrooms
- ¼ cup minced fresh Italian parsley
- 2 tablespoons finely chopped shallot
- 2 teaspoons minced garlic, divided
- 5 teaspoons olive oil, divided
- 1 tablespoon lime juice
- ½ teaspoon salt
- ¼ teaspoon pepper
- 6 beef tenderloin steaks (4 ounces each)
- 2 teaspoons lemon-pepper seasoning
- ⅓ cup balsamic vinegar
- ¼ cup beef broth
- 4 teaspoons butter
- 6 lime slices

1. For salsa, in a small bowl, combine the tomatoes, mushrooms, parsley, shallot, 1 teaspoon garlic, 3 teaspoons oil, lime juice, salt and pepper; set aside.

2. Sprinkle steaks with lemon-pepper. In a large skillet, cook steaks in remaining oil for 4-5 minutes on each side or until meat reaches desired doneness (for medium-rare, a thermometer should read 145°; medium, 160°; well-done, 170°). Remove and keep warm.

3. Combine the vinegar, broth and remaining garlic; add to pan, stirring to loosen browned bits. Cook until liquid is reduced by half, about 2-3 minutes. Stir in butter.

4. Spoon sauce over steaks. Serve with salsa. Garnish with lime slices.

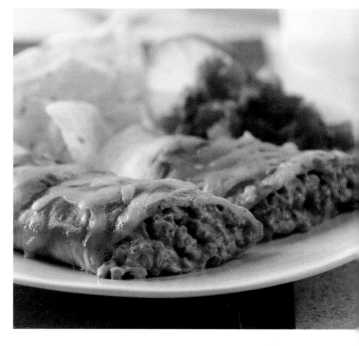

Creamy Beef Enchiladas

These American-style enchiladas are rich, creamy and loaded with cheese. Kids will like the texture and the fact that they have just a touch of south-of-the-border heat.

—BELINDA MORAN WOODBURY, TN

PREP: 25 MIN. • **BAKE:** 20 MIN. • **MAKES:** 12 SERVINGS

- 2 pounds lean ground beef (90% lean)
- 1 cup chopped onion
- 1 can (10¾ ounces) condensed cream of mushroom soup, undiluted
- 1 cup (8 ounces) sour cream
- 1 can (4 ounces) chopped green chilies
- 3 cups (12 ounces) shredded cheddar cheese, divided
- 3 cans (10 ounces each) enchilada sauce, divided
- 12 flour tortillas (8 inches), warmed

1. In a Dutch oven, cook beef and onion over medium heat until meat is no longer pink; drain. Add the soup, sour cream, chilies, 1 cup cheese and ½ cup enchilada sauce; heat through.

2. Spread ¼ cup enchilada sauce into each of two ungreased 13-in. x 9-in. baking dishes. Place ½ cup beef mixture down the center of each tortilla. Roll up and place seam side down in prepared dishes.

3. Pour remaining enchilada sauce over top; sprinkle with remaining cheese. Bake, uncovered, at 350° for 20-25 minutes or until heated through.

ENCHILADA SAUCE

Enchilada sauce is a blend of tomatoes, oil and spices thickened with a little flour or cornstarch. Green enchilada sauce, which is made from tomatillos instead of tomatoes, is also available.

Flatbread Tacos with Ranch Sour Cream

START TO FINISH: 30 MIN. • **MAKES:** 8 SERVINGS

- 1 cup (8 ounces) sour cream
- 2 teaspoons ranch salad dressing mix
- 1 teaspoon lemon juice
- 1½ pounds ground beef
- 1 can (15 ounces) pinto beans, rinsed and drained
- 1 can (14½ ounces) diced tomatoes, undrained
- 1 envelope taco seasoning
- 1 tablespoon hot pepper sauce
- 1 tube (16.3 ounces) large refrigerated buttermilk biscuits
  Optional toppings: sliced ripe olives and shredded lettuce and cheddar cheese

1. In a small bowl, combine the sour cream, dressing mix and lemon juice; chill until serving.

2. In a large skillet, cook beef over medium heat until no longer pink; drain. Add the beans, tomatoes, taco seasoning and pepper sauce; heat through.

3. Meanwhile, roll out each biscuit into a 6-in. circle. In a small nonstick skillet over medium heat, cook each biscuit for 30-60 seconds on each side or until golden brown; keep warm.

4. To serve, spread each flatbread with 2 tablespoons ranch sour cream; top each with ⅔ cup meat mixture. Sprinkle with toppings if desired.

> ❝Made with convenient refrigerated biscuits, these tasty flatbread tacos are ideal for serving buffet-style. Set out the toppings and let everyone make their own.❞
>
> —JENNIFER EGGEBRAATEN BOTHELL, WA

Santa Maria Roast Beef

A zesty dry rub turns a simple beef roast into a real crowd-pleaser. This slightly spicy meat is scrumptious the first and second time around, piled on top of fresh crusty bread.
—**ALLISON ECTOR** ARDMORE, PA

PREP: 20 MIN. + MARINATING • **GRILL:** 1 HOUR + STANDING
MAKES: 6 SERVINGS

- 4 tablespoons paprika
- 3 tablespoons brown sugar
- 2 tablespoons chili powder
- 1 tablespoon garlic powder
- 1 tablespoon white pepper
- 1 tablespoon celery salt
- 1 tablespoon ground cumin
- 1 tablespoon dried oregano
- 1 tablespoon pepper
- 2 teaspoons cayenne pepper
- 1 teaspoon ground mustard
- 1 beef tri-tip roast or beef sirloin tip roast (2 to 3 pounds)
- 2 cups soaked hickory wood chips or chunks
- 2 tablespoons canola oil

1. Combine the first 11 ingredients; rub desired amount over roast. Wrap in plastic wrap and refrigerate overnight. Store leftover dry rub in an airtight container for up to 6 months.

2. Remove roast from the refrigerator 1 hour before grilling. Prepare grill for indirect heat, using a drip pan. Add wood chips according to manufacturer's directions.

3. Unwrap roast and brush with oil; place over drip pan. Grill, covered, over medium-low indirect heat for 1 to 1½ hours or until meat reaches desired doneness (for medium-rare, a thermometer should read 145°; medium, 160°; well-done, 170°). Let stand 10-15 minutes before slicing.

BAKED SANTA MARIA ROAST BEEF *Prepare roast and refrigerate as directed. Unwrap roast and brush with oil and ½ teaspoon liquid smoke. Place on a rack in a shallow roasting pan. Bake, uncovered, at 425° for 55-75 minutes or until meat reaches desired doneness.*

Loaded Spaghetti Bake

We used to go south in our RV for months at a time. One year when we arrived home after being gone for a while, my neighbor Jill came over with a pie plate filled with this wonderful spaghetti bake. Now I make it often for my family. I sometimes use leftover chicken instead of beef.

—**MARIAN PAPPAS** LAKE STEVENS, WA

PREP: 25 MIN. • **BAKE:** 30 MIN. • **MAKES:** 8 SERVINGS

- 12 ounces uncooked spaghetti
- 1 pound lean ground beef (90% lean)
- 1 cup chopped onion
- 1 cup chopped green pepper
- 1 jar (26 ounces) spaghetti sauce
- 1 can (4 ounces) mushroom stems and pieces, drained
- 1 can (2¼ ounces) sliced ripe olives, drained
- 2 cups (8 ounces) shredded cheddar cheese, divided
- 1 can (10¾ ounces) condensed cream of chicken soup, undiluted
- 1 carton (10 ounces) refrigerated Alfredo sauce
- ¼ cup grated Parmesan cheese
- ½ cup cornflake crumbs

1. Preheat oven to 350°. Cook spaghetti according to package directions. Meanwhile, in a large skillet, cook the beef, onion and pepper over medium heat until meat is no longer pink; drain. Add the spaghetti sauce, mushrooms and olives. Drain spaghetti; add to skillet.

2. Transfer to a greased 13x9-in. baking dish. Sprinkle with 1 cup cheddar cheese. In a small bowl, combine the soup, Alfredo sauce and Parmesan cheese; spread over cheddar cheese. In another bowl, combine cornflake crumbs and remaining cheddar cheese; sprinkle over the top.

3. Bake, uncovered, 30 minutes or until bubbly and cheese is melted. Let stand 5 minutes before serving.

Gone-All-Day-Stew

This healthy slow-cooked stew is one of my husband's favorite meals. I always use fresh mushrooms and low-sodium bouillon granules when I make it. No added salt is necessary. It is loaded with satisfying veggies.

—**PATRICIA KILE** ELIZABETHTOWN, PA

PREP: 25 MIN. • **COOK:** 4 HOURS • **MAKES:** 8 SERVINGS

- ¼ cup all-purpose flour
- 1 boneless beef chuck roast (2 pounds), cut into 1-inch cubes
- 2 tablespoons canola oil
- 1 can (10¾ ounces) condensed tomato soup, undiluted
- 1 cup water or red wine
- 2 teaspoons beef bouillon granules
- 3 teaspoons Italian seasoning
- 1 bay leaf
- ½ teaspoon coarsely ground pepper
- 6 medium onions, quartered
- 4 medium potatoes, cut into 1½-inch chunks
- 3 medium carrots, cut into 1-inch slices
- 12 large fresh mushrooms
- ½ cup celery, cut into 1-inch slices
  Hot cooked egg noodles, optional

1. Place the flour in a large resealable plastic bag. Add beef, a few pieces at a time, and shake to coat. In a large skillet, brown meat in oil in batches; drain. Transfer to a 5-qt. slow cooker.

2. In a small bowl, combine the tomato soup, water, bouillon and seasonings; pour over beef. Add the onions, potatoes, carrots, mushrooms and celery.

3. Cover and cook on low for 4-5 hours or until meat is tender. Discard bay leaf. Serve the stew with egg noodles if desired.

Cook perfect spaghetti using this technique.

Carefully ease the spaghetti into boiling water as it softens, pushing it down and around the edge of the pan. When fully immersed, gently stir the spaghetti to separate strands.

SIMMERED ALL DAY
GRAND PRIZE WINNER
★★★★

Fruit-Glazed Pork Chops, page 111

110   117   119

Pork
Entrees

Here is **the comfort food everyone craves**: game-day **pizza**, **prizewinning** ribs, and pork chops **smothered** in old-fashioned pan gravy. From 30-minute dinners to **holiday ham**, versatile pork dishes are **something to celebrate**!

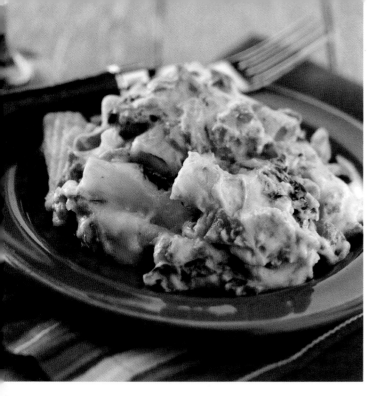

Creamy Spinach Sausage Pasta

So rich and creamy, this pasta dish is wonderfully cheesy and delicious. To save time, I assemble it the night before, then bake it the next day.
—SUSIE SIZEMORE COLLINSVILLE, VA

PREP: 15 MIN. • **BAKE:** 45 MIN. • **MAKES:** 5 SERVINGS

- 3 cups uncooked rigatoni or large tube pasta
- 1 pound bulk Italian sausage
- 1 cup finely chopped onion
- 1 can (14½ ounces) Italian diced tomatoes, undrained
- 1 package (10 ounces) frozen creamed spinach, thawed
- 1 package (8 ounces) cream cheese, softened
- 2 cups (8 ounces) shredded part-skim mozzarella cheese, divided

1. Cook pasta according to package directions. Meanwhile, in a Dutch oven, cook sausage and onion over medium heat until meat is no longer pink; drain. Stir in the tomatoes, spinach, cream cheese and 1 cup mozzarella cheese. Drain pasta; stir into the sausage mixture. Transfer to a greased 11-in. x 7-in. baking dish.
2. Cover and bake at 350° for 35 minutes. Uncover; sprinkle with remaining cheese. Bake 10 minutes longer or until cheese is melted.

Asian Barbecued Pork Loin

The extra kick you get from the Chinese-style mustard is worth the investment when making this dish. I like to serve it with jasmine rice to soak up any extra sauce from the pork.
—MELISSA CARAFA BROOMALL, PA

PREP: 15 MIN. • **BAKE:** 1 HOUR + STANDING
MAKES: 8-10 SERVINGS

- 1 boneless whole pork loin roast (3 to 4 pounds)
- ½ teaspoon garlic salt
- ¼ teaspoon pepper
- ¼ cup finely chopped onion
- 1 tablespoon butter
- ½ cup ketchup
- ⅓ cup honey
- 1 tablespoon hoisin sauce
- 1½ teaspoons Chinese-style mustard
- 1 teaspoon reduced-sodium soy sauce
- ½ teaspoon garlic powder
- ¼ teaspoon ground ginger
- ¼ teaspoon Chinese five-spice powder

1. Sprinkle pork roast with garlic salt and pepper. Place in a shallow roasting pan lined with heavy-duty foil. Bake, uncovered, at 350° for 50 minutes.
2. Meanwhile, in a small saucepan, saute onion in butter until tender. Stir in the remaining ingredients. Bring to a boil. Reduce heat; simmer, uncovered, until sauce is reduced to ¾ cup, about 20-25 minutes, stirring often.
3. Brush sauce over pork. Bake 10-15 minutes longer or until a thermometer reads 145°. Let stand for 10 minutes before slicing.
PER SERVING *232 cal., 8 g fat (3 g sat. fat), 71 mg chol., 348 mg sodium, 14 g carb., trace fiber, 26 g pro.* **Diabetic Exchanges:** *3 lean meat, 1 starch, 1 fat.*

Ham & Cheese Stuffed Potatoes

These hearty potatoes are fully loaded. They can be changed up a zillion different ways, but this is my favorite. It features three kinds of cheese plus cream cheese and cottage cheese.
—**KATHLEEN GILL** PAHRUMP, NV

PREP: 1½ HOURS • **BAKE:** 25 MIN. • **MAKES:** 2 SERVINGS

- 2 large baking potatoes
- ½ cup cubed deli ham
- ¼ cup chopped sweet onion
- ¼ cup chopped celery
- ¼ cup chopped sweet red pepper
- 1 tablespoon olive oil
- 2 ounces reduced-fat cream cheese
- 2 tablespoons cream-style cottage cheese
- ¼ teaspoon salt
- ¼ teaspoon pepper
- ¼ cup shredded sharp cheddar cheese
- 2 tablespoons shredded Swiss cheese
- 2 tablespoons 2% milk
- 1 tablespoon shredded Parmesan cheese
- 1 teaspoon minced fresh basil

1. Scrub and pierce potatoes. Bake at 375° for 1 hour or until tender. When cool enough to handle, cut a thin slice off the top of each potato and discard. Scoop out the pulp, leaving a thin shell.

2. In a large skillet, saute the ham, onion, celery and red pepper in oil until vegetables are tender. Set aside. In a large bowl, mash the pulp with cream cheese, cottage cheese, salt and pepper. Stir in the ham mixture, cheddar cheese, Swiss cheese, milk and Parmesan cheese. Spoon into potato shells.

3. Place on a baking sheet. Bake, uncovered, at 375° for 25-30 minutes or until heated through. Sprinkle with basil.

Speedy Jambalaya

START TO FINISH: 30 MIN. • **MAKES:** 8 SERVINGS

- 1⅓ cups uncooked long grain rice
- 1 large onion, halved and sliced
- 1 medium green pepper, sliced
- 1 medium sweet red pepper, sliced
- 2 teaspoons olive oil
- 3 garlic cloves, minced
- 1 can (28 ounces) diced tomatoes, undrained
- 3 bay leaves
- 1 teaspoon salt
- 1 teaspoon paprika
- ½ teaspoon dried thyme
- ½ teaspoon pepper
- ¼ teaspoon hot pepper sauce
- 2 cans (15½ ounces each) black-eyed peas, rinsed and drained
- ¾ pound fully cooked andouille or smoked sausage, sliced
- ¼ cup minced fresh parsley

1. Cook rice according to package directions. Meanwhile, in a large skillet, saute onion and peppers in oil for 4 minutes. Add garlic; cook 1 minute longer. Stir in the tomatoes, bay leaves, salt, paprika, thyme, pepper and pepper sauce. Bring to a boil.

2. Reduce heat; simmer, uncovered, for 5 minutes. Stir in peas and sausage; heat through. Discard bay leaves. Serve with rice. Sprinkle each serving with parsley.

"Spicy sausage and colorful sweet peppers make this classic Cajun dish look as appetizing as it tastes. It's impossible to say no to seconds!" —**NICOLE FILIZETTI** JACKSONVILLE, FL

Bruschetta Pizza

Loaded with Italian flavor and plenty of fresh tomatoes, this is bound to become a family favorite. It's even better with a homemade whole wheat crust.

—DEBRA KEIL OWASSO, OK

PREP: 25 MIN. • **BAKE:** 10 MIN.
MAKES: 8 SLICES

- ½ **pound reduced-fat bulk pork sausage**
- 1 **prebaked 12-inch pizza crust**
- 1 **package (6 ounces) sliced turkey pepperoni**
- 2 **cups (8 ounces) shredded part-skim mozzarella cheese**
- 1½ **cups chopped plum tomatoes**
- ½ **cup fresh basil leaves, thinly sliced**
- 1 **tablespoon olive oil**
- 2 **garlic cloves, minced**
- ½ **teaspoon minced fresh thyme or ⅛ teaspoon dried thyme**
- ½ **teaspoon balsamic vinegar**
- ¼ **teaspoon salt**
- ⅛ **teaspoon pepper**
  Additional fresh basil leaves, optional

1. In a small skillet, cook the sausage over medium heat until no longer pink; drain. Place crust on an ungreased baking sheet. Top with pepperoni, sausage and cheese. Bake at 450° for 10-12 minutes or until cheese is melted.

2. In a small bowl, combine the tomatoes, sliced basil, oil, garlic, thyme, vinegar, salt and pepper. Spoon over pizza. Garnish with additional basil if desired.

Summertime Spaghetti Sauce

My husband and I look forward to this fresh-tasting sauce when the tomatoes from our garden are at their peak ripeness. It's a real summertime treat.

—**KAY KAEPP** COLDWATER, MI

PREP: 45 MIN. • **COOK:** 30 MIN. • **MAKES:** 5 CUPS

- 3 Italian sausage links (4 ounces each)
- 1 tablespoon olive oil
- 3 medium onions, chopped
- 1 small green pepper, chopped
- 3 cups chopped seeded peeled tomatoes
- 1 jalapeno pepper, seeded and chopped
- 1 tablespoon brown sugar
- 1 tablespoon Italian seasoning
- 1¼ teaspoons salt
- ¼ teaspoon pepper
  Hot cooked pasta

1. Remove casings from sausage; cut sausage into 1-in. pieces. In a large skillet, brown sausage over medium heat. Drain and set aside. Heat oil in the same skillet; add onions and green pepper. Cook and stir until tender.

2. Add tomatoes, jalapeno, brown sugar, Italian seasoning, salt and pepper. Return sausage to the pan. Cook, stirring occasionally, for 12-15 minutes or until meat is no longer pink and sauce is thickened. Serve sauce with pasta.

NOTE *Wear disposable gloves when cutting hot peppers; the oils can burn skin. Avoid touching your face.*

PER (¾-CUP) SERVING *173 cal., 10 g fat (3 g sat. fat), 23 mg chol., 767 mg sodium, 14 g carb., 3 g fiber, 8 g pro. Diabetic Exchanges: 2 vegetable, 2 fat, 1 lean meat.*

Fruit-Glazed Pork Chops

If you've ever eaten applesauce with a pork chop, then you know how beautifully fruit and pork go together. Try this simple recipe with different kinds of fruit preserves to find your own winning flavor combination.

—**EDIE DESPAIN** LOGAN, UT

START TO FINISH: 20 MIN. • **MAKES:** 6 SERVINGS

- ⅓ cup hickory smoke-flavored barbecue sauce
- ½ cup apricot or peach preserves
- 1 tablespoon corn syrup
- 1 teaspoon prepared mustard
- ¼ teaspoon ground cloves
- 6 bone-in pork loin chops (¾ inch thick and 8 ounces each)
- ½ teaspoon salt
- ½ teaspoon pepper

1. In a small bowl, combine the barbecue sauce, preserves, corn syrup, mustard and cloves; set aside.

2. Sprinkle pork chops with salt and pepper. Moisten a paper towel with cooking oil; using long-handled tongs, lightly coat the grill rack.

3. Grill the pork chops, covered, over medium heat or broil 4-5 in. from the heat for 4-5 minutes on each side or until a thermometer reads 145°, basting frequently with the barbecue sauce mixture. Let meat stand for 5 minutes before serving.

Sausage Calzones

Homemade calzones add to the excitement of watching your favorite team on game day. You can make them ahead of time and freeze them once they're cooled. To reheat, bake them at 350° until heated through.

—**JANINE COLASURDO** CHESAPEAKE, VA

PREP: 50 MIN. + RISING • **BAKE:** 20 MIN. • **MAKES:** 6 SERVINGS

- 1 package (¼ ounce) active dry yeast
- ½ cup warm water (110° to 115°)
- ¾ cup warm milk (110° to 115°)
- 2 tablespoons plus 2 teaspoons olive oil, divided
- 1½ teaspoons salt
- 1 teaspoon sugar
- 3 to 3¼ cups all-purpose flour
- 1 pound bulk Italian sausage
- 1 package (10 ounces) frozen chopped spinach, thawed and squeezed dry
- 1 carton (15 ounces) ricotta cheese
- ½ cup grated Parmesan cheese
- 1 tablespoon minced fresh parsley
- ⅛ teaspoon pepper
- 2 tablespoons cornmeal
- ½ teaspoon garlic salt
- 1½ cups pizza sauce, warmed

1. In a large bowl, dissolve yeast in water. Add the milk, 2 tablespoons oil, salt, sugar and 2 cups of flour; beat until smooth. Stir in enough remaining flour to form a soft dough.

2. Turn onto a floured surface; knead until smooth and elastic, about 6-8 minutes. Place in a greased bowl; turn once to grease top. Cover and let rise in a warm place until doubled, about 1 hour.

3. Meanwhile, in a large skillet, cook sausage over medium heat until no longer pink; drain. Add the spinach, cheeses, parsley and pepper; mix well.

4. Punch dough down; divide into six pieces. On a floured surface, roll each piece into an 8-in. circle. Top each with ⅔ cup filling. Fold dough over filling; pinch to seal.

5. Place on greased baking sheets sprinkled with cornmeal. Brush tops lightly with remaining oil; sprinkle with garlic salt. Bake at 400° for 20-25 minutes or until golden brown. Serve with pizza sauce.

Secret's in the Sauce BBQ Ribs

Slow cooking makes these ribs so tender that the meat literally falls off the bones. And the sweet, rich sauce is simply wonderful.

—**TANYA REID** WINSTON SALEM, NC

PREP: 10 MIN. • **COOK:** 6 HOURS • **MAKES:** 5 SERVINGS

- 4½ pounds pork baby back ribs
- 1½ teaspoons pepper
- 2½ cups barbecue sauce
- ¾ cup cherry preserves
- 1 tablespoon Dijon mustard
- 1 garlic clove, minced

1. Cut ribs into serving-size pieces; sprinkle with pepper. Place in a 5- or 6-qt. slow cooker.

2. Combine the remaining ingredients; pour over ribs. Cover and cook on low for 6-8 hours or until meat is tender. Serve with sauce.

Mix a traditional yeast dough in 3 easy steps.

1 Heat liquid to 110° to 115°, using a thermometer. Measure liquid and place in a large mixing bowl. Add active dry yeast; stir until dissolved.

2 Add sugar, salt, fat, eggs (if using) and about half of the flour. Beat with an electric mixer or by hand until smooth.

3 Gradually stir in enough of the remaining flour by hand to form a dough of consistency stated in the recipe.

Pork Chops with Apple Rings

- 6 **pork chops (½ inch thick)**
- ½ **teaspoon celery salt**
- ½ **teaspoon rubbed sage**
- ½ **teaspoon salt**
- ¼ **teaspoon pepper**
- 2 **tablespoons butter**
- 2 **medium unpeeled Golden Delicious apples, cored and cut into ½-inch rings**
- ¼ **cup diced dried apricots**
- 2 **tablespoons golden raisins**
- 2 **tablespoons brown sugar**

Sprinkle pork chops with celery salt, sage, salt and pepper. In a large skillet, brown chops in butter on one side; turn. Top with apple rings. Sprinkle with apricots, raisins and brown sugar. Cover and cook over low heat for 18-22 minutes or until meat juices run clear.

❝With a fruity apricot, raisin and apple topping, these tender chops are simple enough to fix anytime. The best part is that the apples don't have to be peeled–just core and slice and you're ready to go.❞ —**KATHLEEN HARRIS** GALESBURG, IL

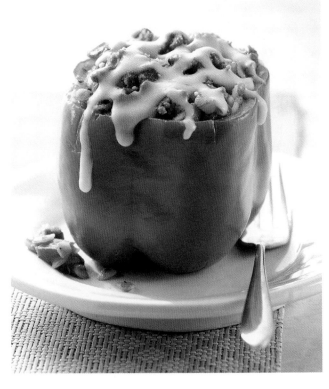

Orzo-Stuffed Peppers

Packed with orzo and Italian sausage, these stuffed peppers make a fun, fast-fixing meal. Use more or less pepper flakes to adjust the level of heat to your liking.
—**KELLY EVANS** DENTON, TX

- 4 **large green peppers**
- 1 **cup uncooked orzo pasta**
- 1 **pound bulk Italian sausage**
- ½ **cup chopped red onion**
- 2 **teaspoons minced garlic**
- 2 **cups marinara or spaghetti sauce**
- 1 **medium tomato, chopped**
- ¼ **cup minced fresh basil or 1 tablespoon dried basil**
- 2 **teaspoons dried rosemary, crushed**
- 1 **teaspoon crushed red pepper flakes**
- ¼ **cup shredded part-skim mozzarella cheese**
- 2 **tablespoons grated Parmesan cheese**

1. Cut tops off peppers and remove seeds. In a Dutch oven, cook peppers in boiling water for 3-5 minutes. Drain and rinse in cold water; set aside.

2. Cook orzo according to package directions. Meanwhile, in a large skillet, cook sausage and onion over medium heat until meat is no longer pink. Add garlic; cook 1 minute longer. Drain.

3. Drain orzo; stir into meat mixture. Add the marinara sauce, tomato, basil, rosemary and pepper flakes. Spoon into peppers.

4. Place in a greased 11-in. x 7-in. baking dish. Cover and bake at 350° for 10 minutes. Uncover; sprinkle with cheeses. Bake 5 minutes longer or until cheese is melted.

German Oktoberfest Pizza

There's a little bit of Deutschland in every slice of this quick and creative pizza. If you like sausage and sauerkraut, you're going to love this dish. It's also a sensational way to use up leftover mashed potatoes.

—**ANGELA SPENGLER** CLOVIS, NM

START TO FINISH: 25 MIN. • **MAKES:** 6 PIECES

- 1 tube (13.8 ounces) refrigerated pizza crust
- 1 pound smoked kielbasa or Polish sausage, cut into ¼-in. slices
- 2 teaspoons butter
- 2 cups leftover or refrigerated mashed potatoes
- 1 cup sauerkraut, rinsed and well drained
- 1 cup (4 ounces) shredded cheddar cheese
- 1 teaspoon caraway seeds

1. Unroll dough into a greased 15-in. x 10-in. x 1-in. baking pan; flatten dough and build up edges slightly. Bake at 425° for 8-10 minutes or until lightly golden brown.

2. Meanwhile, in a large skillet, saute the kielbasa in butter until browned.

3. Spread mashed potatoes over crust. Layer with sauerkraut, kielbasa, cheese and caraway seeds. Bake for 10-15 minutes or until pizza is heated through and the top is lightly browned.

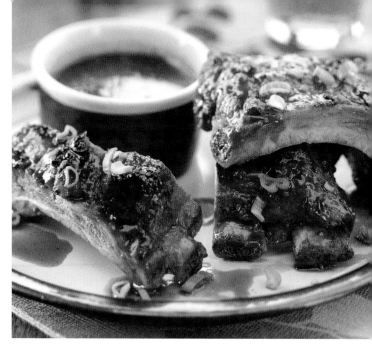

Asian-Style Baby Back Ribs

If you like your ribs tangy and a little sweet, this is the way to go. The molasses and ginger really come through in every bite.

—**ESTHER J. DANIELSON** SAN MARCOS, CA

PREP: 70 MIN. • **GRILL:** 10 MIN. • **MAKES:** 2 SERVINGS

- 1½ pounds pork baby back ribs
- 4½ teaspoons molasses
- 1 tablespoon garlic salt
- 1 teaspoon onion powder
- 1 teaspoon Worcestershire sauce

GLAZE
- ½ cup reduced-sodium soy sauce
- 3 tablespoons thawed pineapple juice concentrate
- 2 tablespoons rice vinegar
- 2 tablespoons hoisin sauce
- 2 tablespoons ketchup
- 1 teaspoon lemon juice
- 1 teaspoon stone-ground mustard
- 1 teaspoon Worcestershire sauce
- 1 teaspoon minced fresh gingerroot
- ½ teaspoon minced garlic
  Chopped green onion

1. Pat ribs dry. Combine the molasses, garlic salt, onion powder and Worcestershire sauce; spoon over meat. Place ribs on a rack in a small shallow roasting pan. Cover and bake at 325° for 50-60 minutes or until tender.

2. In a small saucepan, combine the soy sauce, pineapple juice concentrate, vinegar, hoisin sauce, ketchup, lemon juice, mustard, Worcestershire sauce, ginger and garlic. Bring to a boil. Reduce heat; simmer, uncovered, for 10 minutes or until slightly thickened, stirring occasionally.

3. Moisten a paper towel with cooking oil; using long-handled tongs, rub on grill rack to coat lightly. Brush ribs with some of the glaze; grill, uncovered, over medium heat for 8-12 minutes or until browned, turning frequently and brushing with additional glaze. Serve remaining glaze on the side. Garnish with onion.

His Favorite Ravioli

You can easily turn refrigerated ravioli into a gourmet meal in no time. Just be careful not to overcook the vegetables. I like them to have a little bite.
—**CHRISTA RISPOLI** NEWFOUNDLAND, NJ

START TO FINISH: 30 MIN. • **MAKES:** 4 SERVINGS

- 2 packages (8.8 ounces each) refrigerated pumpkin ravioli or ravioli of your choice
- 1⅔ cups sliced baby portobello mushrooms
- 1 small onion, finely chopped
- 4 thin slices prosciutto or deli ham, chopped
- 1 teaspoon olive oil
- ½ teaspoon minced fresh sage
- 2 cups half-and-half cream
- ½ cup frozen peas, thawed
- 2 tablespoons grated Parmigiano-Reggiano cheese
- ¼ teaspoon salt
- ¼ teaspoon pepper

1. Cook ravioli according to package directions. Meanwhile, in a large skillet, saute the mushrooms, onion and prosciutto in oil until vegetables are tender. Add sage; cook 1 minute longer. Stir in cream. Bring to a boil over medium heat. Reduce heat; simmer, uncovered, for 8-10 minutes or until slightly thickened.
2. Stir in the peas, cheese, salt and pepper; heat through. Drain ravioli; toss with sauce.

Macaroni & Cheese Pizza

What could be better than pizza and mac 'n' cheese combined into one meal? Kids will love it! To make it super-easy, use a can of pizza sauce instead of the tomato sauce, oregano and basil.
—**JENNY STANIEC** OAK GROVE, MN

PREP: 30 MIN. • **BAKE:** 10 MIN. • **MAKES:** 8 SERVINGS

- 1 package (7¼ ounces) macaroni and cheese dinner mix
- 2 eggs, lightly beaten
- ½ pound bulk Italian sausage
- ¼ cup chopped onion
- 1 can (8 ounces) tomato sauce
- 1 teaspoon dried basil
- 1 teaspoon dried oregano
- 1 can (4 ounces) mushroom stems and pieces, drained
- 1 cup (4 ounces) shredded part-skim mozzarella cheese

1. Prepare macaroni and cheese according to package directions; stir in eggs. Spread onto a greased 12-in. pizza pan. Bake at 375° for 10 minutes or until a thermometer reads 160°.
2. Meanwhile, in a large skillet, cook sausage and onion over medium heat until meat is no longer pink; drain.
3. In a small bowl, combine the tomato sauce, basil and oregano. Spread over macaroni mixture. Layer with sausage mixture, mushrooms and cheese. Bake for 10 minutes or until cheese is melted.

Sesame Pork Ribs

No one ever believes how little effort it takes to make these tender, juicy ribs. The lightly sweet and tangy sauce penetrates the ribs as they simmer in the slow cooker.

—SANDY ALEXANDER FAYETTEVILLE, NC

PREP: 15 MIN. • **COOK:** 5 HOURS • **MAKES:** 5 SERVINGS

- ¾ cup packed brown sugar
- ½ cup reduced-sodium soy sauce
- ½ cup ketchup
- ¼ cup honey
- 2 tablespoons white wine vinegar
- 3 garlic cloves, minced
- 1 teaspoon salt
- 1 teaspoon ground ginger
- ¼ to ½ teaspoon crushed red pepper flakes
- 5 pounds bone-in country-style pork ribs
- 1 medium onion, sliced
- 2 tablespoons sesame seeds, toasted
- 2 tablespoons chopped green onions

1. In a large bowl, combine the first nine ingredients. Add ribs and turn to coat. Place the onion in a 5-qt. slow cooker; top with ribs and sauce. Cover and cook on low for 5-6 hours or until meat is tender.
2. Place ribs on a serving platter; sprinkle with sesame seeds and green onions.

Holiday Glazed Ham

I like to serve this juicy, mouthwatering ham with mashed potatoes and colorful vegetables. The apricot glaze is delicious, and the pineapple and cloves assure a truly lovely presentation.

—DIANE FREEMAN FALKLAND, BC

PREP: 20 MIN. • **BAKE:** 2 HOURS • **MAKES:** 16 SERVINGS

- 1 boneless fully cooked ham (about 6 pounds)
- 1 tablespoon whole cloves
- 1 can (20 ounces) sliced pineapple
- 1 cup apricot preserves
- 1 teaspoon ground mustard
- ½ teaspoon ground allspice
   Maraschino cherries

1. Preheat oven to 325°. Place ham on a rack in a shallow roasting pan. Score the surface of ham, making diamond shapes ½ in. deep; insert a clove in each diamond. Bake, uncovered, for 1½ hours.
2. Drain pineapple, reserving juice. In a small saucepan, combine pineapple juice, preserves, mustard and allspice. Bring to a boil; cook and stir for 10 minutes or until slightly thickened.
3. Spoon half of the glaze over ham. Secure pineapple slices and cherries on top and sides of ham with toothpicks.
4. Bake 30-45 minutes or until a thermometer reads 140°, basting twice with remaining glaze.

Barbecue Pork and Penne Skillet

I'm the proud mother of four wonderful and active children. Simple, delicious and quick meals like this are perfect for us to enjoy together following our after-school activities, errands and sports.

—**JUDY ARMSTRONG** PRAIRIEVILLE, LA

START TO FINISH: 25 MIN. • **MAKES:** 8 SERVINGS

- 1 package (16 ounces) penne pasta
- 1 cup chopped sweet red pepper
- ¾ cup chopped onion
- 1 tablespoon butter
- 1 tablespoon olive oil
- 3 garlic cloves, minced
- 1 carton (18 ounces) refrigerated fully cooked barbecued shredded pork
- 1 can (14½ ounces) diced tomatoes with mild green chilies, undrained
- ½ cup beef broth
- 1 teaspoon ground cumin
- 1 teaspoon pepper
- ¼ teaspoon salt
- 1¼ cups shredded cheddar cheese
- ¼ cup chopped green onions

1. Cook pasta according to package directions. Meanwhile, in a large skillet, saute red pepper and onion in butter and oil until tender. Add garlic; saute 1 minute longer. Stir in the pork, tomatoes, broth, cumin, pepper and salt; heat through.

2. Drain pasta. Add pasta and cheese to pork mixture. Sprinkle with green onions.

COOKING PASTA

To prevent pasta from sticking together when cooking, use a large pot and 3 quarts of water for each 8 ounces of pasta you plan to cook. Add 1 tablespoon cooking oil to the water. (This also prevents boiling over.) Bring the water to a full rolling boil before stirring in the pasta. Stir several times to separate the pasta until the water returns to a boil.

Muffuletta Pasta

A friend gave me this recipe when she learned that I love muffuletta sandwiches. It's very rich and filling and goes together quickly for an easy weeknight meal.

—**JAN HOLLINGSWORTH** HOUSTON, MS

START TO FINISH: 25 MIN. • **MAKES:** 8 SERVINGS

- 1 package (16 ounces) bow tie pasta
- 1 bunch green onions, chopped
- 2 teaspoons plus ¼ cup butter, divided
- 1 tablespoon minced garlic
- 1 package (16 ounces) cubed fully cooked ham
- 1 jar (12.36 ounces) tapenade or ripe olive bruschetta topping, drained
- 1 package (3½ ounces) sliced pepperoni
- 1 cup heavy whipping cream
- 2 cups (8 ounces) shredded Italian cheese blend

1. Cook pasta according to package directions. Meanwhile, in a large skillet, saute onions in 2 teaspoons butter until tender. Add garlic; cook 1 minute longer. Add the ham, tapenade and pepperoni; saute 2 minutes longer.

2. Cube remaining butter; stir butter and cream into skillet. Bring to a boil over medium heat. Reduce heat; simmer, uncovered, for 3 minutes.

3. Drain pasta; toss with ham mixture. Sprinkle with cheese.

Pomegranate Pork Tenderloin

Tender slices of pork are paired with a flavorful sweet-tart pomegranate sauce. If you're making this during the week, try using a long grain and wild rice mix, which cooks more quickly than wild rice.

—ELIZABETH DUMONT BOULDER, CO

PREP: 20 MIN. • **COOK:** 20 MIN. • **MAKES:** 4 SERVINGS

- ¼ cup all-purpose flour
- ¼ cup cornmeal
- 2 teaspoons grated lemon peel
- 1½ teaspoons salt, divided
- ½ teaspoon pepper
- 1 to 1¼ pounds pork tenderloin, cut into 2-inch slices
- 2 tablespoons olive oil
- 1 cup reduced-sodium chicken broth
- 1 cup pomegranate juice
- 2 tablespoons sugar
- 1 to 2 garlic cloves, minced
- ¼ teaspoon ground ginger
- ⅛ teaspoon cayenne pepper
- 2 tablespoons cornstarch
- 3 tablespoons cold water
- 2 cups hot cooked wild rice

1. In a large resealable plastic bag, combine the flour, cornmeal, lemon peel, 1 teaspoon salt and pepper. Add pork, a few pieces at a time, and shake to coat.

2. In a large skillet, cook pork in oil for 5-7 minutes on each side or until tender. Remove and keep warm.

3. In the same skillet, combine the broth, juice, sugar, garlic, ginger, cayenne and remaining salt. Bring to a boil. Reduce heat; simmer, uncovered, for 5 minutes.

4. Combine cornstarch and water until smooth; gradually stir into the pan. Bring to a boil; cook and stir for 2 minutes or until thickened. Return pork to the pan and heat through. Serve with rice.

PER SERVING *374 cal., 11 g fat (2 g sat. fat), 63 mg chol., 694 mg sodium, 41 g carb., 2 g fiber, 27 g pro.* **Diabetic Exchanges:** *3 lean meat, 2 starch, 1 fat, ½ fruit.*

Glazed Pork Chops

PREP: 10 MIN. + MARINATING • **GRILL:** 10 MIN. • **MAKES:** 4 SERVINGS

- ⅔ cup apricot preserves
- ½ cup Italian salad dressing
- 2 tablespoons Dijon mustard
- 4 boneless pork loin chops (1 inch thick and 6 ounces each)

1. In a small bowl, combine the preserves, dressing and mustard. Pour ¾ cup marinade into a large resealable bag; add the pork. Seal bag and turn to coat; refrigerate for 8 hours or overnight. Cover and refrigerate remaining marinade for basting.

2. Drain chops and discard marinade. Using long-handled tongs, moisten a paper towel with cooking oil and lightly coat the grill rack.

3. Grill, covered, over medium heat or broil 4-5 in. from the heat for 4-5 minutes on each side or until a thermometer reads 145°, basting frequently with reserved marinade. Let meat stand for 5 minutes before serving.

> ❝I have served these family-favorite chops for birthdays, Easter dinner and everyday meals. The recipe is easy to double or even triple to feed a crowd.❞
>
> **—SONDRA WARSON** MADRID, IA

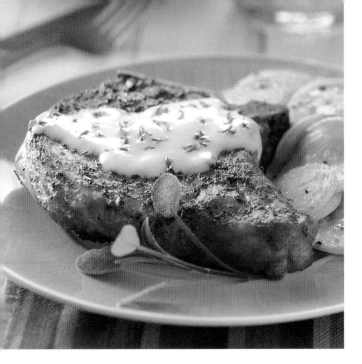

Sage Pork Chops with Cider Pan Gravy

A creamy sauce flavored with apple cider and sage makes for a quick and tasty weeknight dinner. If you like, serve these lightly seasoned chops with couscous, rice or noodles.

—**ERICA WILSON** BEVERLY, MA

START TO FINISH: 30 MIN. • **MAKES:** 4 SERVINGS

- 4 bone-in center-cut pork loin chops (6 ounces each)
  Salt and pepper to taste
- 3 tablespoons dried sage leaves
- ¼ cup all-purpose flour
- 2 tablespoons butter
- 2 tablespoons canola oil
- ½ cup apple cider or juice
- ½ cup reduced-sodium chicken broth
- ¼ cup heavy whipping cream
  Minced fresh parsley

1. Sprinkle pork chops with salt and pepper; rub with sage. Place flour in a small shallow bowl; coat chops with flour.
2. In a large skillet over medium heat, brown chops in butter and oil on both sides. Remove and keep warm.
3. Add cider, stirring to loosen browned bits from pan. Cook, uncovered, for 3 minutes. Stir in the broth; cook for 3 minutes longer. Add cream; cook for 2-3 minutes or until gravy is slightly thickened. Return chops to the pan; cover and cook for 6-8 minutes or until a thermometer reads 160°. Garnish with parsley.

SIMPLE BROTH SUBSTITUTE

If you don't want to open a can of broth for the pork chop recipe, just use ¼ cup water mixed with ¼ teaspoon bouillon granules instead. The gravy will still have plenty of flavor.

Pork Burritos

I have been making this recipe for 20 years—changing it here and there until this delicious version is now what I serve. It's a favorite with our family, and for when we have company.

—**SHARON BELMONT** LINCOLN, NE

PREP: 20 MIN. • **COOK:** 8 HOURS • **MAKES:** 14 SERVINGS

- 1 boneless pork sirloin roast (3 pounds)
- ¼ cup reduced-sodium chicken broth
- 1 envelope reduced-sodium taco seasoning
- 1 tablespoon dried parsley flakes
- 2 garlic cloves, minced
- ½ teaspoon pepper
- ¼ teaspoon salt
- 1 can (16 ounces) refried beans
- 1 can (4 ounces) chopped green chilies
- 14 flour tortillas (8 inches), warmed
  Optional toppings: shredded lettuce, chopped tomatoes, chopped green pepper, guacamole, reduced-fat sour cream and shredded reduced-fat cheddar cheese

1. Cut roast in half; place in a 4- or 5-qt. slow cooker. In a small bowl, combine the broth, taco seasoning, parsley, garlic, pepper and salt. Pour over roast. Cover and cook on low for 8-10 hours or until meat is very tender.
2. Remove pork from the slow cooker; cool slightly. Shred with two forks; set aside. Skim fat from cooking liquid; stir in beans and chilies. Return pork to the slow cooker; heat through.
3. Spoon ½ cup pork mixture down the center of each tortilla; add toppings of your choice. Fold sides and ends over filling and roll up.

TO FREEZE BURRITOS *Roll up burritos without toppings. Wrap individually in paper towels, then foil. Transfer to a resealable plastic bag. May be frozen for up to 2 months. To use frozen burritos, unwrap foil. Place paper towel-wrapped burritos on a microwave-safe plate. Microwave on high for 3-4 minutes or until heated through. Serve with toppings of your choice.*

PER SERVING *320 cal., 9 g fat (3 g sat. fat), 61 mg chol., 606 mg sodium, 33 g carb., 2 g fiber, 26 g pro.* **Diabetic Exchanges:** *2 starch, 2 lean meat, 1 fat.*

Turkey Meat Loaf, page 129

126

133

130

Poultry Entrees

For **healthy** weeknight meals and **special** dinners for company, look to these **best-loved** chicken and turkey recipes. Discover **fresh and fruity** takes on poultry, **irresistible** chicken fingers, **bubbling** casseroles, indulgent **baked mostaccioli** and more.

Sesame Chicken with Ginger Shiitake Cream Sauce

The golden mushroom sauce in this skillet chicken dish is addictive! You may not be able to stop eating it.

—PAMELA GELSOMINI WRENTHAM, MA

PREP: 15 MIN. • **COOK:** 30 MIN.
MAKES: 4 SERVINGS

- 4 **boneless skinless chicken breast halves (6 ounces each)**
- ⅛ **teaspoon salt**
- ⅛ **teaspoon pepper**
- ⅔ **cup sesame seeds**
- 2 **tablespoons peanut oil**
- ½ **pound sliced fresh shiitake mushrooms**
- 4½ **teaspoons minced fresh gingerroot**
- 2 **garlic cloves, minced**
- 4½ **teaspoons soy sauce**
- 1½ **teaspoons butter**
- 1 **cup heavy whipping cream**
- 1½ **teaspoons wasabi mustard**
  Hot cooked rice

1. Flatten chicken to ½-in. thickness; sprinkle with salt and pepper. Place sesame seeds in a shallow bowl; dip chicken in sesame seeds.

2. In a large skillet, cook chicken in oil over medium heat for 6-8 minutes on each side or until a thermometer reads 170°. Remove and keep warm.

3. In the same skillet, cook and stir the mushrooms, ginger and garlic in soy sauce and butter for 3 minutes. Add cream and mustard; cook and stir for 6-8 minutes or until thickened. Serve sauce with chicken and rice.

SHIITAKE SMARTS

Native to Asia and common in Japanese, Korean and Chinese cuisines, shiitake mushrooms have become increasingly popular in U.S. markets. They have a meaty texture and tough stems that should be discarded or reserved for flavoring stock. They can be expensive. To stretch shiitakes in a recipe, try substituting button mushrooms for half of the amount called for.

Mango Chicken with Plum Sauce

A generous serving of this flavorful chicken with crunchy fresh veggies in a sweet Asian sauce will leave you perfectly satisfied.

—CHRISTINE VAUGHT SALEM, OR

PREP: 25 MIN. • **COOK:** 15 MIN. • **MAKES:** 6 SERVINGS

- 1 **tablespoon sugar**
- 1 **tablespoon cornstarch**
- ½ **teaspoon salt**
- ½ **cup chicken broth**
- ¼ **cup teriyaki sauce**
- ½ **pound fresh snow peas, trimmed**
- 2 **large carrots, sliced diagonally**
- 2 **medium zucchini, sliced**
- ½ **cup chopped red onion**
- ½ **medium sweet red pepper, sliced**
- 1 **can (4 ounces) sliced water chestnuts, drained**
- 2 **tablespoons canola oil**
- 3 **cups cubed cooked chicken breasts**
- 2 **medium mangoes, peeled and mashed**
- ½ **cup plum sauce**
- 2 **cups hot cooked brown rice**
- ¼ **cup slivered almonds, toasted**

1. In a small saucepan, combine the sugar, cornstarch and salt; stir in broth and teriyaki sauce until smooth. Cook and stir until thickened. Set aside.

2. In a large skillet or wok, stir-fry the snow peas, carrots, zucchini, onion, pepper and water chestnuts in oil until crisp-tender. Add the chicken, mangoes and broth mixture; heat through. Stir in plum sauce. Serve with rice. Sprinkle with almonds.

Crumb-Coated Chicken & Blackberry Salsa

Maple lends a sweet touch to blackberry salsa. Besides chicken, it's also great with fried fish.

—TAMMY THOMAS MORRISVILLE, VT

START TO FINISH: 25 MIN. • **MAKES:** 2 SERVINGS

- ½ **cup fresh blackberries**
- 1 **jalapeno pepper, seeded and minced**
- 2 **tablespoons minced fresh cilantro**
- 2 **tablespoons chopped red onion**
- 2 **tablespoons maple syrup**
- 2 **tablespoons balsamic vinegar**
- 2 **boneless skinless chicken breast halves (5 ounces each)**
- ⅛ **teaspoon salt**
- ⅛ **teaspoon pepper**
- ¼ **cup all-purpose flour**
- 1 **egg, beaten**
- ½ **cup panko (Japanese) bread crumbs**
- 1 **tablespoon olive oil**

1. In a small bowl, combine the first six ingredients. Cover and refrigerate until serving.

2. Flatten chicken to ¼-in. thickness; sprinkle with salt and pepper. Place the flour, egg and bread crumbs in separate shallow bowls. Coat chicken with flour, dip in egg, then coat with crumbs.

3. In a large skillet, cook chicken in oil over medium heat for 4-6 minutes on each side or until no longer pink. Serve with salsa.

NOTE *Wear disposable gloves when cutting hot peppers; the oils can burn skin. Avoid touching your face.*

Chicken with Rosemary Butter Sauce

START TO FINISH: 25 MIN. • **MAKES:** 4 SERVINGS

- 4 **boneless skinless chicken breast halves (4 ounces each)**
- 4 **tablespoons butter, divided**
- ½ **cup white wine or chicken broth**
- ½ **cup heavy whipping cream**
- 1 **tablespoon minced fresh rosemary**

1. In a large skillet over medium heat, cook chicken in 1 tablespoon butter 4-5 minutes on each side or until a thermometer reads 165°. Remove and keep warm.

2. Add wine to pan; cook over medium-low heat, stirring to loosen browned bits from pan. Add cream and bring to a boil. Reduce heat; cook and stir until slightly thickened. Stir in rosemary and remaining butter until blended. Serve sauce with chicken.

“It only takes a few ingredients to make a rich and creamy sauce with a mellow wine flavor. You can substitute your favorite fresh herb for the rosemary if you prefer.” —**CONNIE MCDOWELL** GREENWOOD, DE

Lasagna Deliziosa

My family loves this lasagna. We often serve it as a birthday dinner. I've lightened it up a lot from the original version by using turkey sausage, lean beef and low-fat cheese. No one can tell the difference!

—**HEATHER O'NEILL** TROY, OH

PREP: 45 MIN. • **BAKE:** 50 MIN. + STANDING
MAKES: 12 SERVINGS

- 9 **uncooked lasagna noodles**
- 1 **package (19½ ounces) Italian turkey sausage links, casings removed**
- ½ **pound lean ground beef (90% lean)**
- 1 **large onion, chopped**
- 2 **garlic cloves, minced**
- 1 **can (28 ounces) diced tomatoes, undrained**
- 1 **can (12 ounces) tomato paste**
- ¼ **cup water**
- 2 **teaspoons sugar**
- 1 **teaspoon dried basil**
- ½ **teaspoon fennel seed**
- ¼ **teaspoon pepper**
- 1 **egg, lightly beaten**
- 1 **carton (15 ounces) reduced-fat ricotta cheese**
- 1 **tablespoon minced fresh parsley**
- ½ **teaspoon salt**
- 2 **cups (8 ounces) shredded part-skim mozzarella cheese**
- ¾ **cup grated Parmesan cheese**

1. Cook noodles according to package directions. Meanwhile, in a Dutch oven, cook the sausage, beef and onion over medium heat until meat is no longer pink. Add garlic; cook 1 minute longer. Drain.

2. Stir in the tomatoes, tomato paste, water, sugar, basil, fennel and pepper. Bring to a boil. Reduce heat; cover and simmer for 15-20 minutes, stirring occasionally.

3. In a small bowl, combine the egg, ricotta cheese, parsley and salt. Drain noodles and rinse in cold water. Spread 1 cup meat sauce into a 13-in. x 9-in. baking dish coated with cooking spray. Top with three noodles, 2 cups meat sauce, ⅔ cup ricotta cheese mixture, ⅔ cup mozzarella and ¼ cup Parmesan. Repeat layers twice.

4. Cover and bake at 375° for 40 minutes. Uncover; bake 10-15 minutes longer or until bubbly. Let stand for 10 minutes before cutting.

PER SERVING *323 cal., 12 g fat (5 g sat. fat), 79 mg chol., 701 mg sodium, 28 g carb., 4 g fiber, 25 g pro.* **Diabetic Exchanges:** *3 lean meat, 2 vegetable, 1 starch, 1 fat.*

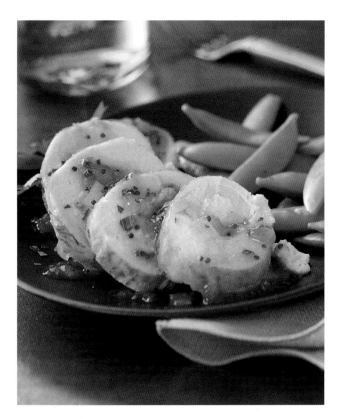

Goat Cheese-Stuffed Chicken with Apricot Glaze

My original version of this recipe used several tablespoons of butter versus the one tablespoon of oil. With a few more tweaks, this rich and filling entree is under 350 calories.

—DAVID DAHLMAN CHATSWORTH, CA

PREP: 20 MIN. • **COOK:** 20 MIN. • **MAKES:** 2 SERVINGS

- 2 boneless skinless chicken breast halves (6 ounces each)
- ¼ teaspoon salt
- ¼ teaspoon pepper
- 2 tablespoons goat cheese
- 2 tablespoons part-skim ricotta cheese
- 4 tablespoons chopped shallots, divided
- 1 teaspoon olive oil
- ⅔ cup reduced-sodium chicken broth
- 2 tablespoons apricot spreadable fruit
- 1 tablespoon lemon juice
- 1 teaspoon spicy brown mustard
- 1 teaspoon minced fresh parsley

1. Flatten chicken to ¼-in. thickness; sprinkle with salt and pepper. Combine the goat cheese, ricotta and 1 tablespoon shallots; spread over the center of each chicken breast. Roll up and secure with toothpicks.
2. In a small nonstick skillet, brown chicken in oil on all sides. Remove and keep warm.
3. In the same skillet, saute remaining shallots until tender. Stir in the broth, spreadable fruit, lemon juice and mustard. Bring to a boil; cook until liquid is reduced by half.
4. Return chicken to the pan; cover and cook for 6-7 minutes or until a no longer pink. Discard toothpicks. Serve chicken with cooking liquid. Sprinkle with parsley.

Southwest Chicken and Rice

START TO FINISH: 10 MIN. • **MAKES:** 4 SERVINGS

- 2 packages (8½ ounces each) ready-to-serve Santa Fe whole grain rice medley
- 2 packages (6 ounces each) ready-to-use Southwestern chicken strips, cut into chunks
- 1 can (10 ounces) diced tomatoes and green chilies, drained
- ½ cup shredded Monterey Jack cheese

1. Heat rice according to package directions. In a 2-qt. microwave-safe dish, combine chicken and tomatoes; stir in rice. Cover and microwave on high for 2-3 minutes.
2. Sprinkle with cheese; cook 1 minute longer or until cheese is melted.
NOTE *This recipe was tested in a 1,100-watt microwave.*

❝This super-fast microwave meal is a tasy way to enjoy family time, no matter how busy you are.❞
—PENNY HAWKINS MEBANE, NC

Turkey Meat Loaf

For a holiday-esque meal any time of year, this tender turkey meat loaf is perfect when complemented with a cranberry glaze. I call it Just-Like-Thanksgiving Meat Loaf.

—**MOLLIE BROWN** LOS ANGELES, CA

PREP: 30 MIN. + STANDING • **BAKE:** 45 MIN. • **MAKES:** 6 SERVINGS

- 1 cup seasoned stuffing cubes
- ½ cup milk
- 1 egg, beaten
- 1 celery rib, finely chopped
- 1 small onion, grated
- 1 small carrot, grated
- ¼ cup dried cranberries
- ½ teaspoon salt
- ¼ teaspoon pepper
- 3 to 4½ teaspoons minced fresh sage, divided
- 3 teaspoons minced fresh rosemary, divided
- 1½ pounds lean ground turkey
- ½ cup whole-berry cranberry sauce
- ½ cup ketchup
- ⅛ teaspoon hot pepper sauce

1. Preheat oven to 375°. In a large bowl, combine stuffing cubes and milk. Let stand 10 minutes; break up stuffing cubes with a fork. Stir in egg, celery, onion, carrot, cranberries, salt and pepper. Combine sage and rosemary; add half to the mixture. Crumble turkey over mixture and mix well. Pat into an ungreased 9x5-in. loaf pan.

2. Bake, uncovered, 25 minutes; drain if necessary. Combine cranberry sauce, ketchup, pepper sauce and remaining herbs; spread over meat loaf. Bake 20-25 minutes or until no pink remains and a thermometer reads 165°.

Chicken Saltimbocca with Mushroom Sauce

I created this recipe to capture the flavors of saltimbocca, but without all the fat and sodium. We really enjoy it.

—**VIRGINIA ANTHONY** JACKSONVILLE, FL

PREP: 20 MIN. • **COOK:** 40 MIN. • **MAKES:** 8 SERVINGS

- ½ cup all-purpose flour
- ¼ teaspoon salt
- ½ teaspoon pepper, divided
- 8 boneless skinless chicken thighs (2 pounds)
- 2 tablespoons olive oil, divided
- 2 cups sliced fresh mushrooms
- 2 thin slices prosciutto or deli ham
- ½ cup chopped shallots
- 2 garlic cloves, minced
- 1 cup white wine or reduced-sodium chicken broth
- 1 cup reduced-sodium chicken broth
- ⅓ cup half-and-half cream
- 3 tablespoons fresh sage or 3 teaspoons dried sage leaves, divided
- 1 can (15 ounces) white kidney or cannellini beans, rinsed and drained, divided
- ¼ cup water

1. In a large resealable plastic bag, combine the flour, salt and ¼ teaspoon pepper. Add chicken, a few pieces at a time, and shake to coat. In a large skillet over medium heat, cook chicken in 1 tablespoon oil for 6-8 minutes on each side or until juices run clear. Remove and keep warm.

2. In the same skillet, saute the mushrooms, prosciutto, shallots and garlic in remaining oil until tender. Stir in wine. Bring to a boil; cook until liquid is reduced to about ⅓ cup, about 10 minutes.

3. Stir in broth. Simmer, uncovered, for 5 minutes or until slightly reduced. Stir in cream and 2 tablespoons sage; heat through (do not boil).

4. Meanwhile, in a small saucepan, lightly mash ½ cup beans; add the water. Stir in the remaining pepper, sage and beans. Heat through.

5. Add chicken to the mushroom mixture and heat through. Serve with beans.

Lemony Spinach-Stuffed Chicken Breasts

This is a favorite of mine to make for dinner guests. I usually serve it with couscous, rice or garlic mashed potatoes along with a vegetable saute or tossed salad.
—**PAM NELSON** BEAVERTON, OR

PREP: 30 MIN. • **COOK:** 20 MIN. • **MAKES:** 4 SERVINGS

- ½ cup chopped sweet onion
- 3 teaspoons olive oil, divided
- 6½ cups fresh baby spinach, chopped
- 1 garlic clove, minced
- 1 tablespoon balsamic vinegar
- ¼ cup crumbled feta cheese
- ½ teaspoon grated lemon peel
- ¼ teaspoon salt
- ¼ teaspoon pepper
- 4 boneless skinless chicken breast halves (6 ounces each)

1. In a large skillet, cook onion in 2 teaspoons oil over medium heat for 15-20 minutes or until golden brown, stirring frequently. Add the spinach, garlic and vinegar; cook until spinach is wilted. Remove from the heat; cool for 5 minutes. Stir in the cheese, lemon peel, salt and pepper.
2. Flatten chicken to ¼-in. thickness. Spread spinach mixture over chicken. Roll up and secure with toothpicks.
3. In a large skillet over medium heat, cook chicken in remaining oil for 8-10 minutes on each side or until a thermometer reads 170°. Discard toothpicks.
PER SERVING *253 cal., 9 g fat (2 g sat. fat), 98 mg chol., 337 mg sodium, 5 g carb., 2 g fiber, 37 g pro.*
Diabetic Exchanges: *5 lean meat, 1 vegetable, 1 fat.*

Orange-Cashew Chicken and Rice

I like to experiment with different ingredients when I make this popular dish. Try celery instead of bok choy or toasted almonds instead of cashews. Each and every combination turns out great!
—**AYSHA SCHURMAN** AMMON, ID

START TO FINISH: 30 MIN. • **MAKES:** 3 SERVINGS

- 1 cup instant brown rice
- 1 can (11 ounces) mandarin oranges
- ¼ cup chopped cashews
- ¼ cup chicken broth
- 2 tablespoons soy sauce
- 2 tablespoons teriyaki sauce
- ¾ pound boneless skinless chicken breasts, cut into ½-inch pieces
- 1 tablespoon canola oil
- ½ cup chopped bok choy
- ¼ cup minced chives

1. Cook rice according to package directions. Meanwhile, drain oranges, reserving ½ cup oranges and 2 tablespoons juice (save remainder for another use).
2. In a small bowl, combine the cashews, broth, soy sauce, teriyaki sauce and reserved juice; set aside. In a large wok or skillet, stir-fry chicken in oil until no longer pink. Add cashew mixture; cook 1 minute longer. Add the bok choy, chives and reserved oranges; cook and stir for 2 minutes.
3. Fluff rice with a fork; serve with chicken mixture.

Pesto Chicken Mostaccioli

I was looking for something new to whip up and decided to invent my own recipe. We love pesto and mac and cheese but who knew what a yummy combination it would be with chicken nuggets! Comfort food to the max, this deliciously different casserole is great for a crowd!

—REBECCA STABLEIN LAKE FOREST, CA

PREP: 25 MIN. • **BAKE:** 25 MIN.
MAKES: 2 CASSEROLES (5 SERVINGS EACH)

    1 package (16 ounces) mostaccioli
    1 package (16 ounces) frozen breaded chicken tenders
    4 cups (16 ounces) shredded cheddar cheese
    1 container (16 ounces) sour cream
    1 carton (15 ounces) ricotta cheese
   ¾ cup prepared pesto
   ⅔ cup heavy whipping cream
   ½ cup grated Parmesan cheese
   ½ cup dry bread crumbs
   ¼ cup butter, melted

1. Cook mostaccioli and chicken according to package directions. Meanwhile, in a large bowl, combine the cheddar cheese, sour cream, ricotta, pesto, cream and Parmesan cheese.
2. Chop chicken tenders and drain mostaccioli; add to cheese mixture. Toss to coat. Transfer to two greased 11-in. x 7-in. baking dishes (dishes will be full). Combine bread crumbs and butter; sprinkle over the top.
3. Bake, uncovered, at 350° for 25-30 minutes or until golden brown.

Maple Chicken 'n' Ribs

With its generous portions, this recipe is great for a potluck or family reunion. I also love this entree because the chicken thighs and country-style ribs are affordable.

—PHYLLIS SCHMALZ KANSAS CITY, KS

PREP: 15 MIN. + MARINATING • **BAKE:** 1½ HOURS
MAKES: 8 SERVINGS

  1½ cups apple cider or juice
   ½ cup maple syrup
    9 garlic cloves, peeled and crushed
    3 tablespoons canola oil
    3 tablespoons soy sauce
    2 cinnamon sticks (3 inches)
    3 whole star anise
   ¾ teaspoon crushed red pepper flakes
    8 pork spareribs
    8 bone-in chicken thighs

1. In a large bowl, combine the first eight ingredients. Divide 1½ cups marinade between two large resealable plastic bags; add spareribs and chicken to separate bags. Seal bags and turn to coat; refrigerate for at least 8 hours or overnight. Cover and refrigerate remaining marinade.
2. Drain and discard marinade. Place ribs and chicken, skin side up, in separate greased shallow roasting pans.
3. Bake at 350° for 1½ to 2 hours or until tender, basting occasionally with reserved marinade.

FOR THE BIRDS
GRAND PRIZE
WINNER
★ ★ ★ ★

Prosciutto Chicken in Wine Sauce

Last year, I decided to grow basil, sage and thyme. The scent of sage is very enticing to me, so I decided to include it in this recipe. The rest just came together naturally.
—**LORRAINE CALAND** SHUNIAH, ON

PREP: 25 MIN. • **COOK:** 30 MIN. • **MAKES:** 6 SERVINGS

- 1 broiler/fryer chicken (3 pounds), cut up and skin removed
- ½ teaspoon salt
- ¼ teaspoon pepper
- 1 tablespoon olive oil
- 1 tablespoon butter
- 1 cup white wine or reduced-sodium chicken broth
- 4 thin slices prosciutto or deli ham, chopped
- 1 shallot, chopped
- 1 tablespoon fresh sage or 1 teaspoon dried sage leaves
- 1 garlic clove, minced

1. Sprinkle chicken with salt and pepper. In a large nonstick skillet coated with cooking spray, brown chicken on all sides in oil and butter.
2. Add the remaining ingredients, stirring to loosen browned bits. Bring to a boil. Reduce heat; cover and simmer for 20-25 minutes or until chicken juices run clear. Remove chicken and keep warm. Bring sauce to a boil; cook for 10-12 minutes or until liquid is reduced to ¾ cup. Serve with chicken.
PER SERVING *231 cal., 11 g fat (4 g sat. fat), 87 mg chol., 456 mg sodium, 2 g carb., trace fiber, 27 g pro.* **Diabetic Exchanges:** *4 lean meat, 1 fat.*

Boost turkey's flavor with skin-deep seasonings.

1 With your fingers, gently loosen the skin from the turkey or turkey breast. Spread half of the mixture over the meat under the skin.

2 Smooth the skin back over the meat and secure with toothpicks if necessary. Spread remaining mixture over the skin.

Roasted Citrus & Herb Turkey

Thanksgiving has never been the same since I tried this recipe. I have made it for the past 3 years, and it never fails to impress us.
—**NANCY NIEMERG** DIETERICH, IL

PREP: 30 MIN. • **BAKE:** 2¾ HOURS + STANDING
MAKES: 14-16 SERVINGS (2 CUPS GRAVY)

- 1 turkey (14 to 16 pounds)
- ¼ cup butter, softened
- 2 tablespoons Italian seasoning
- 2 teaspoons salt
- 2 teaspoons pepper
- 1 large onion, quartered
- 1 medium lemon, quartered
- 1 medium orange, quartered
- 3 fresh rosemary sprigs
- 3 sprigs fresh sage
- 3 cups chicken broth, divided
- ¼ cup all-purpose flour
  Additional citrus fruits and herb sprigs, optional

1. Pat turkey dry. Combine butter and Italian seasoning. With fingers, carefully loosen skin from the turkey breast; rub half of the butter under skin. Rub remaining mixture over the skin. Rub cavity with salt and pepper and fill with onion, lemon, orange, rosemary and sage. Tuck wings under turkey; tie drumsticks together. Place breast side up on a rack in a roasting pan. Pour 2 cups broth into pan.
2. Bake at 325° for 2¾ to 3¼ hours or until a thermometer reads 180°, basting occasionally with pan drippings. Cover loosely with foil if turkey browns too quickly. Cover and let stand for 20 minutes before carving.
3. Pour drippings into a small saucepan; skim fat. Combine flour and remaining broth until smooth; whisk into the pan. Bring to a boil; cook and stir for 2 minutes or until thickened.
4. Discard onion, lemon, orange and herbs from the turkey; transfer turkey to a serving platter. Garnish the platter with additional citrus fruits and herb sprigs if desired. Serve turkey with gravy.

Chorizo-Stuffed Turkey Breast with Mexican Grits

This recipe features a wonderful combination of well-seasoned ingredients. Unique and impressive, it's just perfect for company.
—**VERONICA GANTLEY** NORFOLK, VA

PREP: 30 MIN. • **BAKE:** 1¼ HOURS + STANDING • **MAKES:** 6 SERVINGS

- 1 boneless skinless turkey breast half (2 pounds)
- ½ pound uncooked chorizo, crumbled
- 2 tablespoons olive oil
- 1 teaspoon salt, divided
- 1 teaspoon pepper, divided
- 2 cups water
- 1 cup milk
- 1 cup quick-cooking grits
- 1 can (4 ounces) chopped green chilies
- ½ cup shredded Mexican cheese blend
  Minced fresh parsley, optional

1. Cover turkey with plastic wrap; flatten to ½-in. thickness. Remove plastic. Spread chorizo over turkey to within 1 in. of edges. Roll up jelly-roll style, starting with a short side; tie with kitchen string.

2. Rub with oil. Sprinkle with ½ teaspoon salt and ½ teaspoon pepper. In a large ovenproof skillet, brown turkey on all sides. Bake at 350° for 1¼ to 1½ hours or until a thermometer reads 170°. Cover and let stand for 10 minutes before slicing.

3. In a large saucepan, bring the water, milk and remaining salt to a boil. Slowly stir in grits. Reduce heat; cook and stir for 5-7 minutes or until thickened. Stir in the chilies, cheese and remaining pepper. Serve grits with turkey. Sprinkle with parsley if desired.

Thai Portobello Chicken Stir-Fry

My husband and I never met a mushroom we didn't like. This zesty stir-fry is a favorite of ours. It's loaded with vegetables.
—**SUSAN BAZAN** SEQUIM, WA

PREP: 25 MIN. • **COOK:** 20 MIN. • **MAKES:** 6 SERVINGS

- ½ cup Thai peanut sauce
- ½ cup teriyaki sauce
- ¼ cup chunky peanut butter
- 2 teaspoons Worcestershire sauce
- ¾ pound boneless skinless chicken breasts, cut into thin strips
- 3 tablespoons olive oil, divided
- 1 tablespoon sesame oil
- 3 cups chopped sweet onions
- 4 celery ribs, sliced diagonally
- 2 medium carrots, sliced diagonally
- ½ pound sliced baby portobello mushrooms
- 4½ teaspoons minced fresh gingerroot
- 3 garlic cloves, minced
- ⅓ cup thinly sliced green onions
  Hot cooked rice

1. In a small bowl, combine the peanut sauce, teriyaki sauce, peanut butter and Worcestershire sauce; set aside.

2. In a large skillet or wok, stir-fry chicken in 1 tablespoon olive oil and sesame oil until no longer pink. Remove and keep warm.

3. Stir-fry the sweet onions, celery and carrots in remaining oil for 4 minutes. Add the mushrooms, ginger and garlic; stir-fry 4-6 minutes longer or until vegetables are crisp-tender.

4. Stir sauce mixture and add to the pan. Bring to a boil; cook and stir for 2 minutes or until thickened. Add chicken; heat through. Sprinkle with green onions. Serve with rice.

FREEZE OPTION *Freeze cooled chicken mixture in freezer containers. To use, partially thaw in refrigerator overnight. Heat through in a saucepan, stirring occasionally and adding a little broth or water if necessary. Sprinkle with green onions.*

Chicken Enchilada Bake

A fun new way to serve store-bought rotisserie chicken is to whip up this 5-ingredient casserole. It almost resembles a lasagna, only you're using tortillas instead of noodles.

—**MELANIE BURNS** PUEBLO WEST, CO

PREP: 20 MIN. • **BAKE:** 50 MIN. + STANDING • **MAKES:** 10 SERVINGS

- 4½ cups cubed rotisserie chicken
- 1 can (28 ounces) green enchilada sauce
- 1¼ cups (10 ounces) sour cream
- 9 corn tortillas (6 inches), cut into 1½-inch pieces
- 4 cups (16 ounces) shredded Monterey Jack cheese

1. In a greased 13-in. x 9-in. baking dish, layer half of the chicken, enchilada sauce, sour cream, tortillas and cheese. Repeat layers.

2. Cover and bake at 375° for 40 minutes. Uncover; bake 10 minutes longer or until bubbly. Let stand for 15 minutes before serving.

> **FROM THE WEB**
>
> This was an awesome dish to make! I substituted half pepper jack cheese, and it added just enough spiciness. Also, I couldn't find enchilada sauce, so used green salsa instead. Still, it was delicious and my family enjoyed it. Will definitely make it again!
>
> —**RAINBODELL** TASTEOFHOME.COM

Pecan Chicken with Blue Cheese Sauce

PREP: 15 MIN. • **BAKE:** 20 MIN. • **MAKES:** 4 SERVINGS

- 4 boneless skinless chicken breast halves (5 ounces each)
- ¼ teaspoon salt
- ⅛ teaspoon pepper
- ¼ cup all-purpose flour
- 1 tablespoon minced fresh rosemary or 1 teaspoon dried rosemary, crushed
- ¼ cup butter, melted
- 1 tablespoon brown sugar
- ¾ cup finely chopped pecans

SAUCE
- 1 cup heavy whipping cream
- ⅓ cup crumbled blue cheese
- 1 tablespoon finely chopped green onion
- ¼ teaspoon salt
- ¼ teaspoon pepper

1. Sprinkle chicken with salt and pepper. In a shallow bowl, combine flour and rosemary; in a separate shallow bowl, combine butter and brown sugar. Place pecans in another shallow bowl. Coat chicken with flour mixture, then dip in butter mixture and coat with pecans.

2. Transfer to a greased baking sheet. Bake at 375° for 20-25 minutes or until a thermometer reads 170°.

3. Meanwhile, place cream in a small saucepan. Bring to a boil; cook and stir for 8-10 minutes or until thickened. Stir in the cheese, onion, salt and pepper. Serve with chicken.

"Holiday-special in every way, this tender chicken is coated with pecans and drizzled with a rich blue cheese sauce. It's easy and delicious...a real winner in my book." —**MAGGIE RUDDY** ALTOONA, IA

Mustard Turkey Cutlets

Loaded with protein, turkey cutlets are low in fat and fast to the table. Fragrant rosemary perks up the apple juice, and Dijon cuts the sweetness in the glaze for a family-pleasing blend of flavors.
—**DEBORAH WILLIAMS** PEORIA, AZ

START TO FINISH: 25 MIN. • **MAKES:** 4 SERVINGS

- 2 teaspoons cornstarch
- ½ teaspoon salt, divided
- ⅛ teaspoon plus ¼ teaspoon pepper, divided
- ½ cup thawed apple juice concentrate
- ¼ cup Dijon mustard
- 1½ tablespoons minced fresh rosemary or 1½ teaspoons dried rosemary, crushed
- 1 package (17.6 ounces) turkey breast cutlets
- 1 teaspoon olive oil

1. In a small saucepan, combine the cornstarch, ¼ teaspoon salt and ⅛ teaspoon pepper. Gradually whisk in the concentrate, mustard and rosemary until blended. Cook and stir over medium-high heat until thickened and bubbly. Reduce heat; cook and stir 2 minutes longer. Set aside ¼ cup sauce.
2. Brush turkey with oil; sprinkle with remaining salt and pepper. Using long-handled tongs, moisten a paper towel with cooking oil and lightly coat the grill rack.
3. Grill, covered, over medium heat or broil 4 in. from the heat for 2-3 minutes on each side or until no longer pink, basting occasionally with remaining sauce. Brush with reserved sauce before serving.
PER SERVING *230 cal., 2 g fat (trace sat. fat), 77 mg chol., 725 mg sodium, 19 g carb., trace fiber, 31 g pro.* **Diabetic Exchanges:** *4 lean meat, 1 starch.*

Barbecued Chicken Pizzas

Throw a pizza on the grill at your next cookout and say goodbye to ordinary barbecued chicken. This super-simple recipe is easy to customize, so have fun adding different toppings.
—**ALICIA TREVITHICK** TEMECULA, CA

PREP: 25 MIN. • **GRILL:** 10 MIN. • **MAKES:** 2 PIZZAS (4 PIECES EACH)

- 2 boneless skinless chicken breast halves (6 ounces each)
- ¼ teaspoon salt
- ¼ teaspoon pepper
- 1 cup barbecue sauce, divided
- 1 tube (13.8 ounces) refrigerated pizza crust
- 2 teaspoons olive oil
- 1 medium red onion, thinly sliced
- 2 cups (8 ounces) shredded Gouda cheese
- ¼ cup minced fresh cilantro

1. Sprinkle chicken with salt and pepper. Moisten a paper towel with cooking oil; using long-handled tongs, lightly coat the grill rack. Grill chicken, covered, over medium heat or broil 4 in. from the heat for 5-7 minutes on each side or until a thermometer reads 170°, basting frequently with ½ cup barbecue sauce. Set aside and keep warm.
2. Divide dough in half. On a lightly floured surface, roll each portion into a 12-in. x 10-in. rectangle. Lightly brush both sides of dough with oil; place on grill. Cover and grill over medium heat for 1-2 minutes or until bottoms are lightly browned.
3. Remove from grill. Cut the chicken into ½-in. cubes. Spread the grilled side of each crust with ¼ cup barbecue sauce; layer with chicken, onion, cheese and cilantro. Return to grill. Cover and cook each pizza for 4-5 minutes or until the bottom is lightly browned and cheese is melted.

Swiss Chicken Rolls

I love when my husband asks me to make this elegant dish, because I love it, too.

—TONYA DAUGHERTY MANSFIELD, TX

PREP: 20 MIN. • **BAKE:** 20 MIN.
MAKES: 2 SERVINGS

- 2 **boneless skinless chicken breast halves (5 ounces each)**
- 2 **slices Swiss cheese (¾ ounce each)**
- 2 **thin slices prosciutto or deli ham**
- 1 **tablespoon butter**
- 1 **tablespoon olive oil**
- ¼ **cup chopped onion**
- 1 **small garlic clove, minced**
- 1 **teaspoon all-purpose flour**
- ⅓ **cup Marsala wine or chicken broth**
- 2 **teaspoons minced fresh parsley**
- 1 **teaspoon minced fresh rosemary or ¼ teaspoon dried rosemary, crushed**
- 1 **teaspoon minced fresh thyme or ¼ teaspoon dried thyme**
  Dash salt
  Dash pepper

1. Flatten chicken to ¼-in. thickness; place one cheese and prosciutto slice down the center of each. Roll up jelly-roll style, starting with a short side; secure with toothpicks.

2. In a small skillet, brown chicken in butter and oil on all sides; transfer to an 8-in. square baking dish coated with cooking spray. Cover and bake at 350° for 20-25 minutes or until a thermometer reads 170°.

3. In the same skillet, saute onion and garlic until tender. Stir in flour until blended; gradually add wine. Bring to a boil; cook and stir for 2 minutes or until thickened. Stir in the remaining ingredients. Discard toothpicks from chicken rolls; serve with sauce.

MARSALA WINE

Marsala is a fortified (higher in alcohol) wine from Sicily that's popular in Italian cooking. It's made in dry and sweet styles. Use dry Marsala or cooking Marsala in this recipe. You could also prepare it with sherry if you don't have Marsala.

Honey-Brined Turkey Breast

This recipe will give you a beautifully sweet and spicy, lightly salted turkey roast that also makes great sandwiches, salads and soups. I prefer to use cider or apple juice instead of water for the brine. It makes the turkey so delicious.
—**DEIRDRE DEE COX** KANSAS CITY, KS

PREP: 50 MIN. + CHILLING • **BAKE:** 1¾ HOURS • **MAKES:** 8 SERVINGS

- 2 **quarts apple cider or juice**
- ½ **cup kosher salt**
- ⅓ **cup honey**
- 2 **tablespoons Dijon mustard**
- 1½ **teaspoons crushed red pepper flakes**
- 1 **fresh rosemary sprig**
- 2 **large oven roasting bags**
- 1 **bone-in turkey breast (4 to 5 pounds)**
- 1 **tablespoon olive oil**

1. In a Dutch oven, bring the first five ingredients to a boil. Cook and stir until salt and honey are dissolved. Stir in rosemary. Remove from the heat; cool to room temperature. Refrigerate until chilled.
2. Place a large oven roasting bag inside a second roasting bag; add turkey breast. Carefully pour brine into bag. Squeeze out as much air as possible; seal bags and turn to coat. Place in a roasting pan. Refrigerate for 8 hours or overnight, turning occasionally.
3. Line the bottom of a large shallow roasting pan with foil. Drain turkey and discard brine; place on a rack in prepared pan. Pat dry.
4. Bake, uncovered, at 325° for 30 minutes. Brush with oil. Bake 1½ to 2 hours longer or until a thermometer reads 170°. (Cover loosely with foil if turkey browns too quickly.) Cover and let stand for 15 minutes before carving.
NOTE *This recipe was tested with Morton brand kosher salt. It is best not to use a prebasted turkey breast for this recipe. However, if you do, omit the salt in the recipe.*
PER SERVING *216 cal., 3 g fat (1 g sat. fat), 117 mg chol., 419 mg sodium, 3 g carb., trace fiber, 43 g pro.* **Diabetic Exchange:** *6 lean meat.*

Roast Turkey Breast with Rosemary Gravy

You can serve a dozen people with this juicy turkey breast draped in a smooth rosemary-infused gravy. Tell your guests on a heart-healthy diet to eat up; this one's especially low in sodium and saturated fat.
—**BECKY CLARK** WARRIOR, AL

PREP: 20 MIN. • **BAKE:** 1¾ HOURS + STANDING
MAKES: 12 SERVINGS (1⅓ CUPS GRAVY)

- 2 **medium apples, sliced**
- 1½ **cups sliced leeks (white portion only)**
- 2¼ **cups reduced-sodium chicken broth, divided**
- 1 **bone-in turkey breast (6 pounds)**
- 1 **tablespoon canola oil**
- 2 **teaspoons minced fresh rosemary, divided**
- 3 **tablespoons reduced-fat butter**
- ¼ **cup all-purpose flour**

1. Preheat oven to 325°. Arrange apples and leeks in a roasting pan; add 1 cup broth. Place turkey breast over apple mixture. In a small bowl, combine oil and 1½ teaspoons rosemary. With fingers, carefully loosen skin from the turkey breast; rub rosemary mixture under the skin. Secure skin to underside of breast with toothpicks.
2. Bake, uncovered, 1¾ to 2¼ hours or until a thermometer reads 170°, basting every 30 minutes. Cover loosely with foil if turkey browns too quickly. Remove turkey from oven; tent with foil. Let stand 15 minutes before carving, reserving ¼ cup pan juices. Discard apples and leeks.
3. In a small saucepan, melt butter; add flour and remaining rosemary until blended, stirring constantly. Gradually add pan juices and remaining broth to saucepan. Bring to a boil. Cook and stir for 1 minute or until thickened. Serve with turkey.
NOTE *This recipe was tested with Land O'Lakes light stick butter.*
PER SERVING *227 cal., 5 g fat (1 g sat. fat), 122 mg chol., 204 mg sodium, 3 g carb., trace fiber, 43 g pro.* **Diabetic Exchange:** *6 lean meat.*

Crispy Chicken Fingers

My kids love these crispy yet tender chicken strips. My husband and I cut up the chicken and add them to a lettuce salad with eggs, tomatoes and cheese. Then everybody's happy.

—**RACHEL FIZEL** WOODBURY, MN

PREP: 20 MIN. • **COOK:** 5 MIN./BATCH • **MAKES:** 7 SERVINGS

- 1 **cup all-purpose flour**
- 1 **cup dry bread crumbs**
- 2 **tablespoons grated Parmesan cheese**
- 1 **teaspoon salt**
- ¾ **teaspoon garlic powder**
- ½ **teaspoon baking powder**
- 1 **egg**
- 1 **cup buttermilk**
- 1¾ **pounds boneless skinless chicken breasts, cut into strips**
  Oil for deep-fat frying

1. In a large resealable plastic bag, combine the first six ingredients. In a shallow bowl, whisk egg and buttermilk. Dip a few pieces of chicken at a time in buttermilk mixture, then place in bag; seal and shake to coat.
2. In an electric skillet, heat oil to 375°. Fry chicken, a few strips at a time, for 2-3 minutes on each side or until no longer pink. Drain on paper towels.

Fiesta Chicken Burritos

Looking for some heat with supper but still want a cool kitchen? My burritos have a spicy touch the whole family will love. But if you prefer even more heat, add a teaspoon of cayenne pepper.

—**MARGARET LATTA** PADUCAH, KY

PREP: 30 MIN. • **COOK:** 4¼ HOURS • **MAKES:** 8 SERVINGS

- 1½ **pounds boneless skinless chicken breasts**
- 1 **can (15¾ ounces) whole kernel corn, drained**
- 1 **can (15 ounces) black beans, rinsed and drained**
- 1 **can (10 ounces) diced tomatoes and green chilies, undrained**
- 1 **jalapeno pepper, seeded and finely chopped**
- 3 **tablespoons ground cumin**
- 1 **teaspoon salt**
- 1 **teaspoon paprika**
- ½ **teaspoon pepper**
  Dash cayenne pepper
  Dash crushed red pepper flakes
- 1 **package (8 ounces) reduced-fat cream cheese, cubed**
- 8 **flour tortillas (8 inches), warmed**
  Optional toppings: sour cream, shredded cheddar cheese, shredded lettuce and chopped tomatoes

1. Place chicken in a greased 4-qt. slow cooker. In a large bowl, combine the corn, beans, tomatoes, jalapeno and seasonings; pour over chicken. Cover and cook on low for 4-5 hours or until chicken is tender.
2. Remove chicken; cool slightly. Shred meat with two forks and return to the slow cooker. Stir in cream cheese. Cover and cook for 15 minutes or until heated through.
3. Spoon ¾ cup chicken mixture down the center of each tortilla; add toppings of your choice. Fold sides and ends over filling and roll up.
NOTE *Wear disposable gloves when cutting hot peppers; the oils can burn skin. Avoid touching your face.*

Gingered Chicken Thighs

This recipe was born from my desire to develop a timesaving Asian entree that's easy on the budget. It's a favorite at the girls' camp where I am the head cook. I usually serve it with rice prepared with coconut milk.
—**DEBBIE FLEENOR** MONTEREY, TN

PREP: 20 MIN. + MARINATING • **BAKE:** 20 MIN. • **MAKES:** 6 SERVINGS

- 2 **tablespoons ground ginger**
- 2 **tablespoons orange juice**
- 2 **tablespoons honey**
- 2 **tablespoons reduced-sodium soy sauce**
- 2 **teaspoons curry powder**
- 2 **garlic cloves, minced**
- ½ **teaspoon crushed red pepper flakes**
- 6 **boneless skinless chicken thighs (about 1½ pounds)**
PEANUT SAUCE
- 2 **tablespoons chicken broth**
- 2 **tablespoons orange juice**
- 1 **tablespoon reduced-fat creamy peanut butter**
- ½ **teaspoon ground ginger**

1. In a large resealable plastic bag, combine the first seven ingredients; add the chicken. Seal bag and turn to coat; refrigerate for up to 4 hours.

2. Drain and discard marinade. In a large skillet coated with cooking spray, brown chicken on each side. Transfer to an 11-in. x 7-in. baking dish coated with cooking spray. In a small bowl, whisk sauce ingredients; pour over chicken. Bake, uncovered, at 350° for 20-25 minutes or until no longer pink.

PER SERVING *199 cal., 9 g fat (2 g sat. fat), 76 mg chol., 200 mg sodium, 6 g carb., trace fiber, 22 g pro.* **Diabetic Exchanges:** *3 lean meat, ½ starch.*

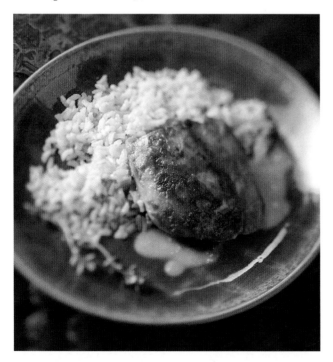

Penne Gorgonzola with Chicken

Having an easy recipe like this in your back pocket will come in handy if you're hosting a dinner party. The simple combination of wine, broth, cream and cheese makes a full-flavored sauce that nicely coats the pasta.
—**GEORGE SCHROEDER** PORT MURRAY, NJ

START TO FINISH: 30 MIN. • **MAKES:** 8 SERVINGS

- 1 **package (16 ounces) penne pasta**
- 1 **pound boneless skinless chicken breasts, cut into ½-inch pieces**
- 1 **tablespoon olive oil**
- 1 **large garlic clove, minced**
- ¼ **cup white wine**
- 1 **cup heavy whipping cream**
- ¼ **cup chicken broth**
- 2 **cups (8 ounces) crumbled Gorgonzola cheese**
- 6 **to 8 fresh sage leaves, thinly sliced**
   Salt and pepper to taste
   Grated Parmigiano-Reggiano cheese and minced fresh parsley

1. Cook pasta according to package directions. Meanwhile, in a large skillet over medium heat, brown chicken in oil on all sides. Add garlic; cook 1 minute longer. Add wine, stirring to loosen browned bits from pan.

2. Add cream and broth; cook until sauce is slightly thickened and chicken is no longer pink. Stir in the Gorgonzola cheese, sage, salt and pepper; cook just until cheese is melted.

3. Drain pasta; toss with sauce. Sprinkle with Parmigiano-Reggiano cheese and parsley.

GORGONZOLA KNOW-HOW

Gorgonzola gets its name from the small Italian town from which it originated. Today, several American dairies also make the creamy cow's milk cheese with distinctive blue-green veins.

For the best results, buy a wedge of Gorgonzola from the cheese section and crumble it yourself for the pasta recipe. Tubs of ready-made crumbles are convenient for salads, but they are expensive and may have additives that will affect their creaminess and melting ability.

Gorgonzola also makes a delectable snack with walnut halves, dried figs, or sliced fresh apples and pears.

AMERICA'S
BEST-LOVED RECIPE
GRAND PRIZE
WINNER
★ ★ ★ ★

Low Country Boil, page 144

153

145

147

Seafood & Meatless Entrees

Savor **heart-healthy** salmon, sweet and **smoky shrimp kabobs**, veggie-packed **black bean cakes** with Mexican salsa, **sensational** tomato quiche and more. It's never been easier to eat more of **the good foods** you should!

Gorgonzola Pasta with Walnuts

START TO FINISH: 30 MIN. • **MAKES:** 2 SERVINGS

- 4 ounces uncooked spaghetti
- 1 large sweet onion, thinly sliced
- 2 tablespoons olive oil
- 1 garlic clove, minced
- 1 cup (4 ounces) crumbled Gorgonzola cheese
- 2 tablespoons balsamic vinegar
- ¼ teaspoon salt
- 1 tablespoon chopped walnuts, toasted

1. Cook spaghetti according to package directions. Meanwhile, in a large skillet, cook onion in oil over medium heat for 15-20 minutes or until golden brown, stirring frequently. Add garlic; cook 2 minutes longer. Remove from the heat.
2. Drain spaghetti; add to the skillet. Stir in the cheese, vinegar and salt. Sprinkle with walnuts.

"Quick, easy and delicious, this appealing pasta dish is a weeknight staple at our house. We never tire of it. It's also excellent alongside fish or grilled chicken."

—TRISHA KRUSE EAGLE, ID

Low Country Boil

Ideal for camping and relaxing trips to the beach, this crowd-pleasing recipe makes an appetizing presentation of perfectly seasoned meats, veggies and seafood.

—MAGESWARI ELAGUPILLAI VICTORVILLE, CA

PREP: 20 MIN. • **COOK:** 40 MIN. • **MAKES:** 4 SERVINGS

- 2 quarts water
- 1 bottle (12 ounces) beer
- 2 tablespoons seafood seasoning
- 1½ teaspoons salt
- 4 medium red potatoes, cut into wedges
- 1 medium sweet onion, cut into wedges
- 4 medium ears sweet corn, cut in half
- ⅓ pound smoked chorizo or kielbasa, cut into 1-inch slices
- 3 tablespoons olive oil
- 6 large garlic cloves, minced
- 1 tablespoon ground cumin
- 1 tablespoon minced fresh cilantro
- ½ teaspoon paprika
- ½ teaspoon pepper
- 1 pound uncooked large shrimp, deveined
- 1 pound uncooked snow crab legs
    Optional condiments: seafood cocktail sauce, lemon wedges and melted butter

1. In a stockpot, combine the water, beer, seafood seasoning and salt; add potatoes and onion. Bring to a boil. Reduce heat; simmer, uncovered, for 10 minutes. Add corn and chorizo; simmer 10-12 minutes longer or until potatoes and corn are tender.
2. Meanwhile, in a small skillet, heat oil. Add the garlic, cumin, cilantro, paprika and pepper. Cook and stir over medium heat for 1 minute.
3. Stir the shrimp, crab legs and garlic mixture into the stockpot; cook for 4-6 minutes or until shrimp and crab turn pink. Drain; transfer seafood mixture to a large serving bowl. Serve with condiments of your choice.

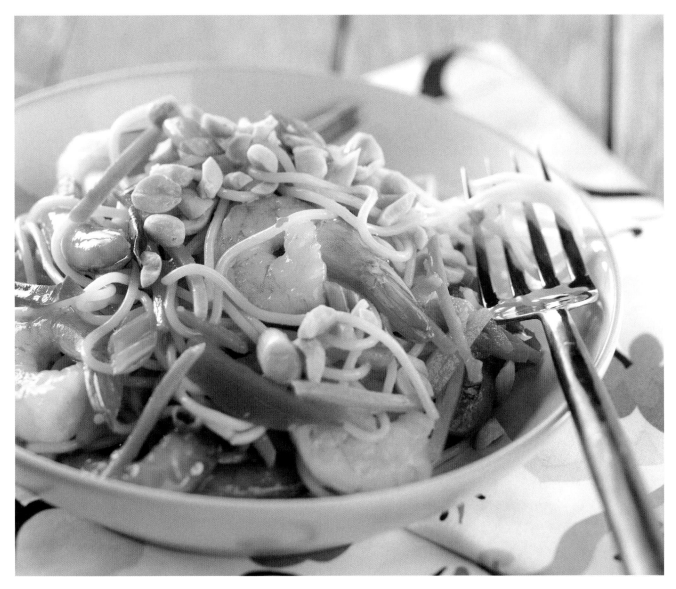

Szechuan Shrimp Noodles

You can use spaghetti to make this Asian-inspired shrimp and noodle bowl. It also keeps well for several days in the refrigerator.

—TISH STEVENSON GRAND RAPIDS, MI

START TO FINISH: 25 MIN. • **MAKES:** 8 SERVINGS

- 10 **ounces uncooked thin spaghetti**
- ⅓ **cup canola oil**
- ⅓ **cup honey**
- 2 **tablespoons rice vinegar**
- 2 **tablespoons sesame oil**
- 2 **tablespoons soy sauce**
- 1 **tablespoon minced fresh gingerroot**
- ½ **teaspoon crushed red pepper flakes**
- 1 **pound cooked medium shrimp, peeled and deveined**
- 1 **package (10 ounces) julienned carrots**
- 2 **cups fresh sugar snap peas**
- 1 **large sweet red pepper, sliced**
- ½ **cup sliced green onions**
- 3 **tablespoons minced fresh cilantro**
- ¾ **cup coarsely chopped dry roasted peanuts**

1. Cook spaghetti according to package directions. Meanwhile, in a small bowl, whisk the canola oil, honey, vinegar, sesame oil, soy sauce, ginger and pepper flakes; set aside.

2. Drain spaghetti; rinse in cold water. Place in a large bowl. Add the shrimp, carrots, peas, red pepper, onions and cilantro. Drizzle with dressing; toss to coat. Sprinkle with peanuts. Chill until serving.

FROM THE WEB

Whenever I serve this to friends and family, I get requests to share the recipe. I add a bit more vinegar, ginger and red pepper than the recipe calls for, depending on my mood and the palates of the others eating the salad. I also serve it with wedges of lime: This adds a lovely flavor to the salad. This dressing is delicious served with similar ingredients, such as napa cabbage, edamame, etc., in a pasta-less salad.

—KGAUDERMAN TASTEOFHOME.COM

SAY CHEESE
GRAND PRIZE
WINNER
★ ★ ★ ★

Shrimp & Macaroni Casserole

I think adding shrimp to this deliciously cheesy casserole is a unique twist on standard macaroni. And you don't have to make a giant batch; this recipe is perfect for two or three.

—**MICHAEL COHEN** LOS ANGELES, CA

PREP: 20 MIN. • **BAKE:** 20 MIN. • **MAKES:** 3 SERVINGS

- 1 cup uncooked elbow macaroni
- 1 egg, beaten
- ¼ cup half-and-half cream
- 2 tablespoons butter, melted
- ½ cup grated Parmesan cheese
- ¾ cup shredded part-skim mozzarella cheese, divided
- 1 garlic clove, minced
- ¼ teaspoon salt
- ⅛ teaspoon pepper
- ¼ pound uncooked shrimp, peeled, deveined and chopped
- ¾ cup chopped fresh spinach

1. Cook macaroni according to package directions. Meanwhile, in a small bowl, combine the egg, cream and butter; set aside. Drain macaroni; transfer to a small bowl. Add the Parmesan cheese, ½ cup mozzarella cheese, garlic, salt, pepper and reserved egg mixture; toss to coat. Stir in shrimp and spinach.

2. Transfer to a 1-qt. baking dish coated with cooking spray. Sprinkle with remaining mozzarella cheese. Bake, uncovered, at 350° for 20-25 minutes or until shrimp turn pink and cheese is melted.

Cedar Plank Salmon with Blackberry Sauce

Here's my favorite entree for a warm-weather cookout. The salmon has a rich grilled taste that's enhanced by the savory blackberry sauce. It's a nice balance of sweet, smoky and spicy.

—**STEPHANIE MATTHEWS** TEMPE, AZ

PREP: 20 MIN. + SOAKING • **GRILL:** 15 MIN.
MAKES: 6 SERVINGS (¾ CUP SAUCE)

- 2 cedar grilling planks
- 2 cups fresh blackberries
- 2 tablespoons white wine
- 1 tablespoon brown sugar
- 1½ teaspoons honey
- 1½ teaspoons chipotle hot pepper sauce
- ¼ teaspoon salt, divided
- ¼ teaspoon pepper, divided
- ¼ cup finely chopped shallots
- 1 garlic clove, minced
- 6 salmon fillets (5 ounces each)

1. Soak grilling planks in water for at least 1 hour.
2. In a food processor, combine the blackberries, wine, brown sugar, honey, hot pepper sauce, ⅛ teaspoon salt and ⅛ teaspoon pepper; cover and process until blended. Strain and discard seeds. Stir shallots and garlic into the sauce; set aside.
3. Place planks on grill over medium-high heat. Cover and heat until planks create a light to medium smoke and begin to crackle, about 3 minutes (this indicates planks are ready). Turn planks over.
4. Sprinkle salmon with remaining salt and pepper. Place on planks. Grill, covered, over medium heat for 12-15 minutes or until fish flakes easily with a fork. Serve with the sauce.

Raise your grill skills with plank cooking.

You can purchase grill-ready cedar, maple, cherry or apple wood planks at grocery, hardware and kitchen specialty stores. To prevent the wood from burning while grilling, first immerse the planks in water and soak for at least 1 hour. (You may have to weigh planks down, such as with a can, to keep them underwater.) For even more flavor, add white wine, beer, apple cider or fresh herbs to the water. When ready to grill, wipe the planks dry and proceed as the recipe directs. Remove the cooked food from the planks. For safety, let the planks cool completely on the grill grate before removing.

Macadamia-Crusted Mahi Mahi

Turn mahi mahi fillets into fancy company fare with a crunchy coating of macadamia nuts and panko, then drizzle it with a yummy, gingery sauce. The whole dish comes together in just 30 minutes.

—IDANA MOONEY CORONA, CA

START TO FINISH: 30 MIN. • **MAKES:** 4 SERVINGS

- 1   cup panko (Japanese) bread crumbs
- ¾   cup macadamia nuts
- ¼   teaspoon salt
- ¼   teaspoon white pepper
- 1   egg
- 2   teaspoons water
- ⅓   cup all-purpose flour
- 4   mahi mahi fillets (4 ounces each)
- ¼   cup canola oil
- 2   tablespoons brown sugar
- 2   tablespoons reduced-sodium soy sauce
- 2   teaspoons minced fresh gingerroot

1. Place the bread crumbs, nuts, salt and pepper in a food processor; cover and pulse until nuts are finely chopped.
2. In a shallow bowl, whisk egg and water. Place flour and nut mixture in separate shallow bowls. Coat fillets with flour, then dip in egg mixture and coat with nut mixture.
3. In a large skillet, heat oil over medium heat; cook fillets for 3-4 minutes on each side or until golden brown.
4. Meanwhile, in a small microwave-safe bowl, combine the brown sugar, soy sauce and ginger. Microwave, uncovered, on high for 30-60 seconds or until sugar is dissolved. Drizzle over fish.

Salmon with Vegetable Salsa

This salsa recipe is great not only with salmon, but also grilled chicken breasts and barbecued shrimp kabobs. The only fresh ingredient not available in my son's garden was the avocado!

—PRISCILLA GILBERT INDIAN HARBOUR BEACH, FL

START TO FINISH: 30 MIN. • **MAKES:** 4 SERVINGS

- 1½   cups grape tomatoes, halved
- 1½   cups chopped peeled cucumber
- 1   medium ripe avocado, peeled and cubed
- 1   small red onion, chopped
- 2   tablespoons minced fresh cilantro
- 1   jalapeno pepper, seeded and minced
- 2   tablespoons lime juice
- ½   teaspoon salt

FISH
- 4   salmon fillets (6 ounces each)
- 1   tablespoon lime juice
- ½   teaspoon salt
- ¼   teaspoon cayenne pepper
- 1   tablespoon butter

1. In a large bowl, combine the tomatoes, cucumber, avocado, onion, cilantro, jalapeno, lime juice and salt; set aside.
2. Drizzle salmon with lime juice. Sprinkle with salt and cayenne pepper. In a large skillet, cook fillets in butter for 3-4 minutes on each side or until fish flakes easily with a fork. Serve with salsa.
NOTE *Wear disposable gloves when cutting hot peppers; the oils can burn skin. Avoid touching your face.*

Cabernet Marinara Pasta

Red wine and fresh herbs accent the sweet sauce in this simple pasta dish. It makes an excellent meatless entree, but you could also serve it with steak.

—SARAH VASQUES MILFORD, NH

PREP: 20 MIN. • **COOK:** 20 MIN. • **MAKES:** 4 SERVINGS

- 1 cup chopped sweet onion
- 2 tablespoons olive oil
- 3 garlic cloves, crushed
- ½ cup Cabernet Sauvignon or other dry red wine
- 1 can (28 ounces) crushed tomatoes
- 3 plum tomatoes, chopped
- 1 tablespoon sugar
- 1 fresh basil sprig
- 1 fresh thyme sprig
- 2 cups uncooked penne pasta
    Parmesan and Romano cheeses

1. In a large saucepan, cook onion in oil over medium heat until tender. Add garlic; cook 1 minute longer. Stir in wine and bring to a boil. Reduce heat; cook for 6-8 minutes or until liquid is reduced by half.
2. Add the crushed tomatoes, plum tomatoes, sugar, basil and thyme; bring to a boil. Reduce heat; cover and simmer for 15 minutes. Meanwhile, cook pasta according to package directions.
3. Discard basil and thyme. Drain pasta; toss with sauce. Top with cheeses.

Spicy Chorizo & Shrimp Rice

Looking for an easy one-skillet meal for dinner tonight? This satisfying dish has a fresh Southwestern flavor your family will warm up to!

—CHERYL PERRY HERTFORD, NC

START TO FINISH: 30 MIN. • **MAKES:** 4 SERVINGS

- ½ pound uncooked chorizo or bulk spicy pork sausage
- 4 tomatillos, husks removed, chopped
- 1 cup uncooked long grain rice
- ¼ cup chopped onion
- ¼ cup chopped celery leaves
- ¼ cup chopped carrot
- ½ teaspoon garlic powder
- ¼ teaspoon pepper
- 2 cups chicken broth
- ½ pound uncooked medium shrimp, peeled and deveined
- ¼ cup crumbled queso fresco or diced part-skim mozzarella cheese
- 2 teaspoons minced fresh cilantro

1. Crumble chorizo into a large skillet; add tomatillos. Cook over medium heat for 6-8 minutes or until meat is fully cooked. Add the rice, onion, celery leaves, carrot, garlic powder and pepper; cook and stir for 2 minutes.
2. Add broth; bring to a boil. Reduce heat; cover and simmer for 10 minutes. Stir in shrimp; cover and cook 5 minutes longer or until shrimp turn pink and rice is tender. Sprinkle with cheese and cilantro.

Apricot-Glazed Salmon with Herb Rice

Salmon lovers will really enjoy this nice and fruity tasting fish with just the right amount of sweetness. If salmon is new to your family, this is a great way to introduce it to them.

—CHARLENE CHAMBERS ORMOND BEACH, FL

PREP: 25 MIN. • **COOK:** 20 MIN. • **MAKES:** 6 SERVINGS

- 6 salmon fillets (4 ounces each)
- ¼ teaspoon salt
- ⅛ teaspoon pepper
- ⅓ cup white wine or reduced-sodium chicken broth
- ⅓ cup apricot spreadable fruit
- ½ teaspoon grated fresh gingerroot
- 2 cups reduced-sodium chicken broth
- 1 cup uncooked long grain rice
- 2 teaspoons butter
- 2 tablespoons chopped dried apricots
- 2 tablespoons minced fresh parsley
- 1 tablespoon minced chives
- 1 teaspoon minced fresh thyme or ¼ teaspoon dried thyme
- 3 tablespoons sliced almonds, toasted

1. Place salmon in a 13-in. x 9-in. baking dish coated with cooking spray. Sprinkle with salt and pepper. In a small bowl, combine the wine, spreadable fruit and ginger; spoon over salmon.

2. Bake at 375° for 15-20 minutes or until fish flakes easily with a fork.

3. Meanwhile, in a small saucepan, bring the broth, rice and butter to a boil. Reduce heat; cover and simmer for 10 minutes. Add apricots; cover and cook 5-8 minutes longer or until liquid is absorbed and rice is tender. Stir in the parsley, chives and thyme. Serve with salmon. Sprinkle each serving with almonds.

Peachy Shrimp Tacos

This simple recipe has become a family favorite. You can use flour tortillas or even hard taco shells, but I like to use corn tortillas because of their slightly higher fiber content.

—VERONICA CALLAGHAN GLASTONBURY, CT

START TO FINISH: 10 MIN. • **MAKES:** 6 SERVINGS

- 1 cup salsa
- 1 cup frozen unsweetened sliced peaches, thawed and diced
- 1 pound cooked medium shrimp, peeled and deveined
- 1 tablespoon minced fresh cilantro
- 1½ cups shredded Chinese or napa cabbage
- 6 corn tortillas (6 inches), warmed

1. In a large skillet, combine salsa and peaches over medium heat until warmed. Add shrimp and cilantro; cook and stir until heated through.

2. Place ¼ cupful cabbage down the center of each tortilla; top with a scant ½ cupful shrimp mixture.

PER SERVING *165 cal., 2 g fat (trace sat. fat), 115 mg chol., 308 mg sodium, 19 g carb., 2 g fiber, 17 g pro.* **Diabetic Exchanges:** *2 lean meat, 1 starch.*

DISCOVER NAPA CABBAGE

Originating in China, napa cabbage has a more elongated, oval-shaped head than our popular head-cabbage varieties. It has crinkly pale green leaves with thick white veins.

Unlike with regular cabbage, napa cabbage's leaves are thin enough to not require cooking or fine shredding. You can thinly slice the cabbage, or even tear the leaves into salad or use whole leaves as a crispy stand-in for your favorite lettuce wrap recipe.

Napa cabbage is also delicious in stir-fried preparations. If substituting it for regular cabbage in other recipes, adjust the cook time downward because it cooks quickly.

Don't confuse napa cabbage with bok choy, another Chinese vegetable. Bok chopy has crispy white stalk-like stems and thicker green tops that generally require cooking.

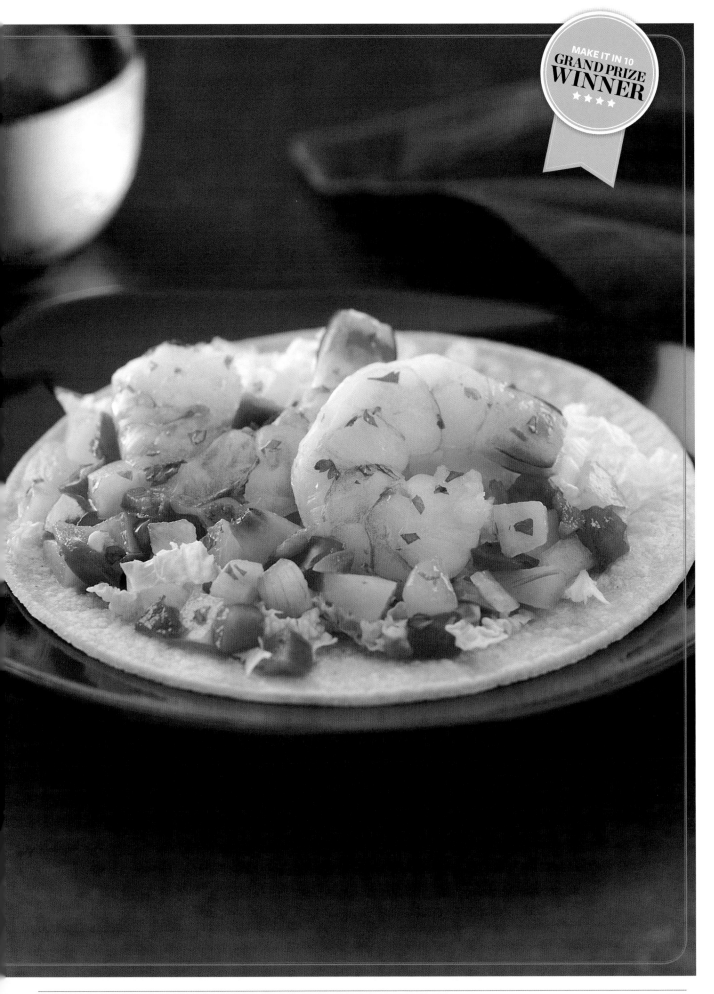

Summer Squash Mushroom Casserole

With its crunchy topping, this rich and creamy dish is wonderful to take to potlucks and picnics.

—JENNIFER WALLACE

CANAL WINCHESTER, OH

PREP: 20 MIN. • **BAKE:** 25 MIN.
MAKES: 6 SERVINGS

- 2   medium yellow summer squash, diced
- 1   large zucchini, diced
- ½   pound sliced fresh mushrooms
- 1   cup chopped onion
- 2   tablespoons olive oil
- 1   can (10¾ ounces) condensed cream of mushroom soup, undiluted
- 2   cups (8 ounces) shredded cheddar cheese
- ½   cup sour cream
- ½   teaspoon salt
- 1   cup crushed butter-flavored crackers (about 25 crackers)
- 1   tablespoon butter, melted

1. In a large skillet, saute the summer squash, zucchini, mushrooms and onion in oil until tender; drain.
2. In a large bowl, combine the vegetable mixture, soup, cheese, sour cream and salt. Transfer to a greased 11-in. x 7-in. baking dish. Combine cracker crumbs and butter. Sprinkle over vegetable mixture.
3. Bake, uncovered, at 350° for 25-30 minutes or until bubbly.

FROM THE WEB

I made a few changes to add a layer of flavor. I dropped the sour cream and cream of mushroom soup. Instead, I made a corn puree from 4 ears fresh corn (corn and skim milk blended in food processor with ¼ cup of flour and a hint of chipotle pepper, cook just until flour is cooked and thickened). Mix everything as called for in the recipe and top with cracker crumbs. This was awesome.

—CARMERKLE TASTEOFHOME.COM

Black Bean Cakes with Mole Salsa

Homemade salsa adds zip to these mouthwatering bean cakes. Serve on a bun for a scrumptious veggie burger!

—ROXANNE CHAN ALBANY, CA

START TO FINISH: 30 MIN. • **MAKES:** 6 SERVINGS (1¼ CUPS SALSA)

- 1 can (15 ounces) black beans, rinsed and drained
- 1 egg, beaten
- 1 cup shredded zucchini
- ½ cup dry bread crumbs
- ¼ cup shredded Mexican cheese blend
- 2 tablespoons chili powder
- ¼ teaspoon salt
- ¼ teaspoon baking powder
- ¼ teaspoon ground cumin
- 2 tablespoons olive oil

SALSA
- 2 medium tomatoes, chopped
- 1 small green pepper, chopped
- 3 tablespoons grated chocolate
- 1 green onion, thinly sliced
- 2 tablespoons minced fresh cilantro
- 1 tablespoon lime juice
- 1 to 2 teaspoons minced chipotle pepper in adobo sauce
- 1 teaspoon honey

1. In a small bowl, mash beans. Add the egg, zucchini, bread crumbs, cheese, chili powder, salt, baking powder and cumin; mix well. Shape into six patties; brush both sides with oil. Place on a baking sheet.

2. Broil 3-4 in. from the heat for 3-4 minutes on each side or until a thermometer reads 160°.

3. Meanwhile, in a small bowl, combine the salsa ingredients. Serve with black bean cakes.

PER SERVING *206 cal., 10 g fat (3 g sat. fat), 39 mg chol., 397 mg sodium, 23 g carb., 6 g fiber, 8 g pro.* **Diabetic Exchanges:** *2 fat, 1½ starch, 1 lean meat.*

Glazed Shrimp & Asparagus

With its spicy Asian flavor, this shrimp and asparagus combo is excellent for a special occasion or a quick-fix weeknight dinner.

—JOAN DUCKWORTH LEES SUMMIT, MO

START TO FINISH: 30 MIN. • **MAKES:** 4 SERVINGS

- 8 ounces uncooked whole wheat angel hair pasta
- 1 tablespoon cornstarch
- ¾ cup cold water
- 1 tablespoon soy sauce
- 1 tablespoon honey
- 1 pound uncooked large shrimp, peeled and deveined
- 3 teaspoons peanut or canola oil, divided
- 1 teaspoon sesame oil
- 1 pound fresh asparagus, trimmed and cut into 2 – to 3-in. lengths
- 1 tablespoon minced fresh gingerroot
- 2 garlic cloves, minced
- ¼ teaspoon crushed red pepper flakes
- 1 tablespoon sesame seeds

1. Cook pasta according to package directions. In a small bowl, combine the cornstarch, water, soy sauce and honey until smooth; set aside.

2. In a large skillet or wok, stir-fry shrimp in 1 teaspoon peanut oil and the sesame oil until shrimp turn pink. Remove and keep warm.

3. Stir-fry asparagus in remaining peanut oil for 2 minutes. Add the ginger, garlic, pepper flakes and sesame seeds; stir-fry 2 minutes longer or until asparagus is crisp-tender.

4. Stir cornstarch mixture and add to the pan. Bring to a boil; cook and stir for 2 minutes or until thickened. Add shrimp; heat through. Drain pasta; serve with shrimp mixture.

Orange Roughy with Tartar Sauce

You'll never buy tartar sauce again once you've tasted my super-easy recipe! Wrapped in a foil packet, the fish comes out flaky and perfect every time, and cleanup is a cinch.

—MICHELLE STROMKO DARLINGTON, MD

START TO FINISH: 30 MIN. • **MAKES:** 6 SERVINGS (1 CUP SAUCE)

- 6 orange roughy fillets (6 ounces each)
- 1 tablespoon seafood seasoning
- 2 tablespoons butter, cubed

TARTAR SAUCE

- ⅔ cup chopped dill pickles
- ½ cup mayonnaise
- 3 tablespoons finely chopped onion
   Dash pepper

1. Place three fillets on a double thickness of heavy-duty foil (about 18 in. square); repeat with remaining fillets. Sprinkle fish with seasoning; dot with butter.

2. Fold foil around fish and seal tightly. Grill packets, covered, over medium heat for 10-15 minutes or until fish flakes easily with a fork. Open foil carefully to allow steam to escape.

3. Combine the sauce ingredients; serve with fish.

Grilled Shrimp with Apricot Sauce

Served on skewers, this is a mouthwatering main attraction for a summertime dinner. Succulent bacon-wrapped shrimp get a tongue-tingling boost from the sweet, slightly hot sauce.

—CAROLE RESNICK CLEVELAND, OH

START TO FINISH: 30 MIN. • **MAKES:** 4 SKEWERS (⅔ CUP SAUCE)

- ½ cup apricot preserves
- 2 tablespoons apricot nectar
- ¼ teaspoon ground chipotle powder
- 12 uncooked large shrimp, peeled and deveined
- 6 slices Canadian bacon, halved

1. In a small bowl, combine the preserves, apricot nectar and chipotle powder. Chill until serving.

2. Thread shrimp and bacon onto four metal or soaked wooden skewers. Grill, covered, over medium heat for 6-8 minutes or until shrimp turn pink, turning once. Serve with sauce.

Tomato Onion Quiche

This scaled-down quiche fills a small pie pan to the brim and is perfect for serving two or three. I think it's best fresh out of the oven when the cheese is wonderfully gooey.

—SHERRI CREWS ST. AUGUSTINE, FL

PREP: 20 MIN. • **BAKE:** 45 MIN. + STANDING
MAKES: 3 SERVINGS

- 1 **sheet refrigerated pie pastry**
- 1 **cup (4 ounces) shredded part-skim mozzarella cheese**
- ½ **cup sliced sweet onion**
- 2 **small plum tomatoes, seeded and thinly sliced**
- 3 **medium fresh mushrooms, thinly sliced**
- ¼ **cup shredded Parmesan cheese**
- 3 **eggs**
- ½ **cup half-and-half cream**
- ½ **teaspoon ground mustard**
- ½ **teaspoon dried basil**
- ½ **teaspoon dried oregano**
- ½ **teaspoon dried thyme**

1. Cut pastry sheet in half. Repackage and refrigerate one half for another use. On a lightly floured surface, roll out remaining half into an 8-in. circle. Place in a 7-in. pie plate; flute edges.
2. Layer half of the mozzarella cheese, onion and tomato in pastry. Top with mushrooms; layer with remaining mozzarella cheese, onion and tomato. Sprinkle with Parmesan cheese. In a small bowl, combine the eggs, cream, mustard and herbs; pour over top.
3. Bake at 350° for 45-55 minutes or until a knife inserted near the center comes out clean. Let stand for 10 minutes before cutting.

EASY APPETIZERS

Make some cute appetizers with the leftover pastry. Roll it into a circle and lightly sprinkle with your favorite nuts and cheeses (such as almonds and Swiss or walnuts and blue cheese). Cut into triangles, roll up from the wide edges, and place point side down on a greased pan. Brush with a little milk for added shine and bake until golden.

Orange Nut Bread & Cream Cheese Spread, page 165

160

167

175

Sides, Breads & Condiments

Cook up a complete dinner with the addition of these **enticing homemade breads**, rustic **roasted** peppers, **old-fashioned** fried tomatoes, down-home **potato dishes, pickles, relishes** and more. These blue-ribbon accompaniments make **a meal to remember**.

Spice Bread with Maple Butter

This whole wheat bread has all the spicy flavors of fall. Served with a cinnamon-spiked maple butter, it's almost too tasty to believe how easy it is to make.

—KATHERINE L. NELSON CENTERVILLE, UT

PREP: 25 MIN. • **BAKE:** 40 MIN. + COOLING
MAKES: 1 LOAF (12 SLICES) AND ½ CUP BUTTER

- ¼ cup butter, softened
- ¾ cup sugar
- 2 eggs
- ½ teaspoon vanilla extract
- 1 cup all-purpose flour
- ½ cup whole wheat flour
- 2 teaspoons baking powder
- ½ teaspoon ground cinnamon
- ¼ teaspoon ground nutmeg
- ¼ teaspoon ground allspice
- ¼ teaspoon salt
- ⅓ cup milk
- ½ cup chopped walnuts

BUTTER

- ½ cup butter, softened
- 2 tablespoons maple syrup
- ½ teaspoon ground cinnamon

1. In a large bowl, cream butter and sugar until light and fluffy. Add eggs, one at a time, beating well after each addition. Beat in vanilla. Combine the flours, baking powder, spices and salt; add to creamed mixture alternately with milk just until moistened. Fold in walnuts.

2. Transfer to a greased 8-in. x 4-in. loaf pan. Bake at 350° for 40-45 minutes or until a toothpick inserted near the center comes out clean. Cool for 10 minutes before removing from pan to a wire rack.

3. Beat butter ingredients until blended; serve with bread.

Country-Style Tomatoes

You've heard of fried green tomatoes, but have you had fried tomato sandwiches? This is always a fun recipe when tomatoes are in season.

—CATHERINE DWYER FREEDOM, NH

PREP: 25 MIN. • **COOK:** 10 MIN./BATCH • **MAKES:** 8 SERVINGS

- 4 large tomatoes
- 1 package (8 ounces) cream cheese, softened
- ¼ cup minced fresh parsley
- 1½ teaspoons minced fresh basil or ½ teaspoon dried basil
- 1 garlic clove, minced
- ¼ teaspoon salt
- ¼ cup all-purpose flour
- 1 cup panko (Japanese) bread crumbs
- 1 egg
- 1 tablespoon 2% milk
- 3 tablespoons butter
- 3 tablespoons olive oil

1. Cut each tomato into four thick slices; place on paper towels to drain. Meanwhile, in a small bowl, beat the cream cheese, parsley, basil, garlic and salt until blended. Spread cream cheese mixture over eight tomato slices; top with remaining tomato slices.

2. Place flour and bread crumbs in separate shallow bowls. In another bowl, whisk egg and milk. Coat the top and bottom of each sandwich with flour, dip into egg mixture, then coat with crumbs.

3. In a large skillet, heat butter and oil over medium-hot heat. Fry tomato sandwiches in batches for 3-4 minutes on each side or until golden brown. Drain on paper towels.

Authentic Boston Brown Bread

PREP: 20 MIN. • **COOK:** 50 MIN. + STANDING
MAKES: 1 LOAF (12 SLICES)

- ½ cup cornmeal
- ½ cup whole wheat flour
- ½ cup rye flour
- ½ teaspoon baking powder
- ½ teaspoon baking soda
- ¼ teaspoon salt
- 1 cup buttermilk
- ⅓ cup molasses
- 2 tablespoons brown sugar
- 1 tablespoon canola oil
- 3 tablespoons chopped walnuts, toasted
- 3 tablespoons raisins
- Cream cheese, softened, optional

1. In a large bowl, combine the first six ingredients. In another bowl, whisk the buttermilk, molasses, brown sugar and oil. Stir into dry ingredients just until moistened. Fold in walnuts and raisins. Transfer to a greased 8-in. x 4-in. loaf pan; cover with foil.

2. Place pan on a rack in a boiling-water canner or other large, deep pot; add 1 in. of hot water to pot. Bring to a gentle boil; cover and steam for 45-50 minutes or until a toothpick inserted near the center comes out clean, adding more water to the pot as needed.

3. Remove pan from the pot; let stand for 10 minutes before removing bread from pan to a wire rack. Serve with cream cheese if desired.

> ❝The rustic, old-fashioned flavor of this hearty bread is out of this world. Recipes like this remind me why I find cooking and baking not only fun, but very fulfilling.❞

—**SHARON DELANEY-CHRONIS** SOUTH MILWAUKEE, WI

Chocolate Chai Mini Loaves

These little breads are irresistible. A friend of mine complains when I give her a loaf because she just can't help but eat the whole thing!

—**LISA CHRISTENSEN** POPLAR GROVE, IL

PREP: 25 MIN. • **BAKE:** 35 MIN. + COOLING
MAKES: 3 MINI LOAVES (6 SLICES EACH)

- 2 ounces semisweet chocolate, chopped
- ½ cup water
- ½ cup butter, softened
- 1 cup packed brown sugar
- 2 eggs
- 1 teaspoon vanilla extract
- 1½ cups all-purpose flour
- 3 tablespoons chai tea latte mix
- 1 teaspoon baking soda
- ½ teaspoon salt
- ½ cup sour cream

FROSTING
- 1 cup confectioners' sugar
- 1 tablespoon butter, softened
- 1 tablespoon chai tea latte mix
- ½ teaspoon vanilla extract
- 4 to 5 teaspoons milk

1. In a microwave, melt chocolate with the water; stir until smooth. Cool slightly. In a large bowl, cream butter and brown sugar until light and fluffy. Add eggs, one at a time, beating well after each addition. Beat in vanilla, then chocolate mixture.

2. Combine the flour, latte mix, baking soda and salt; add to creamed mixture alternately with sour cream.

3. Transfer to three greased 5¾-in. x 3-in. x 2-in. loaf pans. Bake at 350° for 35-40 minutes or until a toothpick inserted near the center comes out clean. Cool for 10 minutes before removing from pans to a wire rack to cool completely.

4. For frosting, combine the confectioners' sugar, butter, latte mix, vanilla and enough milk to achieve desired consistency. Frost tops of loaves.

Texas Garlic Mashed Potatoes

These creamy mashed potatoes get their flavor burst from garlic and caramelized onions. They're great with any meal.

—RICHARD MARKLE MIDLOTHIAN, TX

PREP: 30 MIN. • **BAKE:** 30 MIN. • **MAKES:** 6 SERVINGS

- 1 whole garlic bulb
- 1 teaspoon plus 1 tablespoon olive oil, divided
- 1 medium white onion, chopped
- 4 medium potatoes, peeled and quartered
- ¼ cup butter, softened
- ¼ cup sour cream
- ¼ cup grated Parmesan cheese
- ¼ cup 2% milk
- ½ teaspoon salt
- ¼ teaspoon pepper

1. Remove papery outer skin from garlic (do not peel or separate cloves). Cut top off of garlic bulb. Brush with 1 teaspoon oil. Wrap bulb in heavy-duty foil. Bake at 425° for 30-35 minutes or until softened.
2. Meanwhile, in a large skillet over low heat, cook onion in remaining oil for 15-20 minutes or until golden brown, stirring occasionally. Transfer to a food processor. Cover and process until blended; set aside.
3. Place potatoes in a large saucepan and cover with water. Bring to a boil. Reduce heat; cover and cook for 15-20 minutes or until tender. Drain. Place potatoes in a large bowl. Squeeze softened garlic into bowl; add the butter, sour cream, cheese, milk, salt, pepper and onion. Beat until mashed.

Pina Colada Zucchini Bread

At my husband's urging, I entered this recipe at the Pennsylvania Farm Show and won first place! I think you'll love the cake-like texture and tropical flavors.

—SHARON RYDBOM TIPTON, PA

PREP: 25 MIN. • **BAKE:** 45 MIN. + COOLING
MAKES: 3 LOAVES (12 SLICES EACH)

- 4 cups all-purpose flour
- 3 cups sugar
- 2 teaspoons baking powder
- 1½ teaspoons salt
- 1 teaspoon baking soda
- 4 eggs
- 1½ cups canola oil
- 1 teaspoon each coconut, rum and vanilla extracts
- 3 cups shredded zucchini
- 1 cup canned crushed pineapple, drained
- ½ cup chopped walnuts or chopped pecans

1. Line the bottoms of three greased and floured 8-in. x 4-in. loaf pans with waxed paper and grease the paper; set aside.
2. In a large bowl, combine the flour, sugar, baking powder, salt and baking soda. In another bowl, whisk the eggs, oil and extracts. Stir into dry ingredients just until moistened. Fold in the zucchini, pineapple and walnuts.
3. Transfer to prepared pans. Bake at 350° for 45-55 minutes or until a toothpick inserted near the center comes out clean. Cool for 10 minutes before removing from pans to wire racks. Gently remove waxed paper.

Swiss-Onion Potato Bake

I get a lot of compliments on this cheesy hash brown dish when I take it to potlucks. I also like to serve it at home with our favorite meat loaf.

—**ANNETTA BALLESTEROS** KUTTAWA, KY

PREP: 15 MIN. • **BAKE:** 35 MIN.
MAKES: 12 SERVINGS

- 1 **cup finely chopped sweet onion**
- 2 **tablespoons butter**
- 1 **package (30 ounces) frozen shredded hash brown potatoes, thawed**
- 2 **cups (8 ounces) shredded Swiss cheese**
- 1 **teaspoon salt**
- ¼ **teaspoon pepper**
- 2 **eggs**
- 1 **cup milk**
  Minced fresh parsley, optional

1. In a small skillet, saute onion in butter until tender. In a large bowl, combine the hash browns, cheese, salt, pepper and onion mixture.

2. Transfer to a greased 13-in. x 9-in. baking dish. In a small bowl, whisk eggs and milk; pour over potato mixture.

3. Bake, uncovered, at 350° for 35-40 minutes or until a thermometer reads 160°. Let stand for 5 minutes before cutting. Sprinkle with parsley if desired.

PER SERVING *171 cal., 8 g fat (5 g sat. fat), 59 mg chol., 287 mg sodium, 15 g carb., 1 g fiber, 9 g pro.* **Diabetic Exchanges:** *1 starch, 1 lean meat, 1 fat.*

FROM THE WEB

Very good, very easy. I made it for Easter. This is one of those recipes that is good as it is and could be used for breakfast/ brunch or dinner. I plan to use this dish as a base for other meals, such as changing the Swiss cheese to cheddar and adding green chilies. Or I will use pepper jack cheese and serve the potatoes with brats.

—**TERI396** TASTEOFHOME.COM

Broccoli with Orange Sauce

When serving, I like to arrange broccoli on a platter and drape it with this creamy orange sauce. It's a refreshingly different take on broccoli salad.

—**DORIS HEATH** FRANKLIN, NC

START TO FINISH: 20 MIN. • **MAKES:** 8 SERVINGS

  3 **pounds fresh broccoli, cut into spears**
4½ **teaspoons butter**
4½ **teaspoons all-purpose flour**
 ⅓ **cup orange juice**
 ½ **teaspoon grated orange peel**
 ⅓ **cup canned mandarin oranges**
 ¼ **teaspoon dried tarragon**
 ⅓ **cup plain yogurt**

1. Place broccoli in a large saucepan; add 1 in. of water. Bring to a boil. Reduce heat; cover and cook for 5-8 minutes or until crisp-tender.
2. Meanwhile, in a small saucepan, melt butter. Whisk in flour until smooth. Gradually stir in orange juice. Add the orange peel, mandarin oranges and tarragon. Bring to a boil; cook and stir for 2 minutes or until thickened. Remove from the heat; stir in yogurt.
3. Drain broccoli; serve with sauce.
PER SERVING *100 cal., 3 g fat (2 g sat. fat), 7 mg chol., 90 mg sodium, 16 g carb., 6 g fiber, 5 g pro.* **Diabetic** **Exchanges:** *1 vegetable, ½ starch, ½ fat.*

Caramelized Onions in Mashed Potatoes

My husband came up with this recipe, and I have never tasted a better potato dish! The sweet onions and rich cream cheese make mashed potatoes simply irresistible.

—**KRISTY MCCLELLAN** PHOENIX, AZ

PREP: 20 MIN. • **COOK:** 15 MIN. • **MAKES:** 8 SERVINGS

  4 **large potatoes, peeled and quartered**
 ⅛ **teaspoon seasoned salt**
  6 **tablespoons butter, divided**
 ⅓ **cup chopped onion**
 ⅓ **cup packed brown sugar**
 ⅓ **cup sour cream**
 ¼ **cup half-and-half cream**
  2 **ounces cream cheese, softened**
 ½ **teaspoon salt**
 ⅛ **teaspoon pepper**
    Dash cayenne pepper

1. Place potatoes in a large saucepan and cover with water; add seasoned salt. Bring to a boil. Reduce heat; cover and cook for 15-20 minutes or until tender.
2. Meanwhile, in a small skillet, melt 4 tablespoons butter. Add onion; cook until slightly softened. Sprinkle with brown sugar; cook until brown sugar is bubbly and onion is tender.
3. Drain potatoes; transfer to a large bowl. Add the sour cream, half-and-half, cream cheese, salt, pepper, cayenne and remaining butter; mash until smooth. Stir in the onion mixture.

Sweet Potato Bread & Pineapple Butter

I hope you like my recipe as much as I do. The combination of tangy pineapple with this sweet and spicy loaf is delicious!

—DIANE GOSS CHESTER, VA

PREP: 20 MIN. • **BAKE:** 50 MIN. + COOLING
MAKES: 1 LOAF (16 SLICES) AND 1 CUP BUTTER

- 1¾ cups all-purpose flour
- 1½ cups sugar
- 1½ teaspoons ground cinnamon
- 1 teaspoon ground nutmeg
- ½ teaspoon baking soda
- ½ teaspoon baking powder
- ½ teaspoon salt
- 2 eggs
- 1 cup mashed sweet potatoes
- ½ cup canola oil
- ⅓ cup water

BUTTER

- ½ cup butter, softened
- 1 can (8 ounces) crushed pineapple, well drained

1. In a large bowl, combine the first seven ingredients. In a small bowl, combine the eggs, potatoes, oil and water. Stir into dry ingredients just until moistened.
2. Transfer to a greased 9-in. x 5-in. loaf pan. Bake at 350° for 50-60 minutes or until a toothpick inserted near the center comes out clean. Cool for 10 minutes before removing from pan to a wire rack.
3. In a small bowl, combine butter and pineapple. Serve with bread.

Chili-Cheese Rice Bake

Baked rice with three kinds of cheese is the kind of comforting side dish you could make a meal out of. On occasion, I top it with French-fried onions or crumbled potato chips before baking; it adds a little something extra.

—CATHLENE WILLIS RIGBY, ID

START TO FINISH: 30 MIN. • **MAKES:** 2 SERVINGS

- ½ cup uncooked instant rice
- ½ cup chopped onion
- 1 tablespoon butter
- ½ cup sour cream
- ¼ cup canned chopped green chilies
- 2 tablespoons cream-style cottage cheese
- 2 tablespoons ricotta cheese
- ⅛ teaspoon salt
  Dash pepper
- ½ cup shredded sharp cheddar cheese
- 1 teaspoon minced fresh parsley

1. Cook rice according to package directions. Meanwhile, in a large skillet, saute onion in butter until tender. Remove from the heat; stir in the sour cream, chilies, cottage cheese, ricotta cheese, salt, pepper and rice.
2. Transfer rice mixture to a 2-cup baking dish coated with cooking spray. Sprinkle cheddar cheese over the top. Bake at 375° for 15-20 minutes or until cheese is melted. Sprinkle with parsley.

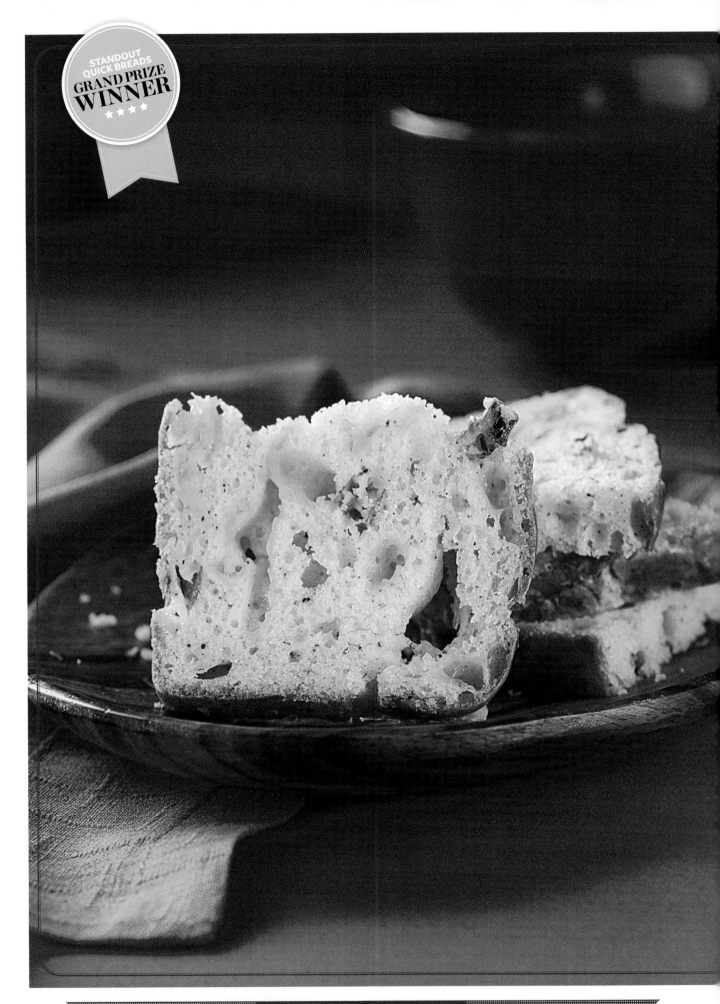

STANDOUT
QUICK BREADS
GRAND PRIZE
WINNER
★ ★ ★ ★

Peppery Cheese Bread

This is my daughter Kendra's favorite savory quick bread. When the warm bread hits your palate, it's just heavenly! It never lasts long in our house.

—**SHARON BOREN** SALEM, OR

PREP: 15 MIN. • **BAKE:** 45 MIN. + COOLING
MAKES: 1 LOAF (16 SLICES)

- 2½ cups all-purpose flour
- 1 tablespoon sugar
- 1½ teaspoons coarsely ground pepper
- 1 teaspoon baking powder
- ¾ teaspoon salt
- ½ teaspoon baking soda
- 2 eggs
- 1 cup (8 ounces) reduced-fat plain yogurt
- ½ cup canola oil
- ¼ cup 2% milk
- 1 tablespoon spicy brown mustard
- 1 cup (4 ounces) shredded cheddar cheese
- 2 green onions, thinly sliced

1. In a large bowl, combine the first six ingredients. In a small bowl, whisk the eggs, yogurt, oil, milk and mustard. Stir into dry ingredients just until moistened. Fold in cheese and onions.

2. Transfer to a greased 9-in. x 5-in. loaf pan. Bake at 350° for 45-55 minutes or until a toothpick inserted near the center comes out clean. Cool for 10 minutes before removing from pan to a wire rack.

STIRRED BATTER SUCCESS

Most quick breads (including loaves, muffins and even pancakes) are made using the stirred batter technique.

Dry ingredients are combined in a large bowl. Wet ingredients are beaten well in a separate bowl, then mixed into the dry ingredients just until they are incorporated. There may even be some lumps left in the batter. Garnishes such as cheese, fruit or veggies are gently folded in with as little mixing as possible.

A very light mixing ensures a tender finished product with a fine crumb, not one that is tough or chewy.

Orange Nut Bread & Cream Cheese Spread

This sweet, delectable bread was my mother's favorite. Every bite gives you a burst of orange and the crunch of walnuts.

—**KAREN SUE GARBACK-PRISTERA** ALBANY, NY

PREP: 40 MIN. • **BAKE:** 35 MIN. + COOLING
MAKES: 3 MINI LOAVES (6 SLICES EACH) AND 1 CUP SPREAD

- ⅓ cup butter, softened
- ⅔ cup sugar
- 2 eggs
- ½ teaspoon orange extract
- ½ teaspoon vanilla extract
- 2 cups all-purpose flour
- 1 teaspoon baking powder
- ½ teaspoon salt
- ¼ teaspoon baking soda
- 1 cup orange juice
- 1 cup chopped walnuts

SPREAD
- 1 package (8 ounces) cream cheese, softened
- 2 tablespoons orange juice
- 1 tablespoon confectioners' sugar
- 1 teaspoon grated orange peel

1. In a large bowl, cream butter and sugar until light and fluffy. Add eggs, one at a time, beating well after each addition. Beat in extracts.

2. Combine the flour, baking powder, salt and baking soda; add to creamed mixture alternately with orange juice. Fold in walnuts.

3. Transfer to three greased 5¾-in. x 3-in. x 2-in. loaf pans. Bake at 350° for 35-40 minutes or until a toothpick inserted near the center comes out clean. Cool for 10 minutes before removing from pans to wire racks.

4. In a small bowl, beat the cream cheese, orange juice, confectioners' sugar and orange peel until well blended. Chill until serving. Serve with bread.

Asparagus and Sun-Dried Tomatoes

START TO FINISH: 25 MIN. • **MAKES:** 12 SERVINGS

- 3 pounds fresh asparagus, trimmed
- ⅓ cup butter, cubed
- ⅓ cup chicken broth
- 3 tablespoons olive oil
- 4 teaspoons grated lemon peel
- ¼ teaspoon salt
- ¼ teaspoon pepper
- ⅓ cup oil-packed sun-dried tomatoes, patted dry and chopped
- ¼ cup minced fresh basil

1. Place asparagus in a steamer basket; place in a large saucepan over 1 in. of water. Bring to a boil; cover and steam for 6-8 minutes or until crisp-tender.

2. Meanwhile, in a small saucepan, melt butter. Stir in the broth, oil, lemon peel and salt.

3. Transfer asparagus to a serving platter; drizzle with butter mixture. Sprinkle with pepper; top with tomatoes and basil.

❝Crisp-tender asparagus is drizzled with lemon butter sauce and sprinkled with flavorful sun-dried tomatoes in this elegant, yet surprisingly quick, dish.❞

—**PAT STEVENS** GRANBURY, TX

Chipotle Sweet Potatoes

Here's a combination you don't normally find with sweet potatoes: balsamic vinaigrette, honey and chipotle peppers. This makes an amazing side dish for a Southwest-inspired meal.
—**KIM JONES** MOUNT JULIET, TN

PREP: 15 MIN. • **BAKE:** 25 MIN. • **MAKES:** 8 SERVINGS

- 3 large sweet potatoes (about 2½ pounds), peeled and cut into ½-inch cubes
- 1 cup balsamic vinaigrette, divided
- ¼ teaspoon salt
- ¼ teaspoon pepper
- ⅓ cup minced fresh cilantro
- 3 tablespoons honey
- 2 chipotle peppers in adobo sauce, minced

1. Place sweet potatoes in two greased 15-in. x 10-in. x 1-in. baking pans. Drizzle with ½ cup vinaigrette and sprinkle with salt and pepper; toss to coat.

2. Bake at 400° for 25-30 minutes or until tender, stirring once. Cool slightly; transfer to a large bowl.

3. In a small bowl, whisk remaining vinaigrette with the cilantro, honey and peppers. Pour over potatoes and gently stir to coat.

PER SERVING *168 cal., 5 g fat (1 g sat. fat), 0 chol., 357 mg sodium, 30 g carb., 3 g fiber, 1 g pro.* ***Diabetic Exchanges:*** *2 starch, 1 fat.*

Blue Cheese & Shallot Bread

You'll definitely want to cut yourself a thick slice of this savory, cheesy bread. Every bite is filled with robust-tasting blue cheese and tender shallots.

—RITA ROWLAND AUBURN, KY

PREP: 20 MIN. • **BAKE:** 50 MIN. + COOLING
MAKES: 1 LOAF (12 SLICES)

- ½ cup chopped shallots
- 3 tablespoons butter
- 2 cups all-purpose flour
- 1 tablespoon sugar
- 2½ teaspoons baking powder
- 1 teaspoon salt
- 1 teaspoon ground mustard
- ¼ cup cold butter
- 1 egg, beaten
- 1 cup 2% milk
- ¾ cup crumbled blue cheese
- 2 tablespoons grated Parmesan cheese

1. In a small skillet, saute the shallots in butter until tender; set aside.

2. In a large bowl, combine the flour, sugar, baking powder, salt and mustard. Cut in butter until mixture resembles coarse crumbs. In a small bowl, combine egg and milk. Stir into crumb mixture just until moistened. Fold in cheeses and reserved shallot mixture.

3. Transfer to a greased 8-in. x 4-in. loaf pan. Bake at 325° for 50-60 minutes or until a toothpick inserted near the center comes out clean. Cool for 10 minutes before removing from pan to wire rack.

Peasant Peppers

My mother-in-law, who lives in Italy, taught me to make this simple casserole. It's considered wholesome peasant fare, but I've never tasted peppers as delicious!

—ROBYN SCOLLO FAIRPORT, NY

PREP: 15 MIN. • **BAKE:** 45 MIN. • **MAKES:** 5 SERVINGS

- 3 large green peppers, thinly sliced
- 3 large sweet red peppers, thinly sliced
- 2 tablespoons olive oil
- 1½ teaspoons salt
- 1 teaspoon pepper
- ½ cup soft bread crumbs

1. Preheat oven to 400°. Place peppers in two 15x10x1-in. baking pans. Drizzle with oil and sprinkle with salt and pepper; toss to coat.

2. Bake 30-35 minutes until tender and skins are slightly blackened; stir. Sprinkle with bread crumbs. Bake 15-20 minutes longer or until lightly browned.

FROM THE WEB

I used sub sandwich dressing instead of olive oil and added half a tablespoon of vegetable oil just in case. I put two pieces of bread in the oven for a few minutes and just crumbled it on top instead of the bread crumbs. Right before serving, I added a little Parmesan. Nothing fancy, just the kind in the jar. This dish is delicious and satisfying, with a simple flavor that is very pleasing. —GLASSROSE352 TASTEOFHOME.COM

Sweet Potato Spice Bread

It's a good thing this recipe makes two mini loaves because they'll go fast! For a small household, eat one loaf now and freeze the other for later.

—**RONNIE LITTLES** VIRGINIA BEACH, VA

PREP: 15 MIN. • **BAKE:** 25 MIN. + COOLING
MAKES: 2 MINI LOAVES (6 SLICES EACH)

- 1 **cup all-purpose flour**
- 1½ **teaspoons baking powder**
- ¼ **teaspoon each ground cinnamon, nutmeg and allspice**
- ⅛ **teaspoon salt**
- 1 **egg**
- ⅓ **cup mashed sweet potato**
- ⅓ **cup honey**
- 3 **tablespoons canola oil**
- 2 **tablespoons molasses**
- ⅓ **cup chopped walnuts**

1. In a small bowl, combine the flour, baking powder, spices and salt. In another small bowl, whisk the egg, sweet potato, honey, oil and molasses. Stir into dry ingredients just until moistened. Fold in walnuts.

2. Transfer to two 5¾-in. x 3-in. x 2-in. loaf pans coated with cooking spray. Bake at 325° for 25-30 minutes or until a toothpick inserted near the center comes out clean. Cool for 10 minutes before removing from pans to wire racks.

PER SERVING *142 cal., 6 g fat (1 g sat. fat), 18 mg chol., 85 mg sodium, 20 g carb., 1 g fiber, 3 g pro.* **Diabetic Exchanges:** *1½ starch, 1 fat.*

SWEET IDEA

I've always added grated orange peel to my mashed sweet potatoes. To save time and mess, I now just cut a 2- to 3-inch strip of orange peel and add it to the boiling water as the sweet potatoes cook. Then I mash the softened peel right along with the potatoes for a bright and fresh, wonderful flavor.

—**PAT W.** NEW BLOOMFIELD, MO

Flavorful Red Potatoes

I like to make this recipe with both baby red and Yukon Gold potatoes. If you can't find those, use larger potatoes cut into quarters. I'd be satisfied eating just these for dinner.
—**WOLFGANG HANAU** WEST PALM BEACH, FL

START TO FINISH: 30 MIN. • **MAKES:** 6 SERVINGS

- 12 **small red potatoes**
- ½ **cup grated Parmesan cheese**
- ½ **cup olive oil**
- 2 **tablespoons minced fresh parsley**
- 2 **tablespoons capers, drained**
- 2 **tablespoons sliced Greek olives**
- 1 **tablespoon thinly sliced green onion**
- 1 **teaspoon white wine vinegar**
- ¼ **teaspoon pepper**

1. Place potatoes in a large saucepan and cover with water. Bring to a boil. Reduce heat; cover and cook for 15-20 minutes or until tender.
2. Meanwhile, in a small bowl, combine the remaining ingredients. Drain potatoes; cool slightly. Cut each in half; place in a serving bowl. Add cheese mixture and toss gently to coat.

Triple Cranberry Sauce

Cranberry fans will ask for this sauce again and again. It's loaded with their favorite fruit—in fresh, dried and juice form. Orange and allspice make it awesome
—**ARLENE SMULSKI** LYONS, IL

PREP: 10 MIN. • **COOK:** 15 MIN. + CHILLING • **MAKES:** 3 CUPS

- 1 **package (12 ounces) fresh or frozen cranberries**
- 1 **cup thawed cranberry juice concentrate**
- ½ **cup dried cranberries**
- ⅓ **cup sugar**
- 3 **tablespoons orange juice**
- 3 **tablespoons orange marmalade**
- 2 **teaspoons grated orange peel**
- ¼ **teaspoon ground allspice**

1. In a small saucepan, combine the cranberries, juice concentrate, dried cranberries and sugar. Cook over medium heat until the berries pop, about 15 minutes.
2. Remove from the heat; stir in the orange juice, marmalade, orange peel and allspice. Transfer to a small bowl; refrigerate until chilled.

Green Beans with Pecans

I collect cookbooks from all over the world, and I love to try new recipes for my husband or for entertaining. When I come across a recipe like this, I make a copy and put it in a protective sleeve so we can make it again and again.

—**SHARON DELANEY-CHRONIS** SOUTH MILWAUKEE, WI

PREP: 20 MIN. • **COOK:** 15 MIN. • **MAKES:** 8 SERVINGS

- 1 tablespoon butter
- 1 cup chopped pecans
- 2 tablespoons maple syrup
- ⅛ teaspoon salt

BEANS
- ¼ cup finely chopped shallots
- 2 tablespoons butter
- 2 teaspoons all-purpose flour
- ½ teaspoon grated orange peel
  Dash cayenne pepper
- 1½ pounds fresh green beans, trimmed
- ⅔ cup reduced-sodium chicken broth
- ⅓ cup orange juice
- 1 teaspoon fresh sage or ¼ teaspoon dried sage leaves
- ¼ teaspoon salt
- ⅛ teaspoon pepper

1. In a small heavy skillet, melt butter. Add pecans; cook over medium heat until toasted, about 4 minutes. Add syrup and salt; cook and stir for 2-3 minutes or until pecans are glossy. Spread on foil to cool.
2. Meanwhile, in a large skillet, saute shallots in butter until tender; stir in the flour, orange peel and cayenne. Add the remaining ingredients; cover and cook for 5 minutes. Uncover; cook and stir 4-5 minutes longer or until the beans are crisp-tender. Transfer to a serving bowl and sprinkle with pecans.

Savory Dill and Caraway Scones

These tender, tasty scones practically melt in your mouth. The herb-and-spice flavors make them stand out from typical fruit scones.

—**SALLY SIBTHORPE** SHELBY TOWNSHIP, MI

PREP: 20 MIN. • **BAKE:** 15 MIN. • **MAKES:** 1 DOZEN

- 2 cups all-purpose flour
- 4½ teaspoons sugar
- 1 tablespoon onion powder
- 1 tablespoon snipped fresh dill or 1 teaspoon dill weed
- 2 teaspoons caraway seeds
- 1 teaspoon baking powder
- ¾ teaspoon salt
- ½ teaspoon baking soda
- ½ teaspoon coarsely ground pepper
- 6 tablespoons cold butter
- 1 egg yolk
- ¾ cup sour cream
- ½ cup ricotta cheese
- 4 teaspoons heavy whipping cream
  Additional caraway seeds, optional

1. In a large bowl, combine the first nine ingredients. Cut in butter until mixture resembles coarse crumbs. Combine the egg yolk, sour cream and ricotta cheese; stir into crumb mixture just until moistened. Turn onto a floured surface; knead 10 times.
2. Pat into two 6-in. circles. Cut each into six wedges. Separate wedges and place on a greased baking sheet. Brush tops with cream; sprinkle with additional caraway seeds if desired. Bake at 400° for 15-18 minutes or until golden brown. Serve warm.

Tomato & Olive Bread

I like to serve this special bread with spaghetti and meatballs or a good steak. Pesto and black olives give this loaf a distinctive flavor that complements almost any meal.

—**ANN BAKER** TEXARKANA, TX

PREP: 30 MIN. + RISING • **BAKE:** 15 MIN. + COOLING
MAKES: 1 MINI LOAF (6 SLICES)

- 1⅛ teaspoons active dry yeast
- ¼ cup warm water (110° to 115°)
- 1 tablespoon grated Parmesan cheese
- 1 tablespoon chopped ripe olives
- 1 tablespoon olive oil
- 1 tablespoon sun-dried tomato pesto
- 1 tablespoon egg white
- 2¼ teaspoons sugar
- ⅛ teaspoon salt
- 1 to 1¼ cups all-purpose flour

1. In a small bowl, dissolve yeast in warm water. Add the cheese, olives, oil, pesto, egg white, sugar, salt and ¾ cup flour. Beat until smooth. Stir in enough remaining flour to form a soft dough.
2. Turn onto a lightly floured surface; knead until smooth and elastic, about 6-8 minutes. Place in a bowl coated with cooking spray, turning once to coat the top. Cover and let rise in a warm place until doubled, about 1 hour.
3. Punch dough down; shape into a loaf. Place in a 5¾-in. x 3-in. x 2-in. loaf pan coated with cooking spray. Cover and let rise until doubled, about 20 minutes.
4. Bake at 350° for 15-20 minutes or until golden brown. Remove from pan to a wire rack to cool.
PER SERVING *114 cal., 3 g fat (1 g sat. fat), 1 mg chol., 105 mg sodium, 18 g carb., 1 g fiber, 3 g pro.* **Diabetic Exchanges:** *1 starch, ½ fat.*

Corn Bread with a Kick

To me, nothing says Southern cooking like crisp corn bread made in a cast-iron skillet. I use a very old skillet that belonged to my great-aunt.

—**GEORDYTH SULLIVAN** CUTLER BAY, FL

PREP: 20 MIN. • **BAKE:** 20 MIN. • **MAKES:** 8 SERVINGS

- ⅔ cup all-purpose flour
- ⅔ cup cornmeal
- 1 tablespoon sugar
- ½ teaspoon baking powder
- ½ teaspoon salt
- ¼ teaspoon baking soda
- 1 egg
- 1 cup buttermilk
- 3 tablespoons butter
- 3 chipotle peppers in adobo sauce, drained and chopped
- 6 bacon strips, cooked and crumbled

1. In a large bowl, combine the first six ingredients. In another bowl, whisk egg and buttermilk.
2. Place butter in an 8-in. ovenproof skillet; heat skillet in a 425° oven for 3-5 minutes or until butter is melted. Meanwhile, stir egg mixture into dry ingredients just until moistened. Fold in peppers and bacon.
3. Carefully swirl the butter in the skillet to coat the sides and bottom of pan; add batter. Bake at 425° for 18-22 minutes or until a toothpick inserted near the center comes out clean. Cut into wedges; serve warm.

Peanut Butter Banana Bread

My family literally comes running when they smell this bread baking. Between the thick chocolate layer and the peanutty topping, this bread is simply scrumptious!

—**SHERRY LEE** COLUMBUS, OH

PREP: 25 MIN. • **BAKE:** 45 MIN. + COOLING
MAKES: 2 LOAVES (12 SLICES EACH)

TOPPING
- ½ cup all-purpose flour
- ½ cup packed brown sugar
- ¼ cup creamy peanut butter
- ½ teaspoon ground cinnamon

BATTER
- ½ cup butter, softened
- 1 package (8 ounces) cream cheese, softened
- 1¼ cups sugar
- 2 eggs
- 1 cup mashed ripe bananas
- 1 teaspoon vanilla extract
- 2¼ cups all-purpose flour
- 1½ teaspoons baking powder
- ½ teaspoon baking soda
- 1 teaspoon ground cinnamon
- 1½ cups semisweet chocolate chips

1. In a small bowl, stir the flour, brown sugar, peanut butter and cinnamon until crumbly; set aside.
2. In a large bowl, cream the butter, cream cheese and sugar until light and fluffy. Add eggs, one at a time, beating well after each addition. Beat in bananas and vanilla. Combine the flour, baking powder, baking soda and cinnamon; stir into creamed mixture just until moistened.
3. Divide half of the batter between two greased 8-in. x 4-in. loaf pans; sprinkle with half of the topping. Top with chocolate chips. Repeat layers of batter and topping.
4. Bake at 350° for 45-55 minutes or until a toothpick inserted near the center comes out clean. Cool for 10 minutes before removing from pans to wire racks.
NOTE *Reduced-fat peanut butter is not recommended for this recipe.*

Bread & Butter Peppers

If your pepper plants are as prolific as mine, this recipe will come in handy. The crunchy mix of sliced peppers makes a zesty picnic side or sandwich topping.

—**STARR MILAM** SHELDON, WI

PREP: 20 MIN. + STANDING • **COOK:** 5 MIN. + CHILLING
MAKES: 1 QUART

- 2½ cups seeded sliced banana peppers (about 7 peppers)
- 1 medium green pepper, julienned or 1 medium green tomato, halved and sliced
- 1 jalapeno pepper, seeded and sliced
- 1 small onion, sliced
- ¼ cup canning salt
- 12 to 15 ice cubes
- 2 cups sugar
- 1 cup white vinegar
- 1 tablespoon mustard seed
- ½ teaspoon celery seed

1. In a large bowl, combine the peppers, onion and salt; top with ice. Let stand for 2 hours. Rinse and drain well.
2. In a large saucepan, combine the sugar, vinegar, mustard seed and celery seed. Bring to a boil; cook and stir just until sugar is dissolved. Pour over pepper mixture; cool. Cover tightly and refrigerate for at least 24 hours. Store in the refrigerator for up to 3 months.
NOTE *Wear disposable gloves when cutting hot peppers; the oils can burn skin. Avoid touching your face.*

Know quick bread is done with this simple test.

Insert a toothpick near the center of the bread. If the toothpick comes out clean—without any crumbs—the bread is done.

Garden Tomato Relish

Here's a great way to use up your garden harvest, and to have a tasty relish on hand for the burgers and dogs of fall tailgating season. Why not share a jar with a friend or neighbor?

—KELLY MARTEL TILLSONBURG, ON

PREP: 1½ HOURS + SIMMERING
PROCESS: 20 MIN. • **MAKES:** 10 PINTS

- 10 **pounds tomatoes**
- 3 **large sweet onions, finely chopped**
- 2 **medium sweet red peppers, finely chopped**
- 2 **medium green peppers, finely chopped**
- 2 **teaspoons mustard seed**
- 1 **teaspoon celery seed**
- 4½ **cups white vinegar**
- 2½ **cups packed brown sugar**
- 3 **tablespoons canning salt**
- 2 **teaspoons ground ginger**
- 2 **teaspoons ground cinnamon**
- 1 **teaspoon ground allspice**
- 1 **teaspoon ground cloves**
- 1 **teaspoon ground nutmeg**

1. In a large saucepan, bring 8 cups water to a boil. Add tomatoes, a few at a time; boil for 30 seconds. Drain and immediately place tomatoes in ice water. Drain and pat dry; peel and finely chop. Place in a stockpot. Add onions and peppers.

2. Place mustard and celery seed on a double thickness of cheesecloth; bring up corners of cloth and tie with string to form a bag. Add spice bag and the remaining ingredients to the pot. Bring to a boil. Reduce heat and simmer, uncovered, for 60-75 minutes or until slightly thickened. Discard spice bag.

3. Carefully ladle relish into hot 1-pint jars, leaving ½-in. headspace. Remove air bubbles; wipe rims and adjust lids. Process in boiling-water canner for 20 minutes.

NOTE *The processing time listed is for altitudes of 1,000 feet or less. For altitudes up to 3,000 feet, add 5 minutes; 6,000 feet, add 10 minutes; 8,000 feet, add 15 minutes; 10,000 feet, add 20 minutes.*

Potato Bacon Casserole

Bacon and potatoes are a terrific combination. My hearty and super-easy side goes with most main dishes. Everyone enjoys it so much that it's a regular at our table.
—**JOANNE PANZETTA** BUSHNELL, FL

PREP: 20 MIN. • **BAKE:** 35 MIN. • **MAKES:** 8 SERVINGS

  4 **cups frozen shredded hash brown potatoes, thawed**
  ½ **cup finely chopped onion**
  8 **bacon strips, cooked and crumbled**
  1 **cup (4 ounces) shredded cheddar cheese**
  1 **egg**
  1 **can (12 ounces) evaporated milk**
  ½ **teaspoon seasoned salt**

1. In a greased 8-in. square baking dish, layer half of the potatoes, onion, bacon and cheese. Repeat layers.
2. In a small bowl, whisk the egg, milk and seasoned salt; pour over potato mixture. Cover and bake at 350° for 30 minutes. Uncover; bake 5-10 minutes longer or until a knife inserted near the center comes out clean.

Cowboy Corn Bread

This corn bread is richer and sweeter than others I've tried. It's especially luscious alongside ham and beans.
—**KAREN ANN BLAND** GOVE, KS

PREP: 15 MIN. • **BAKE:** 25 MIN. • **MAKES:** 12 SERVINGS

  2 **cups biscuit/baking mix**
  1 **cup yellow cornmeal**
  ¾ **cup sugar**
  ½ **teaspoon baking soda**
  ½ **teaspoon salt**
  2 **eggs**
  1 **cup butter, melted**
  1 **cup half-and-half cream**

1. In a large bowl, combine the first five ingredients. In another bowl, combine the eggs, butter and cream; stir into the dry ingredients just until moistened. Spread into a greased 13-in. x 9-in. baking pan.
2. Bake at 350° for 25-30 minutes or until a toothpick inserted near the center comes out clean. Serve warm.

Peanut Butter Turtle Candies, page 181

180

186

185

Cookies, Bars & Candy

Share the **joy** of fresh-baked cookies, **delightfully gooey caramel** bars, **wholesome** lunch box **treats**, and **irresistible** candies sure to **capture hearts**. Nothing beats these **winning goodies** for a little **home-cooked love on the go**.

Cherry Chocolate Chip Cookies

My husband and I love homemade cookies, so I concocted these oatmeal cookies with chocolate chips and dried cherries. Chocolate-covered-cherry lovers have to try these.

—DENISE FRITZ ORMOND BEACH, FL

PREP: 20 MIN. • **BAKE:** 15 MIN./BATCH • **MAKES:** 15 COOKIES

- ½ cup butter, softened
- ⅔ cup packed brown sugar
- ⅓ cup sugar
- 1 egg
- 1 teaspoon vanilla extract
- 1 cup all-purpose flour
- ¾ cup quick-cooking oats
- ¾ teaspoon baking soda
- ½ teaspoon salt
- ⅔ cup dried cherries, chopped
- ½ cup semisweet chocolate chips

1. In a small bowl, cream butter and sugars until light and fluffy. Beat in egg and vanilla. Combine the flour, oats, baking soda and salt; gradually add to creamed mixture and mix well. Stir in cherries and chocolate chips.

2. Drop by scant ¼ cupfuls 3 in. apart onto ungreased baking sheets. Bake at 350° for 14-16 minutes or until golden brown. Cool for 1 minute before removing from baking sheets to wire racks. Store in an airtight container.

PER SERVING *203 cal., 8 g fat (5 g sat. fat), 30 mg chol., 194 mg sodium, 31 g carb., 1 g fiber, 2 g pro.* **Diabetic Exchanges:** *2 starch, 1 fat.*

Blondie Nut Bars

Full of nuts and chocolate chips, these blondies definitely have more fun. With a subtle vanilla and coffee flavor, they make a sweet treat for potlucks, office parties and picnics.

—LORI PHILLIPS CORONA, CA

PREP: 15 MIN. • **BAKE:** 25 MIN. + COOLING • **MAKES:** 2 DOZEN

- 4 eggs
- 2 tablespoons heavy whipping cream
- 2 tablespoons butter, melted
- 2 teaspoons instant coffee granules
- 1 teaspoon vanilla extract
- 2 cups all-purpose flour
- 2 cups sugar
- 2 teaspoons baking powder
- ¼ teaspoon salt
- 1 cup chopped almonds
- 1 cup chopped walnuts
- 1 cup (6 ounces) semisweet chocolate chips
  Confectioners' sugar

1. In a large bowl, beat the eggs, cream, butter, coffee granules and vanilla until blended. Combine the flour, sugar, baking powder and salt; gradually add to butter mixture. Stir in the almonds, walnuts and chocolate chips (batter will be stiff).

2. Spread into a greased 13-in. x 9-in. baking pan. Bake at 350° for 25-30 minutes or until lightly browned. Cool on a wire rack. Cut into bars. Dust with confectioners' sugar.

Maple Walnut Crisps

If you like maple, you'll love these sweet-and-salty crackers full of buttery, nutty flavor. If not, you can substitute corn syrup for maple syrup and vanilla extract for the maple flavoring.

—MARY SHIVERS ADA, OK

PREP: 15 MIN. • **BAKE:** 10 MIN. + COOLING • **MAKES:** 44 CRISPS

 44 **Club crackers (2½ inches x 1 inch)**
 1 **cup unsalted butter, cubed**
 1 **cup packed brown sugar**
 2 **tablespoons maple syrup**
 ½ **cup chopped pecans**
 ½ **cup chopped walnuts**
 ⅓ **cup finely chopped almonds**
 ¼ **teaspoon maple flavoring**

1. Place crackers in a single layer in a parchment paper-lined 15-in. x 10-in. x 1-in. baking pan. Set aside.
2. In a small heavy saucepan, melt butter over medium heat. Stir in brown sugar and syrup. Bring to a boil; cook and stir for 3-4 minutes or until sugar is dissolved. Stir in remaining ingredients. Spread evenly over crackers.
3. Bake at 350° for 10-12 minutes or until top appears dry. Cool completely on a wire rack. Break into pieces. Store in an airtight container.

PER SERVING *104 cal., 8 g fat (3 g sat. fat), 11 mg chol., 47 mg sodium, 9 g carb., trace fiber, 1 g pro.* **Diabetic Exchanges:** *1 fat, ½ starch.*

Diamond Almond Bars

Making these chewy almond bar cookies has been a tradition in our family for generations. They're especially popular at the holidays, but be sure to freeze several dozen extra to enjoy into the New Year.

—LIZ GREEN TAMWORTH, ON

PREP: 20 MIN. • **BAKE:** 25 MIN. + COOLING • **MAKES:** 5 DOZEN

 1 **cup butter, softened**
 1 **cup plus 1 tablespoon sugar, divided**
 1 **egg, separated**
 1 **teaspoon almond extract**
 2 **cups all-purpose flour**
 ½ **cup blanched sliced almonds**
 ¼ **teaspoon ground cinnamon**

1. In a large bowl, cream butter and 1 cup sugar until light and fluffy. Beat in egg yolk and extract. Gradually add flour to creamed mixture and mix well.
2. Press into a greased 15-in. x 10-in. x 1-in. baking pan. Beat egg white until foamy; brush over dough. Top with almonds. Combine cinnamon and remaining sugar; sprinkle over the top.
3. Bake at 350° for 25-30 minutes or until lightly browned (do not overbake). Cool on a wire rack for 10 minutes. Cut into diamond-shaped bars. Cool completely.

PER SERVING *64 cal., 4 g fat (2 g sat. fat), 12 mg chol., 23 mg sodium, 7 g carb., trace fiber, 1 g pro.* **Diabetic Exchanges:** *½ starch, ½ fat.*

Gooey Butterscotch Bars

The name says it all for these finger-lickin' good bars! And just imagine the fun you could have experimenting with different flavors of pudding, chips and cookie mixes.

—CAROL BREWER FAIRBORN, OH

PREP: 20 MIN. • **BAKE:** 20 MIN. + COOLING
MAKES: ABOUT 3 DOZEN

- 1 package (17½ ounces) sugar cookie mix
- 1 package (3.4 ounces) instant butterscotch pudding mix
- ½ cup butter, softened
- 1 egg
- 14 ounces caramels
- ½ cup evaporated milk
- 2 cups mixed nuts
- 1 teaspoon vanilla extract
- 1 cup butterscotch chips

1. In a large bowl, combine the sugar cookie mix, pudding mix, butter and egg. Press into an ungreased 13-in. x 9-in. baking pan. Bake at 350° for 20-25 minutes or until set.

2. In a large saucepan, combine caramels and milk. Cook and stir over medium-low heat until melted. Remove from the heat. Stir in nuts and vanilla. Pour over crust. Sprinkle with butterscotch chips.

3. Cool completely. Cut into bars. Store in an airtight container.

Nutty Orange Snowballs

An old recipe from my mom in North Dakota, these orange-flavored cookies are popular for weddings and special occasions. They're especially great at Christmastime because they look just like snowballs!

—JUDITH WEIDNER SPEARFISH, SD

PREP: 30 MIN. • **BAKE:** 10 MIN./BATCH + COOLING
MAKES: 3 DOZEN

- 1 cup butter, softened
- 1¼ cups confectioners' sugar, divided
- 1 teaspoon grated orange peel
- ½ teaspoon orange extract
- ½ teaspoon vanilla extract
- 2 cups all-purpose flour
- ¼ teaspoon salt
- ½ cup finely chopped walnuts
- ½ cup finely chopped hazelnuts

1. In a large bowl, cream butter and ¾ cup confectioners' sugar until light and fluffy. Beat in orange peel and extracts. Combine flour and salt; gradually add to creamed mixture and mix well. Stir in nuts.

2. Shape into ¾-in. balls. Place 1 in. apart on ungreased baking sheets. Bake at 350° for 10-12 minutes or until bottoms are lightly browned. Remove to wire racks to cool completely.

3. Place remaining confectioners' sugar in a large resealable plastic bag. Add cookies, a few at a time, and shake to coat. Store in an airtight container.

PER SERVING *107 cal., 7 g fat (3 g sat. fat), 13 mg chol., 52 mg sodium, 10 g carb., trace fiber, 1 g pro.* **Diabetic Exchanges:** *1 fat, ½ starch.*

Peanut Butter Turtle Candies

PREP: 30 MIN. + CHILLING • **MAKES:** 2 DOZEN

- 72 pecan halves (about 1¾ cups)
- ¼ cup peanut butter
- 2 tablespoons butter, softened
- ½ cup confectioners' sugar
- 5 ounces milk chocolate candy coating, coarsely chopped
- 2 teaspoons shortening

1. On waxed paper-lined pans, arrange pecan halves in clusters of three.

2. In a small bowl, beat peanut butter and butter until blended; gradually beat in confectioners' sugar. In a microwave, melt candy coating and shortening; stir until smooth.

3. Spoon ¼ teaspoon of melted chocolate into the center of each pecan cluster. Place teaspoonfuls of peanut butter mixture in the center of each cluster; press down slightly. Spoon remaining melted chocolate over tops. Chill for 10 minutes or until set. Store in an airtight container in the refrigerator.

PER SERVING *97 cal., 7 g fat (3 g sat. fat), 3 mg chol., 19 mg sodium, 8 g carb., 1 g fiber, 1 g pro.* **Diabetic Exchanges:** *1 fat, ½ starch.*

> ❝Every year at the holidays, these candy turtles are a huge hit with family, friends and co-workers. I get lots of requests for more and have even been told not to bother with a holiday visit if I don't bring my turtles. Yikes!❞ —MISTY SCHWOTZER GROVEPORT, OH

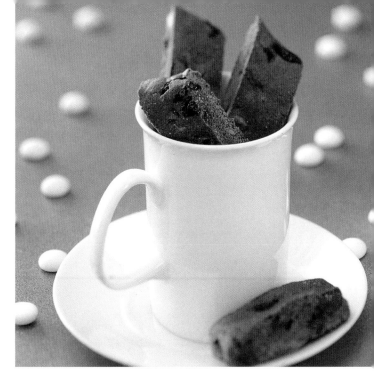

Chocolate Pistachio Biscotti

Chocolate, pistachios and cranberries are great together, especially during the holiday season! Warm your friends and neighbors with hot coffee and these festive treats.
—GILDA LESTER MILLSBORO, DE

PREP: 30 MIN. • **BAKE:** 30 MIN. + COOLING • **MAKES:** 40 COOKIES

- ⅓ cup butter, softened
- 1 cup plus 1 tablespoon sugar, divided
- 3 eggs
- 2 teaspoons vanilla extract
- 2¾ cups all-purpose flour
- ⅓ cup baking cocoa
- 2½ teaspoons baking powder
- ½ teaspoon ground cinnamon
- 1 cup (6 ounces) semisweet chocolate chips
- ½ cup pistachios
- ½ cup dried cranberries

1. In a large bowl, cream butter and 1 cup sugar until light and fluffy. Add eggs, one at a time, beating well after each addition. Beat in vanilla. Combine the flour, cocoa, baking powder and cinnamon; add to the creamed mixture and mix well (dough will be sticky). Stir in the chips, pistachios and cranberries.

2. Divide dough into four portions. On ungreased baking sheets, shape portions into 10-in. x 2½-in. rectangles. Sprinkle with remaining sugar. Bake at 350° for 20-25 minutes or until set. Carefully remove to wire racks; cool for 5 minutes.

3. Transfer to a cutting board; cut each rectangle into 10 slices. Place cut side down on ungreased baking sheets. Bake for 5-8 minutes on each side or until lightly browned. Remove to wire racks to cool. Store in an airtight container.

PER SERVING *107 cal., 4 g fat (2 g sat. fat), 20 mg chol., 48 mg sodium, 17 g carb., 1 g fiber, 2 g pro.* **Diabetic Exchanges:** *1 starch, 1 fat.*

Lemon Stars

These awesome little cookies have a light, crunchy texture and a citrusy zing. The star theme makes them ideal for the Christmas season. You could also make bunnies or chicks for Easter.

—JACQUELINE HILL NORWALK, OH

PREP: 45 MIN. + CHILLING
BAKE: 10 MIN./BATCH + COOLING
MAKES: 9 DOZEN

- ½ cup butter-flavored shortening
- 1 cup sugar
- 1 egg
- 1½ teaspoons lemon extract
- ½ cup sour cream
- 1 teaspoon grated lemon peel
- 2¾ cups all-purpose flour
- ½ teaspoon baking soda
- ½ teaspoon salt

FROSTING
- 1½ cups confectioners' sugar
- 6 tablespoons butter, softened
- ¾ teaspoon lemon extract
- 3 drops yellow food coloring, optional
- 3 to 4 tablespoons 2% milk
  Yellow colored sugar, optional

1. In a large bowl, cream shortening and sugar until light and fluffy. Beat in egg and extract. Stir in sour cream and peel. Combine the flour, baking soda and salt; gradually add to creamed mixture and mix well. Divide dough into three balls; cover and refrigerate for 3 hours or until easy to handle.

2. Remove one portion of dough from the refrigerator at a time. On a lightly floured surface, roll out dough to ¼-in. thickness. Cut with a floured 2-in. star cookie cutter. Place 1 in. apart on ungreased baking sheets.

3. Bake at 375° for 6-8 minutes or until edges are lightly browned. Remove to wire racks to cool.

4. For frosting, in a small bowl, combine the confectioners' sugar, butter, extract, food coloring if desired and enough milk to achieve a spreading consistency.

5. Frost cookies; sprinkle with colored sugar if desired.

Cherry Mocha Balls

My mother-in-law gave me this recipe before my wedding, and I've made mocha balls nearly every Christmas since. Because they freeze so well, I'll frequently bake some early and put them away to call on as last-minute holiday treats.

—**JEANA CROWELL** WHITEWATER, KS

PREP: 15 MIN. + CHILLING • **BAKE:** 15 MIN./BATCH + COOLING
MAKES: ABOUT 6 DOZEN

- 1 **cup butter, softened**
- ½ **cup sugar**
- 4 **teaspoons vanilla extract**
- 2 **cups all-purpose flour**
- ¼ **cup baking cocoa**
- 1 **tablespoon instant coffee granules**
- ½ **teaspoon salt**
- 1 **cup finely chopped pecans**
- ⅔ **cup chopped red candied cherries**
  Confectioners' sugar

1. In a large bowl, cream butter and sugar until light and fluffy. Beat in vanilla. In another bowl, whisk flour, cocoa, coffee granules and salt; gradually beat into creamed mixture. Stir in pecans and cherries. If necessary, cover and refrigerate dough until firm enough to shape.
2. Preheat oven to 350°. Shape dough into 1-in. balls; place 2 in. apart on ungreased baking sheets. Bake 15 minutes or until cookies are set. Cool completely on wire racks. Dust with confectioners' sugar.

Eggnog Logs

A lady at church passed on this old-fashioned recipe. I always include these logs in holiday food gifts to family and friends.

—**KIM JORDAN** DUNSMUIR, CA

PREP: 30 MIN. + CHILLING • **BAKE:** 15 MIN./BATCH + COOLING
MAKES: 4½ DOZEN

- 1 **cup butter, softened**
- ¾ **cup sugar**
- 1¼ **teaspoons ground nutmeg**
- 1 **egg**
- 2 **teaspoons vanilla extract**
- ½ **to 1 teaspoon rum extract**
- 3 **cups all-purpose flour**

FROSTING

- ¼ **cup butter, softened**
- 3 **cups confectioners' sugar**
- 1 **teaspoon vanilla extract**
- ½ **to 1 teaspoon rum extract**
- 2 **tablespoons half-and-half cream**
  Ground nutmeg

1. In a bowl, cream butter and sugar. Add the nutmeg, egg and extracts; mix thoroughly. Stir in flour. If necessary, chill dough for easier handling.
2. On a lightly floured surface, shape dough into ½-in.-diameter rolls; cut each into 3-in.-long pieces. Place 2 in. apart on ungreased baking sheets. Bake at 350° for 15 minutes or until lightly browned. Cool on wire racks.
3. For frosting, beat butter until light and fluffy. Add 2 cups confectioners' sugar and extracts; mix well. Beat in cream and remaining confectioners' sugar. Frost cookies. With tines of a small fork, make lines down the frosting to simulate bark. Sprinkle with nutmeg.

Chewy Date Pinwheels

For a lovely addition to your holiday cookie tray, make a batch of these pretty pinwheel cookies. The date-and-pecan filling will bring back memories of Christmases past.

—NAOMI CROSS OWENTON, KY

PREP: 25 MIN. + CHILLING • **BAKE:** 15 MIN./BATCH
MAKES: ABOUT 4 DOZEN

FILLING
- 1½ cups chopped dates
- 1 cup sugar
- 1 cup water
- ½ cup chopped pecans

COOKIE DOUGH
- 1 cup butter, softened
- 2 cups packed brown sugar
- ½ cup sugar
- 3 eggs
- 4½ cups all-purpose flour
- 1 teaspoon baking soda
- 1 teaspoon salt
- 1 teaspoon ground cinnamon

1. In a large saucepan, combine the dates, sugar and water. Cook and stir over medium heat for 7-9 minutes or until thickened. Stir in nuts; set aside to cool.

2. In a large bowl, cream butter and sugars until light and fluffy. Add eggs, one at a time, beating well after each addition. Combine the flour, soda, salt and cinnamon; gradually add to creamed mixture and mix well. Divide dough in half.

3. On a floured surface, roll out one portion of dough into a ¼-in.-thick rectangle. Spread with half of filling. Roll up jelly-roll style, starting with a long side. Repeat with remaining dough and filling. Wrap each roll in plastic wrap; refrigerate overnight.

4. Unwrap dough; cut into ½-in. slices. Place 2 in. apart on greased baking sheets. Bake at 375° for 12-14 minutes. Remove to wire racks to cool.

Gooey Chocolate Cookies

PREP: 15 MIN. + CHILLING • **BAKE:** 10 MIN./BATCH
MAKES: 4½ DOZEN

- 1 package (8 ounces) cream cheese, softened
- ½ cup butter, softened
- 1 egg
- 1 teaspoon vanilla extract
- 1 package chocolate cake mix (regular size)

1. In a large bowl, beat cream cheese and butter until light and fluffy. Beat in egg and vanilla. Add cake mix and mix well (dough will be sticky). Cover and refrigerate for 2 hours.

2. Roll rounded tablespoonfuls of dough into balls. Place 2 in. apart on ungreased baking sheets. Bake at 350° for 9-11 minutes or until tops are cracked. Cool for 2 minutes before removing from pans to wire racks.

PER SERVING *69 cal., 4 g fat (2 g sat. fat), 13 mg chol., 90 mg sodium, 8 g carb., trace fiber, 1 g pro.* **Diabetic Exchanges:** *½ starch, ½ fat.*

❝These soft and chewy cookies couldn't be easier to make. Jazz them up with a chocolate kiss in the center or substitute a different flavored cake mix.❞

—ANGELA BAILEY SAN PIERRE, IN

Finnish Pinwheels

When my sister was hosting an exchange student from Finland, she served my pinwheel cookies to her guest. The young lady instantly recognized what they were. I felt good knowing they're still being made in our ancestors' country.
—**ILONA BARRON** ONTONAGON, MI

PREP: 1 HOUR • **BAKE:** 15 MIN./BATCH • **MAKES:** ABOUT 7 DOZEN

FILLING
- ½ **pound pitted dried plums, chopped**
- ½ **pound pitted dates, chopped**
- 1 **cup water**
- 2 **tablespoons sugar**
- 1 **tablespoon butter**

PASTRY
- 3 **cups all-purpose flour**
- 1 **cup sugar**
- 2 **teaspoons baking powder**
- ½ **teaspoon salt**
- 1 **cup cold butter**
- 1 **egg, beaten**
- 3 **tablespoons heavy whipping cream**
- 1 **teaspoon vanilla extract**

1. In a saucepan, combine dried plums, dates, water and sugar. Cook over low heat, stirring constantly, until thickened. Remove from the heat and stir in butter. Cool.
2. Meanwhile, in a bowl, sift together flour, sugar, baking powder and salt. Cut in butter as for a pie pastry. Blend in egg, cream and vanilla. Form into two balls.
3. Place one ball at a time on a floured surface and roll to ⅛-in. thickness. Cut into 2-in. squares. Place on ungreased baking sheets. Make 1-in. slits in corners. Place ½ teaspoon of filling in the center of each square. Bring every other corner up into center to form a pinwheel and press lightly. Bake cookies at 325° for 12 minutes or until the points are light golden brown.

Whipped Shortbread

This version of shortbread is tender, not too sweet and melts in your mouth. Mostly I make it for the holidays, but I'll also prepare it year-round for wedding showers and afternoon tea parties.
—**JANE FICIUR** BOW ISLAND, AB

PREP: 50 MIN. • **BAKE:** 20 MIN./BATCH • **MAKES:** 16-18 DOZEN

- 3 **cups butter, softened**
- 1½ **cups confectioners' sugar, sifted**
- 4½ **cups all-purpose flour**
- 1½ **cups cornstarch**
  Nonpareils and/or halved candied cherries

1. In a large bowl, cream butter and confectioners' sugar until light and fluffy. Gradually add flour and cornstarch, beating until well blended.
2. With hands lightly dusted with additional cornstarch, roll dough into 1-in. balls. Place 1 in. apart on ungreased baking sheets. Press lightly with a floured fork. Top with nonpareils or cherry halves.
3. Bake at 300° for 20-22 minutes or until the bottoms are lightly browned. Cool for 5 minutes before removing from pans to wire racks.

S'more Bars

Once school starts, it can be hard for kids to let go of summer. But these rich, gooey, great-tasting bars will bring back sweet campfire memories—and smiles—whether they're served for dessert or as an after-school snack.

—LISA MORIARTY WILTON, NH

PREP: 20 MIN. • **BAKE:** 25 MIN. + COOLING • **MAKES:** 1½ DOZEN

- ½ cup butter, softened
- ¾ cup sugar
- 1 egg
- 1 teaspoon vanilla extract
- 1⅓ cups all-purpose flour
- ¾ cup graham cracker crumbs
- 1 teaspoon baking powder
- ⅛ teaspoon salt
- 5 milk chocolate candy bars (1.55 ounces each)
- 1 cup marshmallow creme

1. In a large bowl, cream butter and sugar until light and fluffy. Beat in egg and vanilla. Combine the flour, cracker crumbs, baking powder and salt; gradually add to creamed mixture. Set aside ½ cup for topping.

2. Press remaining mixture into a greased 9-in.-square baking pan. Place candy bars over crust; spread with marshmallow creme. Crumble remaining graham cracker mixture over top.

3. Bake at 350° for 25-30 minutes or until golden brown. Cool on a wire rack. Cut into bars. Store in an airtight container.

PER SERVING *213 cal., 9 g fat (5 g sat. fat), 28 mg chol., 114 mg sodium, 30 g carb., 1 g fiber, 3 g pro.* **Diabetic Exchanges:** *2 starch, 1 fat.*

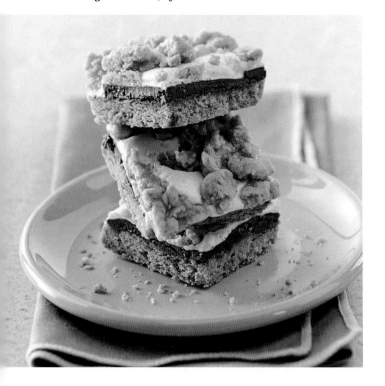

Oatmeal Surprise Cookies

Chocolate-covered raisins and the warming fall-like flavor of pumpkin pie spice turn these oatmeal cookies into prize-winning gourmet treats! Tuck one into your child's lunch for a special surprise.

—BECKY CLARK WARRIOR, AL

PREP: 20 MIN. • **BAKE:** 15 MIN./BATCH • **MAKES:** 3 DOZEN

- 1 cup butter, softened
- ¾ cup packed brown sugar
- ½ cup sugar
- 2 eggs
- 1½ cups all-purpose flour
- 1 teaspoon baking soda
- 1 teaspoon pumpkin pie spice
- 2¾ cups quick-cooking oats
- 1½ cups chocolate-covered raisins

1. In a large bowl, cream butter and sugars until light and fluffy. Beat in eggs. Combine the flour, baking soda and pumpkin pie spice; gradually add to creamed mixture and mix well. Stir in oats and raisins.

2. Drop by tablespoonfuls 2 in. apart onto greased baking sheets. Flatten slightly. Bake at 350° for 13-15 minutes or until golden brown. Cool for 5 minutes before removing to wire racks. Store in an airtight container.

PER SERVING *149 cal., 7 g fat (4 g sat. fat), 25 mg chol., 80 mg sodium, 21 g carb., 1 g fiber, 2 g pro.* **Diabetic Exchanges:** *1½ starch, 1 fat.*

Use softened butter for baking success.

1 Butter that's fresh from the fridge is too firm to use in recipes where it will be creamed with sugar. Proceeding before it's ready could result in lumps.

2 Properly softened butter offers little resistance when pressed. It is ready to use.

Trail Mix Clusters

PREP: 25 MIN. + CHILLING • **MAKES:** 4 DOZEN

- 2 cups (12 ounces) semisweet chocolate chips
- ½ cup unsalted sunflower kernels
- ½ cup salted pumpkin seeds or pepitas
- ½ cup coarsely chopped cashews
- ½ cup coarsely chopped pecans
- ¼ cup flaked coconut
- ¼ cup finely chopped dried apricots
- ¼ cup dried cranberries
- ¼ cup dried cherries or blueberries

1. In a large microwave-safe bowl, melt chocolate chips; stir until smooth. Stir in the remaining ingredients.

2. Drop by tablespoonfuls onto waxed paper-lined baking sheets. Refrigerate until firm. Store in an airtight container in the refrigerator.

PER SERVING *79 cal., 6 g fat (2 g sat. fat), 0 chol., 26 mg sodium, 8 g carb., 1 g fiber, 2 g pro.* **Diabetic Exchanges:** *1 fat, ½ starch.*

> ❝They may look naughty, but these wholesome chocolaty clusters couldn't be nicer! And the dried fruits, seeds and nuts are good for you, too.❞

—**ALINA NIEMI** HONOLULU, HI

Macadamia Nut Fudge

My aunt lives in Hawaii, and she keeps our family supplied with fresh pineapples, mangoes and macadamia nuts, as well as recipes like this one. My neighbors like this fudge so much that they have started calling me the Candy Lady of Cleveland.

—**VICKI FIORANELLI** CLEVELAND, MS

PREP: 15 MIN. + CHILLING • **MAKES:** ABOUT 5 POUNDS

- 2 teaspoons plus ½ cup butter, divided
- 4½ cups granulated sugar
- 1 can (12 ounces) evaporated milk
- 3 cups chopped macadamia nuts, divided
- 12 ounces German sweet chocolate, chopped
- 1 package (12 ounces) semisweet chocolate chips
- 1 jar (7 ounces) marshmallow creme
- 2 teaspoons vanilla extract
- ½ teaspoon salt, optional

1. Line two 9-in.-square pans with foil; butter the foil with the 2 teaspoons butter. Set aside.

2. In a large heavy saucepan, combine the sugar, milk and remaining butter. Bring to a gentle boil. Cook for 5 minutes, stirring constantly. Remove from the heat; stir in 2 cups of nuts, the chopped chocolate, chocolate chips, marshmallow creme, vanilla and salt if desired.

3. Pour fudge into prepared pans; sprinkle remaining nuts over top and press in lightly. Refrigerate until firm. Using foil, lift fudge out of pans. Discard foil; cut fudge into 1-in. squares. Store in an airtight container.

PECAN NUT FUDGE *Use 3 cups chopped toasted pecans in place of the macadamia nuts.*

PER SERVING *72 cal., 4 g fat (1 g sat. fat), 2 mg chol., 14 mg sodium, 10 g carb., trace fiber, 1 g pro.* **Diabetic Exchanges:** *1 fat, ½ starch.*

Maple Nut Truffles

Let the kids help you roll these simple no-bake treats. They make wonderful gifts, and you need only five ingredients.

—REBEKAH RADEWAHN WAUWATOSA, WI

PREP: 25 MIN. + CHILLING • **MAKES:** 2½ DOZEN

1½ cups semisweet chocolate chips
4 ounces cream cheese, softened
1½ cups confectioners' sugar
¾ teaspoon maple flavoring
1 cup chopped walnuts

1. In a small microwave-safe bowl, melt chocolate chips. Set aside to cool. In another bowl, beat cream cheese and confectioners' sugar until smooth. Add melted chocolate and maple flavoring; beat until well blended. Chill for 15 minutes or until firm enough to handle.
2. Shape into 1-in. balls; roll in walnuts. Store in an airtight container in the refrigerator.

PER SERVING *103 cal., 6 g fat (2 g sat. fat), 4 mg chol., 12 mg sodium, 12 g carb., 1 g fiber, 2 g pro.* **Diabetic Exchanges:** *1 starch, 1 fat.*

Chocolate Shortbread

This chocolate-flavored shortbread is so easy to put together with ingredients I always have on hand. The recipe is a popular choice when the occasion calls for a cookie.

—KATHERINE BOTH ROCKY MOUNTAIN HOUSE, AB

PREP: 15 MIN. + CHILLING • **BAKE:** 20 MIN./BATCH
MAKES: ABOUT 4 DOZEN

1 cup butter, softened
1½ cups all-purpose flour
⅔ cup confectioners' sugar
⅓ cup baking cocoa
Dash salt

1. In a large bowl, beat butter until light and fluffy. Combine the remaining ingredients; gradually beat into the butter. Chill for 1 hour.
2. Drop by rounded teaspoonfuls 2 in. apart on greased baking sheets. Bake at 300° for 20 minutes or until set.

EASY COOKIE ASSORTMENT

If you make several kinds of cookies during the holidays for parties or to give as gifts, here's a tip that is sure to simplify your baking. I spend a couple of weekends before the holiday rush (sometimes as early as October) mixing up my different cookie doughs. Then I freeze the dough in large freezer bags. When I'm ready to bake, I just thaw the dough in the refrigerator overnight. **—CINDI P.** ANCHORAGE, AK

Triple-Berry Crumb Pie, page 203

197

200

205

Cakes & Pies

Capture hearts with **towering** layer cakes, **fun** freezer pies, **bursting-with-berries** summertime treats and **irresistible** cupcakes. When these **prizewinning beauties** grace the table, everyone will **celebrate**!

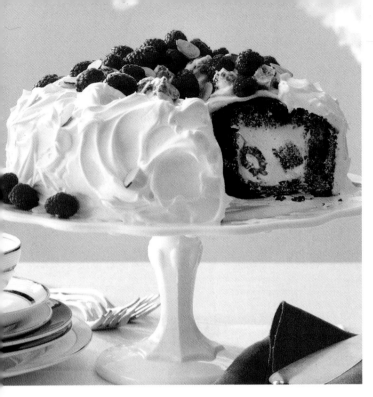

Chocolate Raspberry Tunnel Cake

Slice into this beautiful cake and get ready for a wonderful surprise. The fluffy raspberry filling in the tunnel gives chocolate cake a luscious twist.

—**ED LELAND** VAN WERT, OH

PREP: 50 MIN. • **BAKE:** 45 MIN. + CHILLING • **MAKES:** 12 SERVINGS

- ⅔ cup butter, softened
- 1⅔ cups sugar
- 3 eggs
- ½ teaspoon vanilla extract
- 2 cups all-purpose flour
- ⅔ cup baking cocoa
- 1¼ teaspoons baking powder
- ¼ teaspoon baking soda
- 1⅓ cups 2% milk

FILLING

- 2 packages (3 ounces each) cream cheese, softened
- 1 can (14 ounces) sweetened condensed milk
- ⅓ cup lemon juice
- ½ teaspoon almond extract
- 2 to 4 drops red food coloring, optional
- 1 carton (12 ounces) frozen whipped topping, thawed, divided
- 1 cup fresh raspberries
  Toasted sliced almonds and additional fresh raspberries, optional

1. In a large bowl, cream butter and sugar until light and fluffy. Add eggs, one at a time, beating well after each addition. Beat in vanilla. Combine the flour, cocoa, baking powder and baking soda; add to the creamed mixture alternately with milk, beating well after each addition.

2. Transfer to a greased and floured 10-in. tube pan. Bake at 350° for 45-55 minutes or until a toothpick inserted near the center comes out clean.

3. Cool 10 minutes before removing from pan to a wire rack to cool completely. Cut a 1-in. slice off top of cake; set aside. Hollow out the bottom portion of cake, leaving a 1-in. shell. Cube the removed cake to measure 1 cup; set aside. (Save remaining cake for another use.)

4. Beat cream cheese until fluffy. Gradually beat in milk, lemon juice, extract and food coloring if desired. Fold in 1 cup whipped topping. Fold berries and reserved cake cubes into mixture. Fill tunnel with cake cube mixture; replace cake top.

5. Spoon cake cube mixture over top of cake to within 1 in. of edge and into center hole of cake. Frost top edge and sides of cake with remaining whipped topping. Sprinkle with almonds and additional raspberries if desired. Chill.

Mayan Chocolate Pecan Pie

This started off as a regular pecan pie for Thanksgiving Day, but it evolved into something even tastier and more special!

—**CHRIS MICHALOWSKI** DALLAS, TX

PREP: 20 MIN. • **BAKE:** 55 MIN. + COOLING • **MAKES:** 8 SERVINGS

- ½ cup chopped pecans
- ½ cup dark chocolate chips
- 1 frozen pie shell (9 inches)
- 3 eggs
- 1 cup sugar
- 1 cup dark corn syrup
- 2 tablespoons butter, melted
- 1 tablespoon coffee liqueur
- 1 teaspoon ground ancho chili pepper
- 1 teaspoon vanilla extract
- 1 cup pecan halves

1. Sprinkle chopped pecans and chocolate chips into pastry shell. In a small bowl, whisk the eggs, sugar, corn syrup, butter, liqueur, pepper and vanilla. Pour into pastry; arrange pecan halves over filling.

2. Bake at 350° for 55-60 minutes or until set. Cool on a wire rack. Refrigerate leftovers.

Grandma's Christmas Cake

One bite of my old-fashioned spice cake will bring back memories. Loaded with raisins and nuts, it tastes extra-special drizzled with a rich, buttery sauce.

—LINDA STEMEN MONROEVILLE, IN

PREP: 25 MIN. • **BAKE:** 45 MIN. + COOLING • **MAKES:** 12 SERVINGS

- 2 cups sugar
- 2 cups raisins
- 2 cups water
- 1 cup butter, cubed
- 3½ cups all-purpose flour
- 1 teaspoon baking soda
- 1 teaspoon ground cinnamon
- ½ teaspoon each ground nutmeg and cloves
- 1 cup chopped pecans

BRANDY BUTTER SAUCE

- 1 cup heavy whipping cream
- 1 cup butter, cubed
- 1 cup sugar
- 4 egg yolks, lightly beaten
- ¼ cup brandy

1. In a large saucepan, combine the sugar, raisins, water and butter. Bring to a boil. Reduce heat to medium; cook, uncovered, for 5 minutes or until sugar is dissolved. Remove from the heat; cool.

2. In a large bowl, combine flour, baking soda, cinnamon, nutmeg and cloves. Add raisin mixture; beat until blended. Fold in pecans.

3. Pour into a greased and floured 10-in. fluted tube pan. Bake at 350° for 45-55 minutes or until cake springs back when lightly touched. Cool for 10 minutes before removing from pan to a wire rack to cool completely.

4. For sauce, in a large saucepan, bring cream to a boil; stir in butter and sugar until smooth. Reduce heat; stir a small amount of hot liquid into egg yolks. Return all to the pan, stirring constantly. Cook until sauce is slightly thickened and coats the back of a spoon (do not boil). Remove from the heat; stir in brandy. Serve warm with cake.

Chocolate Bliss Marble Cake

I serve this cake at all our family parties. I started making it in 1985 when my husband had heart surgery and had to watch what he ate. It's low in fat, but delicious—and beautiful.

—JOSEPHINE PIRO EASTON, PA

PREP: 40 MIN. • **BAKE:** 30 MIN. + COOLING • **MAKES:** 16 SERVINGS

- 5 egg whites
- ¼ cup baking cocoa
- ¼ cup hot water
- 1 cup sugar, divided
- 1 cup fat-free milk
- 3 tablespoons canola oil
- 1 teaspoon vanilla extract
- ¾ teaspoon almond extract
- 2½ cups all-purpose flour
- 3 teaspoons baking powder
- ½ teaspoon salt
- 1½ cups reduced-fat whipped topping
- 4 ounces semisweet chocolate, chopped
- 1½ cups fresh raspberries

1. Let the egg whites stand at room temperature for 30 minutes. Dissolve cocoa in water; let stand until cool.

2. In a large bowl, beat ¾ cup sugar, milk, oil and extracts until well blended. Combine the flour, baking powder and salt; gradually beat into sugar mixture until blended.

3. In another bowl with clean beaters, beat egg whites on medium speed until soft peaks form. Beat in remaining sugar, 1 tablespoon at a time, on high until stiff peaks form. Gradually fold into batter. Remove 2 cups batter; stir in reserved cocoa mixture.

4. Coat a 10-in. fluted tube pan with cooking spray. Alternately spoon the plain and chocolate batters into pan. Cut through batter with a knife to swirl.

5. Bake at 350° for 30-35 minutes or until a toothpick inserted near the center comes out clean. Cool for 10 minutes before removing from pan to a wire rack to cool completely.

6. For topping, in a microwave, melt whipped topping and chocolate; stir until smooth.

7. Place cake on a serving plate. Drizzle with topping. Arrange raspberries in center of cake.

Lemon-Mint Pound Cake with Strawberries

Fresh mint and strawberries are two ingredients that shout "summer" to me. This lemony twist on shortcake is great when you want to impress.
—**NICHOLE JONES** PLEASANT GROVE, UT

PREP: 45 MIN. • **BAKE:** 1 HOUR + COOLING
MAKES: 12 SERVINGS

- ¼ **cup sugar**
- ¼ **cup loosely packed fresh mint leaves**
- ¾ **cup butter, softened**
- 2½ **cups confectioners' sugar, divided**
- 3 **eggs**
- 1½ **cups all-purpose flour**
- 2¼ **cups heavy whipping cream, divided**
- 2 **tablespoons lemon juice**
- 2 **teaspoons grated lemon peel**
- 1 **jar (10 ounces) lemon curd**
- 1 **quart fresh strawberries, sliced**

1. Place sugar and mint in a small food processor; cover and process until blended. Set aside.

2. In a large bowl, cream butter and 1¾ cups confectioners' sugar until light and fluffy. Beat in 4½ teaspoons of the reserved mint mixture. Add eggs, one at a time, beating well after each addition. Add flour alternately with ¼ cup of the cream. Stir in lemon juice and peel.

3. Pour into a greased and floured 8x4-in. loaf pan. Bake at 325° for 60-70 minutes or until a toothpick inserted near the center comes out clean. Cool for 10 minutes before removing from pan to a wire rack to cool completely.

4. In a large bowl, beat remaining cream until it begins to thicken. Add ½ cup of the confectioners' sugar and 1 tablespoon mint mixture; beat until stiff peaks form. Fold in lemon curd; set aside.

5. In another bowl, combine the strawberries with remaining mint mixture and confectioners' sugar. Slice cake; serve with strawberry mixture and lemon cream.

Mixed Nut 'n' Fig Pie

Can't decide on a favorite nut? My recipe settles the question by calling for deluxe mixed nuts. A hint of orange enhances this sweet, crunchy pie.

—**BARBARA ESTABROOK** RHINELANDER, WI

PREP: 30 MIN. • **BAKE:** 1 HOUR + COOLING • **MAKES:** 8 SERVINGS

    Pastry for single-crust pie (9 inches)
- ½ **cup chopped dried figs**
- 3 **tablespoons water**
- 2 **tablespoons orange marmalade**
- ¾ **cup packed brown sugar**
- 1 **tablespoon cornstarch**
- 1 **cup corn syrup**
- 3 **eggs**
- 6 **tablespoons butter, melted**
- 2 **teaspoons vanilla extract**
- 1½ **cups deluxe mixed nuts**

TOPPING
- 1 **cup heavy whipping cream**
- 2 **tablespoons sugar**
- 1 **tablespoon orange marmalade**

1. Line a 9-in. pie plate with pastry; trim and flute edges. Line pastry with a double thickness of heavy-duty foil. Bake at 450° for 8 minutes. Remove foil; bake 5 minutes longer. Cool on a wire rack. Reduce heat to 300°.

2. In a small saucepan, combine figs and water. Cook and stir over low heat until water is absorbed. Remove from the heat; stir in marmalade. In a large bowl, combine brown sugar and cornstarch. Add the corn syrup, eggs, butter, vanilla and fig mixture; stir in nuts. Pour into crust.

3. Bake at 300° for 1 to 1¼ hours or until set. Cover edges with foil during the last 30 minutes to prevent overbrowning if necessary. Cool on a wire rack.

4. In a small bowl, beat cream until it begins to thicken. Add sugar and marmalade; beat until soft peaks form. Serve with pie. Refrigerate leftovers.

Raspberry Cream Pie

This recipe is delicious with either fresh-picked or frozen raspberries, which means you can make it year-round. One bite of cool, creamy raspberry pie instantly turns winter into summer.

—**JULIE PRICE** NASHVILLE, TN

PREP: 30 MIN. + CHILLING • **MAKES:** 8 SERVINGS

- 1½ **cups crushed vanilla wafers (about 45 wafers)**
- ⅓ **cup chopped pecans**
- ¼ **cup butter, melted**

FILLING
- 1 **package (8 ounces) cream cheese, softened**
- ⅔ **cup confectioners' sugar**
- 2 **tablespoons orange liqueur**
- 1 **teaspoon vanilla extract**
- 1 **cup heavy whipping cream, whipped**

TOPPING
- 1 **cup sugar**
- 3 **tablespoons cornstarch**
- 3 **tablespoons water**
- 2½ **cups fresh or frozen raspberries, divided**

1. Combine the wafer crumbs, pecans and butter. Press onto the bottom and up the sides of a greased 9-in. pie plate.

2. In a large bowl, beat the cream cheese, confectioners' sugar, liqueur and vanilla until light and fluffy. Fold in whipped cream. Spread into crust. Chill until serving.

3. In a small saucepan, combine sugar and cornstarch; stir in water and 1½ cups raspberries. Bring to a boil; cook and stir for 2 minutes or until thickened. Transfer to a bowl; refrigerate until chilled.

4. Spread topping over filling. Garnish with remaining berries.

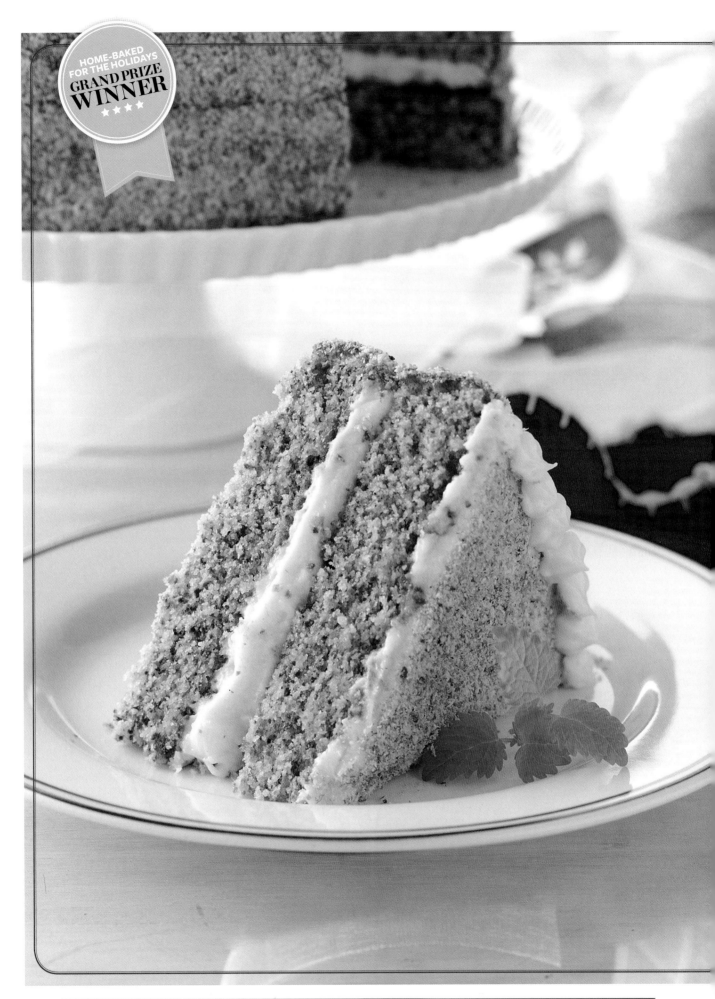

Holiday Walnut Torte

This torte is one of my grandma's best-loved recipes—tender layers of nut-filled cake put together with apricot glaze and cream cheese frosting. It is just divine!

—**EILEEN KORECKO** HOT SPRINGS VILLAGE, AR

PREP: 40 MIN. • **BAKE:** 25 MIN. + COOLING
MAKES: 10-12 SERVINGS

- 3 eggs
- 1½ cups sugar
- 3 teaspoons vanilla extract
- 1¾ cups all-purpose flour
- 1 cup ground walnuts
- 2 teaspoons baking powder
- ½ teaspoon salt
- 1½ cups heavy whipping cream

GLAZE
- ⅔ cup apricot preserves
- 1 tablespoon sugar

FROSTING
- ½ cup butter, softened
- 1 package (3 ounces) cream cheese, softened
- 2 cups confectioners' sugar
- 1 teaspoon vanilla extract
- ¾ cup ground walnuts, divided

1. In a large bowl, beat the eggs, sugar and vanilla on high speed for 5 minutes or until thick and lemon-colored. Combine the flour, walnuts, baking powder and salt; beat into egg mixture. Beat cream until stiff peaks form; fold into batter.

2. Pour into two greased and floured 9-in. round baking pans. Bake at 350° for 25-30 minutes or until a toothpick inserted near the center comes out clean. Cool for 10 minutes before removing from pans to wire racks to cool completely.

3. In a small saucepan over medium heat, cook and stir preserves and sugar until sugar is dissolved. Set aside ½ cup. Brush remaining glaze over cake tops.

4. In a large bowl, beat butter and cream cheese until fluffy. Add confectioners' sugar and vanilla; beat until smooth. Spread ½ cup frosting over one cake; top with second cake and ¾ cup frosting. Sprinkle ½ cup walnuts over the top.

5. Brush reserved glaze over sides of cake; press the remaining walnuts onto sides. Pipe remaining frosting around top edge of cake. Store in the refrigerator.

Apricot-Raspberry Angel Torte

No one needs to know you used a prepared angel food cake and canned pie filling to create this gorgeous torte. Fresh raspberries lend a from-scratch touch.

—**SALLY SIBTHORPE** SHELBY TOWNSHIP, MI

PREP: 20 MIN. • **BAKE:** 35 MIN. + COOLING • **MAKES:** 12 SERVINGS

- 1 package (16 ounces) angel food cake mix
- 2 packages (one 8 ounces, one 3 ounces) cream cheese, softened
- ⅓ cup sugar
- 1¼ teaspoons almond extract
- 1 carton (8 ounces) frozen whipped topping, thawed
- 1 can (21 ounces) apricot or peach pie filling
- 1½ cups fresh raspberries
- 1 cup sliced almonds
   Fresh mint leaves

1. Prepare and bake cake according to package directions, using an ungreased 10-in. tube pan. Cool.

2. In a large bowl, beat the cream cheese, sugar and extract until light and fluffy; fold in whipped topping.

3. Split cake into three layers. Place bottom layer on a serving plate; spread with a third of the cream cheese mixture. Top with a third of the pie filling, raspberries and almonds. Repeat layers twice. Garnish with mint. Refrigerate leftovers.

Sour Cream Peach Pecan Pie

Fresh peaches, good Southern pecans and real vanilla make this pie impossible to resist!

—SHERRELL DIKES HOLIDAY ISLE, AR

PREP: 30 MIN. • **BAKE:** 45 MIN. + COOLING • **MAKES:** 8 SERVINGS

    Pastry for single-crust pie (9 inches)
4 **cups sliced peeled peaches**
2 **tablespoons peach preserves**
1 **cup sugar**
1 **cup (8 ounces) sour cream**
3 **egg yolks**
¼ **cup all-purpose flour**
1 **teaspoon vanilla extract**

TOPPING
½ **cup all-purpose flour**
½ **cup packed brown sugar**
¼ **cup sugar**
3 **tablespoons chopped pecans**
1 **teaspoon ground cinnamon**
¼ **cup cold butter, cubed**

1. Line a 9-in. pie plate with pastry; trim and flute edges. In a large bowl, combine peaches and preserves. Transfer to pastry shell. In a small bowl, whisk the sugar, sour cream, egg yolks, flour and vanilla. Pour over peaches.
2. Bake at 425° for 30 minutes. Meanwhile, in a small bowl, combine the flour, sugars, pecans and cinnamon. Cut in butter until crumbly; sprinkle over pie.
3. Bake for 15-20 minutes or until a knife inserted in the center comes out clean and topping is golden brown. Cover edges with foil during the last 15 minutes to prevent overbrowning if necessary. Cool completely on a wire rack for 3 hours before serving. Store in the refrigerator.

Peanut Butter Pies

I absolutely love peanut butter, and peanut butter pie is one of my favorites. But I'm a registered dietitian, so I knew just how high my original recipe was in fat and calories. I finally came up with a lighter version that meets my pie expectations.

—LISA VARNER EL PASO, TX

PREP: 15 MIN. + FREEZING • **MAKES:** 2 PIES (8 SERVINGS EACH)

1 **package (8 ounces) fat-free cream cheese**
¾ **cup reduced-fat creamy peanut butter**
1 **can (14 ounces) fat-free sweetened condensed milk**
1 **teaspoon vanilla extract**
1 **carton (12 ounces) frozen fat-free whipped topping, thawed**
2 **reduced-fat graham cracker crusts (8 inches)**
¼ **cup chocolate syrup**
¼ **cup finely chopped unsalted peanuts**

1. In a large bowl, beat cream cheese and peanut butter until smooth. Beat in milk and vanilla until blended. Fold in whipped topping. Pour into crusts. Cover and freeze for 8 hours or overnight.
2. Remove from the freezer 10 minutes before serving. Drizzle with syrup and sprinkle with peanuts. Store leftovers in the freezer.

POTLUCK PIES

I often double my pumpkin pie recipe so I have extra pies for potlucks. I wrap the additional pies three times in plastic wrap and once in aluminum foil, then freeze. This wrapping makes it easy to transport the frozen pies. At the potluck, I simply unwrap, garnish and thaw the pies for a convenient dessert.

—ELIZABETH W. SPENCER, IN

Vermont Maple Oatmeal Pie

This yummy pie has an old-fashioned feeling, but is so easy to prepare. Serve it with ice cream drizzled with maple syrup or top it with maple- or cinnamon-flavored whipped cream.

—BARB MILLER OAKDALE, MN

PREP: 20 MIN. • **BAKE:** 50 MIN. + COOLING • **MAKES:** 8 SERVINGS

- 1 sheet refrigerated pie pastry
- 4 eggs
- 1 cup sugar
- 3 tablespoons all-purpose flour
- 1 teaspoon ground cinnamon
- ½ teaspoon salt
- 1 cup quick-cooking oats
- ¾ cup corn syrup
- ½ cup maple syrup
- ¼ cup butter, melted
- 3 teaspoons vanilla extract
- 1 cup flaked coconut
  Vanilla ice cream, optional

1. Unroll pastry into a 9-in. pie plate; flute edges. In a large bowl, combine the eggs, sugar, flour, cinnamon and salt. Stir in the oats, syrups, butter and vanilla; pour into crust. Sprinkle with coconut.

2. Bake at 350° for 50-60 minutes or until set. Cover edges with foil during the last 15 minutes to prevent overbrowning if necessary. Cool on a wire rack. Serve with ice cream if desired. Refrigerate leftovers.

German Chocolate Cream Pie

I've won quite a few awards in recipe contests over the past 10 years, and I was delighted when this luscious pie sent me to the Great American Pie Show finals in Branson, Missouri.

—MARIE RIZZIO INTERLOCHEN, MI

PREP: 20 MIN. • **BAKE:** 45 MIN. + COOLING • **MAKES:** 8 SERVINGS

  Pastry for single-crust pie (9 inches)
- 4 ounces German sweet chocolate, chopped
- ¼ cup butter, cubed
- 1 can (12 ounces) evaporated milk
- 1½ cups sugar
- 3 tablespoons cornstarch
  Dash salt
- 2 eggs
- 1 teaspoon vanilla extract
- 1⅓ cups flaked coconut
- ½ cup chopped pecans

TOPPING
- 2 cups heavy whipping cream
- 2 tablespoons confectioners' sugar
- 1 teaspoon vanilla extract
  Additional flaked coconut and chopped pecans

1. Line a 9-in. pie plate with pastry; trim and flute edges.

2. Place the chocolate and butter in a small saucepan. Cook and stir over low heat until smooth. Remove from the heat; stir in milk. In a large bowl, combine the sugar, cornstarch and salt. Add the eggs, vanilla and chocolate mixture; mix well. Pour into crust. Sprinkle with coconut and pecans.

3. Bake at 375° for 45-50 minutes or until a knife inserted near the center comes out clean. Cool pie completely on a wire rack.

4. For topping, in a large bowl, beat cream until it begins to thicken. Add confectioners' sugar and vanilla; beat until stiff peaks form. Spread over pie; sprinkle with additional coconut and pecans. Refrigerate until serving.

Candy Bar Cupcakes

Everyone in my family loves cupcakes, so I experimented to create these cream cheese-filled treats with a sweet Snickers surprise inside. I also lightened them up without anyone knowing.
—**EDIE DESPAIN** LOGAN, UT

PREP: 40 MIN. • BAKE: 20 MIN. + COOLING • MAKES: 1½ DOZEN

- 1 cup sugar
- 1 cup buttermilk
- ¼ cup canola oil
- 1 teaspoon vanilla extract
- 1½ cups all-purpose flour
- ⅓ cup baking cocoa
- 1 teaspoon baking soda
- ½ teaspoon salt

FILLING
- 6 ounces fat-free cream cheese
- 2 tablespoons confectioners' sugar
- 1 egg
- 2 Snickers candy bars (2.07 ounces each), finely chopped

FROSTING
- ⅓ cup butter, cubed
- ⅓ cup packed brown sugar
- 3 tablespoons fat-free milk
- 1½ cups confectioners' sugar

1. In a large bowl, beat the sugar, buttermilk, oil and vanilla until well blended. Combine the flour, cocoa, baking soda and salt; gradually beat into sugar mixture until blended.
2. For filling, in a small bowl, beat cream cheese and confectioners' sugar until light and fluffy. Add egg; mix well. Stir in the candy bars.
3. Fill paper-lined muffin cups one-third full with batter. Drop filling by tablespoonfuls into the center of each cupcake (cups will be about half full). Bake at 350° for 20-25 minutes or until a toothpick inserted in the filling comes out clean. Cool for 10 minutes before removing from pans to wire racks to cool completely.
4. For frosting, in a small saucepan, melt butter. Stir in brown sugar. Bring to a boil; cook for two minutes, stirring occasionally. Remove from the heat; stir in the milk, then confectioners' sugar. Cool until frosting reaches spreading consistency. Frost cupcakes.

Chocolate Sour Cream Torte

My mother started serving this torte many years ago and only shared her original recipe with two people. This is my lightened-up version, which is stilly yummy, chocolaty and delicious!
—**KAREN RAMES** HICKORY HILLS, IL

PREP: 40 MIN. • BAKE: 20 MIN. + COOLING • MAKES: 16 SERVINGS

- ¼ cup shortening
- 1¼ cups sugar
- 2 eggs
- 2 ounces bittersweet chocolate, melted and cooled
- 1½ teaspoons vanilla extract
- 1½ cups all-purpose flour
- ⅓ cup baking cocoa
- 1 teaspoon baking powder
- ½ teaspoon baking soda
- ½ teaspoon salt
- 1 cup (8 ounces) reduced-fat sour cream
- 1 cup fat-free milk
- ¼ cup plain yogurt

FROSTING
- 1 cup (8 ounces) reduced-fat sour cream
- ⅔ cup sugar
- 1 carton (12 ounces) frozen reduced-fat whipped topping, thawed

1. In a large bowl, beat shortening and sugar until crumbly, about 2 minutes. Add eggs, one at a time, beating well after each addition. Beat in chocolate and vanilla.
2. Combine the flour, cocoa, baking powder, baking soda and salt. Combine the sour cream, milk and yogurt; add to the shortening mixture alternately with dry ingredients, beating well after each addition.
3. Line two 9-in. round baking pans with waxed paper; coat pans with cooking spray and sprinkle with flour. Add the batter.
4. Bake at 350° for 18-22 minutes or until a toothpick inserted near the center comes out clean. Cool for 10 minutes before removing from pans to wire racks to cool completely.
5. For frosting, in a large bowl, combine sour cream and sugar. Fold in whipped topping. Place the bottom layer on a serving plate; top with a third of the frosting. Top with the remaining cake layer. Frost top and sides of cake. Refrigerate until serving.

Blueberry Bounty Cake

You'll have a hard time deciding whether to serve this blueberry beauty for dessert, breakfast or brunch. Don't worry if the berries sink to the bottom; it makes a lovely presentation when the cake is inverted out of the pan.

—ALICE TESCH WATERTOWN, WI

PREP: 20 MIN. • **BAKE:** 45 MIN. + COOLING
MAKES: 12 SERVINGS (1 CUP SAUCE)

1½ cups butter, softened
1¾ cups sugar
 4 eggs
 1 tablespoon grated lemon peel
 2 teaspoons vanilla extract
 3 cups cake flour
2½ teaspoons baking powder
 ¼ teaspoon salt
 1 cup lemonade
1½ cups fresh or frozen blueberries

BLUEBERRY SAUCE
 2 teaspoons cornstarch
 ¼ cup sugar
 ¼ cup water
 1 cup fresh or frozen blueberries, thawed

1. In a large bowl, cream butter and sugar until light and fluffy. Add the eggs, one at a time, beating well after each addition. Beat in the lemon peel and vanilla.

2. Combine the flour, baking powder and salt; add to creamed mixture alternately with lemonade, beating well after each addition. Fold in blueberries.

3. Pour into a greased and floured 10-in. fluted tube pan. Bake at 350° for 45-50 minutes or until a toothpick inserted near the center comes out clean. Cool for 20 minutes before removing from pan to a wire rack to cool completely.

4. In a small saucepan, combine cornstarch and sugar. Stir in water until smooth. Add blueberries; bring to a boil over medium heat, stirring constantly. Cook and stir 1 minute longer or until thickened. Serve warm with cake.

NOTE *If using frozen blueberries, use without thawing to avoid discoloring the batter.*

Wonderful Carrot Cake

I trim the sugar and replace some of the oil with applesauce to lighten up my carrot cake. I also use some whole wheat flour instead of all white. But in my opinion, there's no substitute for real cream cheese in the frosting.

—**BRENDA RANKHORN** NEW MARKET, AL

PREP: 25 MIN. • **BAKE:** 40 MIN. + COOLING • **MAKES:** 24 SERVINGS

- ¾ cup sugar
- ¾ cup packed brown sugar
- 3 eggs
- ½ cup canola oil
- ½ cup unsweetened applesauce
- 1 teaspoon vanilla extract
- 1½ cups all-purpose flour
- ½ cup whole wheat flour
- 2 teaspoons baking powder
- 1 teaspoon salt
- 1 teaspoon ground cinnamon
- ½ teaspoon ground allspice
- ¼ teaspoon baking soda
- 3 cups finely shredded carrots
- ½ cup chopped walnuts

FROSTING

- 3 ounces cream cheese, softened
- 1 tablespoon fat-free milk
- 1 teaspoon vanilla extract
- 2½ cups confectioners' sugar
  Dash salt

1. In a large bowl, beat the first six ingredients until well blended. Combine flours, baking powder, salt, cinnamon, allspice and baking soda; gradually beat into sugar mixture until blended. Stir in carrots and walnuts.

2. Pour into a 13x9-in. baking pan coated with cooking spray. Bake at 350° for 40-45 minutes or until a toothpick inserted near the center comes out clean. Cool completely on a wire rack.

3. For frosting, beat the cream cheese, milk and vanilla until fluffy. Add confectioners' sugar and salt; beat until smooth. Spread over top of cake. Store in the refrigerator.

Raspberry-Lemon Pie

PREP: 25 MIN. + CHILLING • **MAKES:** 10 SERVINGS

- 24 chocolate wafers, divided
- ¼ cup butter, melted
- 2 tablespoons sugar
- 1 package (3 ounces) raspberry gelatin
- 1 cup boiling water
- ¾ cup (6 ounces) lemon yogurt
- 1 cup heavy whipping cream
- 3 tablespoons confectioners' sugar
- 1 cup fresh or frozen raspberries, thawed
  Grated lemon peel and additional fresh raspberries, optional

1. Cut a thin slice from a wafer so that wafer will stand flat against side of pie plate; repeat nine times. Set aside. Crush remaining wafers and trimmed portions.

2. Combine wafer crumbs, butter and sugar; press onto the bottom of an ungreased 9-in. pie plate. Arrange trimmed wafers around edge of pie plate, lightly pressing into crust. Refrigerate until set.

3. In a large bowl, dissolve gelatin in boiling water. Cover and refrigerate for 45 minutes or until partially set. Beat on medium speed for 5 minutes or until fluffy. Fold in yogurt.

4. In another bowl, beat cream until it begins to thicken. Add confectioners' sugar; beat until stiff peaks form. Fold whipped cream and raspberries into gelatin mixture. Spread into crust.

5. Chill for at least 4 hours. Garnish with lemon peel and additional raspberries if desired.

> **"Expecting company?** This no-fuss pie is easy to make in advance, and it's perfect for a party or get-together.**"** —**JAN LOUDEN** BRANSON, MO

Greek Honey Nut Pie

I love baklava, so I thought, *Why not use phyllo, honey and nuts to make a pie? Then you can have a bigger piece!* Fans of the Greek pastry will enjoy this twist.

—**ROSALIND JACKSON** STUART, FL

PREP: 30 MIN. • **BAKE:** 40 MIN. + COOLING • **MAKES:** 8 SERVINGS

- 4 cups chopped walnuts
- ¼ cup packed brown sugar
- 1 teaspoon ground cinnamon
- 1 package (16 ounces, 14-inch x 9-inch sheet size) frozen phyllo dough, thawed
- 1 cup butter, melted

SYRUP
- ¾ cup sugar
- ½ cup water
- ½ cup honey
- 1 teaspoon vanilla extract

1. In a large bowl, combine the walnuts, brown sugar and cinnamon; set aside. Brush a 9-in. pie plate with some of the butter; set aside.
2. Unroll phyllo dough; keep covered with plastic wrap and a damp towel to prevent it from drying out. Layer eight sheets of phyllo in prepared pan, brushing each layer with butter and rotating sheets to cover the pie plate. Let edges of dough hang over the sides. Sprinkle a third of the nut mixture onto the bottom.
3. Layer four sheets of phyllo over nut mixture in the same manner; sprinkle with a third of the nut mixture. Repeat these last two steps. Top with an additional eight sheets of phyllo, again brushing with butter and rotating sheets. Fold ends of phyllo up over top of pie; brush with butter.
4. Using a sharp knife, cut pie into eight wedges. Cut 1-2 additional sheets of phyllo into thin strips, rolling into rose shapes if desired; arrange decoratively over top. (Save remaining phyllo for another use.) Bake at 350° for 40-45 minutes or until golden brown.
5. Meanwhile, in a saucepan, combine the sugar, water and honey; bring to a boil. Reduce heat; simmer, uncovered, for 10 minutes. Add vanilla. Pour over warm pie. Cool on a wire rack. Refrigerate leftovers.

Triple-Berry Crumb Pie

Berries and hazelnuts are plentiful here in the Pacific Northwest, so ingredients for this treat are often at my fingertips. I like to freeze a couple of pies to enjoy in winter.

—**KATHERINE BARRETT** BELLEVUE, WA

PREP: 25 MIN. • **BAKE:** 55 MIN. + COOLING • **MAKES:** 8 SERVINGS

- 1½ cups all-purpose flour
- 1½ cups ground hazelnuts
- 1 cup sugar, divided
- ¾ cup cold butter, cubed
- 2 cups fresh blackberries
- 2 cups fresh blueberries
- 2 cups fresh strawberries, sliced
- 3 tablespoons cornstarch

1. In a large bowl, combine the flour, hazelnuts and ½ cup sugar; cut in butter until crumbly. Set aside 1½ cups crumb mixture for topping. Press remaining mixture onto the bottom and up the sides of an ungreased 9-in. deep-dish pie plate.
2. Place berries in a large bowl; sprinkle with cornstarch and remaining sugar. Stir until well blended. Spoon into crust. Sprinkle with reserved crumb mixture.
3. Bake at 375° for 55-60 minutes or until crust is golden brown and filling is bubbly (cover edges with foil during the last 15 minutes to prevent overbrowning if necessary). Cool on a wire rack.

Marshmallow-Almond Key Lime Pie

It's great to see that many grocers now carry Key limes, which give the signature pie its sweet-tart flavor. My version gets an unusual treatment with a creamy marshmallow topping.

—**JUDY CASTRANOVA** NEW BERN, NC

PREP: 40 MIN. • **BAKE:** 15 MIN. + CHILLING
MAKES: 8 SERVINGS

- 1 cup all-purpose flour
- 3 tablespoons brown sugar
- 1 cup slivered almonds, toasted, divided
- ¼ cup butter, melted
- 1 tablespoon honey
- 1 can (14 ounces) sweetened condensed milk
- 1 package (8 ounces) cream cheese, softened, divided
- ½ cup Key lime juice
- 1 tablespoon grated Key lime peel
  Dash salt
- 1 egg yolk
- 1¾ cups miniature marshmallows
- 4½ teaspoons butter
- ½ cup heavy whipping cream

1. Place the flour, brown sugar and ½ cup almonds in a food processor. Cover and process until blended. Add melted butter and honey; cover and process until crumbly. Press onto the bottom and up the sides of a greased 9-in. pie plate. Bake at 350° for 8-10 minutes or until crust is lightly browned. Cool on a wire rack.

2. In a large bowl, beat the milk, 5 ounces cream cheese, lime juice, peel and salt until blended. Add egg yolk; beat on low speed just until combined. Pour into crust. Bake for 15-20 minutes or until center is almost set. Cool on a wire rack.

3. In a large saucepan, combine the marshmallows and butter. Cook and stir over medium-low heat until melted. Transfer to a large bowl. Add cream and remaining cream cheese; beat until smooth. Cover and refrigerate until chilled.

4. Beat marshmallow mixture until light and fluffy. Spread over pie; sprinkle with remaining almonds.

Chocolate Zucchini Cupcakes

Our grandkids love these cupcakes and don't believe us when we tell them there are veggies in them! I'm always asked to share this recipe.

—**CAROLE FRASER** NORTH YORK, ON

PREP: 25 MIN. • **BAKE:** 20 MIN. + COOLING • **MAKES:** 21 CUPCAKES

- 1¼ cups butter, softened
- 1½ cups sugar
- 2 eggs
- 1 teaspoon vanilla extract
- 2½ cups all-purpose flour
- ¾ cup baking cocoa
- 1 teaspoon baking powder
- 1 teaspoon baking soda
- ½ teaspoon salt
- ½ cup plain yogurt
- 1 cup grated zucchini
- 1 cup grated carrots
- 1 can (16 ounces) chocolate frosting

1. In a large bowl, cream butter and sugar until light and fluffy. Add eggs, one at a time, beating well after each addition. Stir in vanilla. Combine the flour, baking cocoa, baking powder, baking soda and salt; add to the creamed mixture alternately with yogurt, beating well after each addition. Fold in zucchini and carrots.

2. Fill paper-lined muffin cups two-thirds full. Bake at 350° for 18-22 minutes or until a toothpick inserted near the center comes out clean. Cool for 10 minutes before removing from pans to wire racks to cool completely. Frost cupcakes.

Frosty Coffee Pie

This pie was inspired by my husband, who loves coffee ice cream, and his mom, who makes a cool, creamy dessert using pudding mix. Cooking is a way to show others that I care for them.

—**APRIL TIMBOE** SILOAM SPRINGS, AR

PREP: 15 MIN. + FREEZING • **MAKES:** 8 SERVINGS

- ¼ cup hot fudge ice cream topping, warmed
- 1 chocolate crumb crust (9 inches)
- 3 cups coffee ice cream, softened
- 1 package (5.9 ounces) instant chocolate pudding mix
- ½ cup cold strong brewed coffee
- ¼ cup cold 2% milk
- 1¾ cups whipped topping
- 1 cup marshmallow creme
- ¼ cup miniature semisweet chocolate chips

1. Spread ice cream topping into crust. In a large bowl, beat the ice cream, dry pudding mix, coffee and milk until blended; spoon into crust.

2. In another bowl, combine the whipped topping and marshmallow creme; spread over top. Sprinkle with chocolate chips. Cover and freeze until firm.

FROM THE WEB

Very rich and very good! I made my own coffee ice cream so I could make it decaf.

—**KAFAUGHN** TASTEOFHOME.COM

Easy Tiramisu, page 223

211

222

225

Just Desserts

From **bread pudding** dripping with **chocolate and caramel** to frosty cheesecake **ice cream**, crunchy, buttery **tarts**, iced **cinnamon buns** and perennial-favorite **fruit crisps**, this **star-studded chapter** is **bursting** with sweet possibilities.

Turtle Bread Pudding

Transform yesterday's bread into the most amazing dessert you'll ever eat. Every bite of this yummy, gooey, oh-so-chocolaty bread pudding will have you wondering how you managed before you tried this recipe!
—**GLORIA BRADLEY** NAPERVILLE, IL

PREP: 25 MIN. • **BAKE:** 35 MIN. + STANDING • **MAKES:** 10 SERVINGS

- 7 cups cubed day-old French bread (1-inch cubes)
- ⅓ cup semisweet chocolate chips
- 4 tablespoons chopped pecans, divided
- 3 cups fat-free milk, divided
- ½ cup packed brown sugar
- ¼ cup baking cocoa
- 8 caramels
- 2 teaspoons butter
- ¼ teaspoon chili powder
- 3 eggs, beaten
- 1 teaspoon vanilla extract
- ¼ cup caramel ice cream topping
- ¼ cup milk chocolate chips

1. Place bread cubes in an 11-in. x 7-in. baking dish coated with cooking spray. Sprinkle with semisweet chips and 2 tablespoons pecans. In a large saucepan, combine 1 cup of milk, the brown sugar, cocoa, caramels, butter and chili powder. Cook and stir over medium-low heat until caramels are melted. Add remaining milk; heat through.
2. Stir a small amount of mixture into the eggs; return all to the pan, stirring constantly. Stir in vanilla. Pour mixture over bread cubes; let stand for 10 minutes or until the bread is softened.
3. Bake, uncovered, at 350° for 35-40 minutes or until a knife inserted near the center comes out clean. Drizzle with caramel topping and sprinkle with remaining pecans; bake 2-3 minutes longer or until caramel topping is heated through. Let stand for 10 minutes.
4. In a microwave, melt milk chocolate chips; stir until smooth. Drizzle over bread pudding. Refrigerate leftovers.

Lemon Blueberry Tart

Lemon adds a zesty counterpoint to this blueberry tart's fruit topping and rich, buttery crust.
—**ERIN CHILCOAT** CENTRAL ISLIP, NY

PREP: 40 MIN. + CHILLING • **BAKE:** 15 MIN. + CHILLING
MAKES: 12 SERVINGS

- 1¼ cups all-purpose flour
- ⅓ cup sugar
- ¼ teaspoon salt
- ½ cup cold butter, cubed
- 1 egg yolk
- 2 tablespoons cold water
- 1 teaspoon vanilla extract

FILLING
- 1 can (14 ounces) sweetened condensed milk
- ½ cup lemon juice
- 4 egg yolks
- 4 teaspoons grated lemon peel
  Dash salt

TOPPING
- 2 cups fresh blueberries
- ½ cup blueberry spreadable fruit

1. In a large bowl, combine the flour, sugar and salt; cut in butter until mixture resembles coarse crumbs. Whisk the egg yolk, water and vanilla; add to crumb mixture. Stir until dough forms a ball. Cover and refrigerate for at least 30 minutes.
2. On a floured surface, roll dough into an 11-in. circle. Transfer to a greased 9-in. fluted tart pan with a removable bottom; trim even with edge of pan. Place pan on a baking sheet.
3. Line unpricked pastry shell with a double thickness of heavy-duty foil. Bake at 375° for 15 minutes. Remove foil; bake 5 minutes longer.
4. In a small bowl, beat filling ingredients; pour into crust. Bake 12-15 minutes or until set. Cool on a wire rack.
5. For topping, microwave blueberries and spreadable fruit on high for 1-2 minutes or until bubbly around the edges; stir. Cool for 5-10 minutes. Gently spoon over filling. Refrigerate until chilled.

CUTTING IN BUTTER

Cutting butter into dry ingredients results in tiny bits of flour-coated butter throughout the dough, creating a cookie crust that is both tender and crumbly at the same time. If you don't have a pastry blender, use two knives to cut in the cold butter.

Jeweled Plum Tartlets

When living in Michigan, I developed these tarts as a way to enjoy the seasonal plums there. The red plums shine just like jewels in the creamy custard when they emerge from the oven.

—**NICOLE FILIZETTI** JACKSONVILLE, FL

PREP: 30 MIN. • **BAKE:** 20 MIN. + COOLING • **MAKES:** 2 SERVINGS

- ½ cup plus 2 teaspoons all-purpose flour, divided
- 4 teaspoons sugar
- ⅛ teaspoon salt
- ¼ cup cold butter, cubed
- 2 medium plums, sliced
- 1 egg yolk
- 1 tablespoon 2% milk
- 4 teaspoons brown sugar, divided
   Vanilla ice cream

1. In a small bowl, combine ½ cup flour, sugar and salt; cut in butter until mixture resembles coarse crumbs. Press onto the bottom and up the sides of two 4-in. fluted tart pans with removable bottoms. Bake at 325° for 10 minutes or until set.
2. Arrange plum slices in crusts. In another bowl, combine the egg yolk, milk, 2 teaspoons of brown sugar and the remaining flour. Spoon over the plums; sprinkle with remaining brown sugar.
3. Bake for 20-25 minutes or until a knife inserted near the center comes out clean. Cool on a wire rack. Serve tartlets with ice cream.

Hot Fudge Pudding Cake

My mom used to make a recipe like this when I was younger. I decided to make some healthy changes, and this version is as good, if not better, than the original. Being a dietitian, I love to lighten up desserts.

—**JACKIE TERMONT** RUTHER GLEN, VA

PREP: 15 MIN. • **BAKE:** 30 MIN. • **MAKES:** 9 SERVINGS

- 1 cup all-purpose flour
- 1 cup sugar, divided
- 3 tablespoons plus ¼ cup baking cocoa, divided
- 2 teaspoons baking powder
- ¼ teaspoon salt
- ½ cup fat-free milk
- ⅓ cup prune baby food
- 1½ teaspoons vanilla extract
- ¼ cup plus 2 tablespoons packed brown sugar
- 1¼ cups boiling water

1. In a large bowl, combine the flour, ¾ cup sugar, 3 tablespoons of cocoa, the baking powder and salt. In another bowl, combine the milk, baby food and vanilla. Stir into dry ingredients just until moistened. Spread into an 8-in.-square baking dish coated with cooking spray.
2. Combine brown sugar with the remaining sugar and cocoa; sprinkle over the batter. Carefully pour water over the top (do not stir). Bake, uncovered, at 350° for 28-32 minutes or until top is set and edges pull away from sides of dish. Serve warm.

Chocolate Berry Tarts

I sometimes use ready-made graham tart shells if I'm short on time. Either way, this rich berry dessert is an elegant treat.
—**LOUISE GILBERT** QUESNEL, BC

PREP: 20 MIN. + CHILLING • **MAKES:** 2 SERVINGS

    5 tablespoons butter, divided
    1 cup chocolate graham cracker crumbs (about 5 whole
       crackers)
    2 teaspoons sugar
    3 tablespoons heavy whipping cream
   ⅛ teaspoon ground cinnamon
   ⅔ cup semisweet chocolate chips
   ⅓ cup fresh blackberries
   ⅓ cup fresh raspberries
       Confectioners' sugar

1. In a small microwave-safe bowl, melt 4 tablespoons butter; stir in cracker crumbs and sugar. Press onto the bottom and up the sides of two 4-in. fluted tart pans with removable bottoms. Freeze for 1 hour or until firm.
2. In a small saucepan, combine the cream, cinnamon and remaining butter. Bring to a boil over medium heat, stirring constantly. Remove from the heat; stir in chocolate chips until melted. Pour into crusts. Refrigerate until firm, about 1 hour.
3. Just before serving, arrange berries over filling; sprinkle with confectioners' sugar.

Strawberry & Wine Sorbet

Here's a bright and refreshing treat that tastes like you're biting into a just-picked strawberry! White wine and lemon juice enhance its not-too-sweet flavor.
—**DONNA LAMANO** OLATHE, KS

PREP: 20 MIN. + FREEZING • **MAKES:** 1 QUART

   ¾ cup sugar
   ½ cup water
 1½ pounds fresh strawberries, hulled
    1 cup white wine
   ½ cup honey
   ¼ cup lemon juice

1. In a small saucepan, bring sugar and water to a boil. Cook and stir until sugar is dissolved; set aside to cool.
2. Place the remaining ingredients in a food processor; add sugar syrup. Cover and process for 2-3 minutes or until smooth. Strain and discard seeds and pulp. Transfer the puree to a 13-in. x 9-in. dish. Freeze for 1 hour or until edges begin to firm. Stir and return to freezer. Freeze 2 hours longer or until firm.
3. Just before serving, transfer to a food processor; cover and process for 2-3 minutes or until smooth.

Strawberry Cheesecake Mousse

Indulge your sweet tooth with this easy and refreshing berry dessert. I've been making it for years. It's like a no-bake cheesecake without the crust.

—VIRGINIA ANTHONY JACKSONVILLE, FL

PREP: 20 MIN. + CHILLING • **MAKES:** 6 SERVINGS

- ½ teaspoon unflavored gelatin
- ¼ cup cold water
- 1 quart fresh strawberries, halved
- 2 tablespoons reduced-sugar strawberry preserves
- 1 package (8 ounces) reduced-fat cream cheese
- ½ cup sugar, divided
- ¼ cup reduced-fat sour cream, divided
- ½ cup heavy whipping cream

1. Sprinkle gelatin over cold water; let stand for 1 minute. Microwave on high for 20 seconds. Stir and let stand for 1 minute or until gelatin is completely dissolved. Meanwhile, combine strawberries and preserves; set aside.

2. In a large bowl, beat the cream cheese, ¼ cup sugar and 2 tablespoons of sour cream until blended; set aside.

3. In another bowl, beat whipping cream and remaining sour cream until it begins to thicken. Add the gelatin mixture and remaining sugar; beat until stiff peaks form. Fold into cream cheese mixture.

4. In each of six dessert dishes, layer ½ cup strawberry mixture and ⅓ cup cream cheese mixture. Refrigerate until chilled.

Glazed Pear Shortcakes

Family and friends will savor every last crumb of this lickety-split dessert. The pound cake absorbs the apricot flavor and the warm sweetness of the pears.

—FRAN THOMAS SAINT JAMES CITY, FL

START TO FINISH: 10 MIN. • **MAKES:** 4 SERVINGS

- 2 medium pears, sliced
- 2 tablespoons butter
- 4 teaspoons apricot spreadable fruit
- 8 thin slices pound cake
- 4 teaspoons chopped walnuts
- 4 tablespoons whipped topping

1. In a small skillet, saute pears in butter until tender. Remove from the heat; stir in spreadable fruit.

2. Place cake slices on four dessert dishes; top with pear mixture, walnuts and whipped topping.

SWITCH IT UP

Experiment with different fruit-and-nut flavor combinations to top the pound cake, such as peaches and pecans; apples and walnuts; cherries and almonds; or pineapple and macadamia nuts. In the summer, quickly grill the pound cake for a toasty flavor boost.

Rhubarb Berry Tart

This tart sets up beautifully. The crust has a delicate almond flavor and the fruit filling has the perfect amount of sweetness. What a tasty way to show off fresh spring and summer produce!

—**MARY ANN LEE** CLIFTON PARK, NY

PREP: 30 MIN. • **BAKE:** 55 MIN. + COOLING • **MAKES:** 12 SERVINGS

- ½ cup sugar
- 4 teaspoons quick-cooking tapioca
- 3 cups sliced fresh or frozen rhubarb
- 2 cups sliced fresh strawberries
- 2 tablespoons orange liqueur or juice
- 1 teaspoon grated lemon peel

CRUST
- ½ cup butter, softened
- ½ cup sugar
- 1 egg
- ½ teaspoon almond extract
- 1½ cups all-purpose flour
- 1½ teaspoons baking powder

TOPPING
- 2 cups (16 ounces) sour cream
- ½ cup sugar
- 2 egg yolks
- 1 teaspoon vanilla extract

1. In a large bowl, combine sugar and tapioca. Add rhubarb and strawberries; toss to coat. Stir in liqueur and lemon peel. Let stand for 15 minutes.

2. Meanwhile, in a small bowl, cream butter and sugar until light and fluffy. Beat in egg and almond extract. Combine flour and baking powder; gradually add to the creamed mixture and mix well.

3. Press dough onto the bottom of a greased 10-in. springform pan. Top with fruit mixture.

4. Combine the topping ingredients; spoon over fruit. Place pan on a baking sheet. Bake at 350° for 55-60 minutes or until set. Cool on a wire rack for 10 minutes. Carefully run a knife around edge of pan to loosen. Cool completely. Store in the refrigerator.

NOTE *If using frozen rhubarb, measure rhubarb while still frozen, then thaw completely. Drain in a colander, but do not press liquid out.*

> **This recipe is a variation of an original I've been making for years. The tangy pineapple-cream cheese filling cuts the sweetness of the pecan topping.**

—**MARILYN BLANKSCHIEN** CLINTONVILLE, WI

Pineapple Pecan Cups

PREP: 25 MIN. • **BAKE:** 25 MIN. + COOLING • **MAKES:** 6 SERVINGS

- 3 tablespoons butter, softened
- 1½ ounces cream cheese, softened
- ½ cup all-purpose flour

FILLING
- 1 package (3 ounces) cream cheese, softened
- 1 tablespoon sugar
- ¼ cup crushed pineapple, drained

TOPPING
- 1 egg
- ¼ cup packed brown sugar
- 2 tablespoons light corn syrup
- 1 tablespoon butter, melted
- 1 teaspoon all-purpose flour
- ½ teaspoon vanilla extract
- ¼ cup chopped pecans

1. In a small bowl, beat butter and cream cheese until smooth. Add flour; mix well. Divide dough into six portions; press onto the bottom and ¾ in. up the sides of six muffin cups coated with cooking spray. Set aside.

2. In another bowl, beat cream cheese and sugar until smooth; stir in pineapple. Spread into each cup. Combine the egg, brown sugar, corn syrup, butter, flour and vanilla; stir in pecans. Spoon over filling.

3. Bake at 350° for 25-30 minutes or until topping is set. Cool for 10 minutes before carefully removing from pan to a wire rack to cool completely.

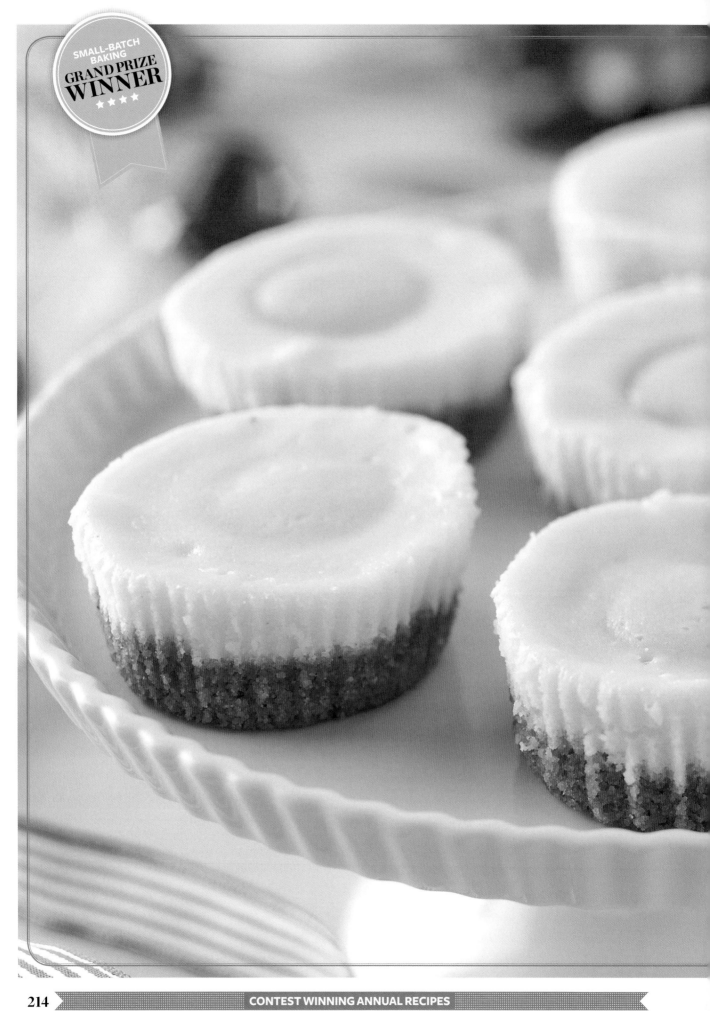

Miniature Peanut Butter Cheesecakes

The recipe for these yummy treats with a peanut butter cup inside was handed down to me from my mother. They're perfect for holidays or any special occasion.
—**MARY ANN DELL** PHOENIXVILLE, PA

PREP: 20 MIN. • **BAKE:** 15 MIN. + CHILLING • **MAKES:** 6 SERVINGS

- ⅓ cup graham cracker crumbs
- 1 tablespoon sugar
- 5 teaspoons butter, melted

FILLING
- 4 ounces cream cheese, softened
- ¼ cup sugar
- 2 teaspoons all-purpose flour
- 2 tablespoons beaten egg
- ¼ teaspoon vanilla extract
- 6 miniature peanut butter cups

1. In a small bowl, combine the cracker crumbs, sugar and butter. Press onto the bottoms of six paper-lined muffin cups; set aside.

2. In a small bowl, beat the cream cheese, sugar and flour until smooth. Add egg and vanilla; beat on low speed just until combined. Place a peanut butter cup in the center of each muffin cup; fill with cream cheese mixture.

3. Bake at 350° for 15-18 minutes or until center is set. Cool on a wire rack for 10 minutes before removing from pan to a wire rack to cool completely. Refrigerate for at least 2 hours.

CANDY BAR BONANZA

Have fun with this easy and versatile recipe by tucking different types of chopped or whole miniature candy bars (such as Heath, Snickers or Krackel) inside.

Also try the recipe in miniature muffin cups and place a Rolo, flavored chocolate kiss candy, Milk Dud, or a few holiday-colored M&Ms inside. (Be sure to decrease the bake time if using miniature muffin cups.)

For a fun decoration, pipe a star of homemade ganache or canned chocolate frosting on top of the cheesecakes and garnish each with the candy that guests will find inside.

Raspberry Mint Shakes

I think this is the perfect way to cool down and relax at warm-weather outdoor gatherings. The creamy combo of raspberry and mint just can't be beat.
—**TIFFANIE WRIGHT** KEMPNER, TX

START TO FINISH: 10 MIN. • **MAKES:** 2 SERVINGS

- ¼ cup 2% milk
- ¼ cup heavy whipping cream
- ¼ teaspoon almond extract
- ⅓ cup honey
- 2 cups fresh or frozen raspberries
- 1 cup vanilla ice cream
- 2 tablespoons chopped fresh mint leaves

In a blender, combine all ingredients; cover and process for 30 seconds or until blended. Pour into chilled glasses and serve immediately.

Caramel Praline Tart

This rich dessert is my own creation, and I'm very proud of it. It's easy enough to make for everyday, but special enough for company or a potluck.
—**KATHLEEN SPECHT** CLINTON, MT

PREP: 35 MIN. + CHILLING • **MAKES:** 16 SERVINGS

  1 sheet refrigerated pie pastry
 36 caramels
  1 cup heavy whipping cream, divided
 3½ cups pecan halves
  ½ cup semisweet chocolate chips, melted

1. Unroll pastry on a lightly floured surface. Transfer to an 11-in. fluted tart pan with removable bottom; trim edges.
2. Line unpricked pastry shell with a double thickness of heavy-duty foil. Bake at 450° for 8 minutes. Remove foil; bake 5-6 minutes longer or until light golden brown. Cool on a wire rack.
3. In a large saucepan, combine caramels and ½ cup of the cream. Cook and stir over medium-low heat until caramels are melted. Stir in pecans. Spread filling evenly into crust. Drizzle with melted chocolate.
4. Refrigerate for 30 minutes or until set. Whip remaining cream; serve with tart.

Strawberries with Chocolate Cream Filling

Simple and delicious, these little gems are the ideal "something sweet" to serve with coffee, tea or champagne.
—**LISA HUFF** WILTON, CT

START TO FINISH: 30 MIN. • **MAKES:** 3 DOZEN

 1½ ounces semisweet chocolate, grated, divided
  1 package (8 ounces) cream cheese, softened
  1 teaspoon vanilla extract
  1 cup whipped topping
 18 large fresh strawberries, halved

1. Set aside 2 tablespoons of chocolate. In a microwave, melt remaining chocolate; stir until smooth. Cool to room temperature.
2. In a small bowl, beat cream cheese and vanilla until smooth. Beat in melted chocolate. Fold in whipped topping and 1 tablespoon grated chocolate. Cut a small hole in the corner of pastry or plastic bag; insert #21 star pastry tip. Fill the bag with cream cheese mixture.
3. Place strawberries cut side up on a serving platter. Pipe cream cheese mixture onto strawberries. Sprinkle with remaining grated chocolate. Refrigerate leftovers.

Berry Delicious Rhubarb Crisp

I sometimes grate about a tablespoonful of fresh orange or lemon zest and add to the crumb mixture for extra flavor. This is the kind of dessert that reminds me of summer nights.

—SHANNON HADINGER-ARTHUR
LUCASVILLE, OH

PREP: 15 MIN. • **BAKE:** 25 MIN.
MAKES: 9 SERVINGS

- 1 **cup all-purpose flour**
- 1 **cup packed brown sugar**
- ¾ **cup old-fashioned oats**
- ½ **cup butter, melted**
- 1½ **teaspoons vanilla extract, divided**
- 1 **teaspoon ground cinnamon**
- 1½ **cups diced fresh or frozen rhubarb**
- 1½ **cups sliced fresh strawberries**
- 1½ **cups fresh blackberries**
- ½ **cup sugar**
- 1 **tablespoon cornstarch**
- ½ **cup cold water**
  Vanilla ice cream

1. In a small bowl, combine the flour, brown sugar, oats, butter, 1 teaspoon vanilla and cinnamon. Set aside 1 cup for topping; press remaining crumb mixture into a greased 8-in. square baking dish. Top with rhubarb, strawberries and blackberries.
2. In a small saucepan, combine sugar and cornstarch. Stir in water. Bring to a boil; cook and stir for 1-2 minutes or until thickened. Stir in remaining vanilla. Pour over fruit; sprinkle with remaining crumb mixture.
3. Bake at 350° for 25-30 minutes or until bubbly. Serve with ice cream.
NOTE *If using frozen rhubarb, measure rhubarb while still frozen, then thaw completely. Drain in a colander, but do not press liquid out.*

FROM THE WEB

Excellent recipe! I used all fresh fruit and substituted blueberries for the blackberries, as they are cheaper and more widely available. I received many compliments and requests for the recipe! **—HALLMARKCHICK88**
TASTEOFHOME.COM

Hungarian Nut Rolls

It isn't officially Christmas until I've made this treasured recipe from my husband's grandmother. The apple-walnut filling has the most amazing flavor.

—DONNA BARDOCZ HOWELL, MI

PREP: 40 MIN. + RISING • **BAKE:** 30 MIN. + COOLING
MAKES: 4 LOAVES (12 SLICES EACH)

- 2 packages (¼ ounce each) active dry yeast
- ½ cup warm 2% milk (110° to 115°)
- ¼ cup plus 2 tablespoons sugar
- ¾ teaspoon salt
- 1 cup butter, softened
- 1 cup (8 ounces) sour cream
- 3 eggs, lightly beaten
- 6 to 6½ cups all-purpose flour

FILLING

- 1¼ cups sugar
- ½ cup butter, cubed
- 1 egg
- ½ teaspoon ground cinnamon
- 4½ cups ground walnuts
- 1 large apple, peeled and grated

ICING

- 2 cups confectioners' sugar
- 2 to 3 tablespoons 2% milk

1. In a large bowl, dissolve yeast in warm milk. Add the sugar, salt, butter, sour cream, eggs and 3 cups of flour. Beat on medium speed for 3 minutes. Beat until smooth. Stir in enough remaining flour to form a soft dough (dough will be sticky).

2. Turn onto a floured surface; knead until smooth and elastic, about 6-8 minutes. Place in a greased bowl, turning once to grease top. Cover and let rise in a warm place until doubled, about 1 hour.

3. Meanwhile, in a large saucepan, combine the sugar, butter, egg and cinnamon. Cook and stir over medium heat until mixture is thick enough to coat the back of a spoon. Remove from the heat; gently stir in walnuts and apple. Cool completely.

4. Punch dough down. Turn onto a lightly floured surface; divide into four portions. Roll each into a 12-in. x 10-in. rectangle. Spread filling to within ½ in. of edges. Roll up jelly-roll style, starting with a long side; pinch seams to seal. Place seam side down on greased baking sheets. Cover and let rise until doubled, about 30 minutes.

5. Bake at 350° for 30-40 minutes or until lightly browned. Remove from pans to wire racks to cool. Combine icing ingredients; drizzle over loaves..

Citrus-Melon Sorbet

PREP: 15 MIN. + FREEZING • **MAKES:** 2 CUPS

- ¼ cup orange juice
- 2 tablespoons lime juice
- 3 cups diced cantaloupe
- ¾ cup sugar
- 1 teaspoon grated lemon peel
- 1 teaspoon grated lime peel

1. In a blender, combine all ingredients. Cover and process for 1-2 minutes or until smooth. Transfer puree to a 13-in. x 9-in. dish. Cover and freeze for 45 minutes or until edges begin to firm; stir.

2. Freeze 2 hours longer or until firm. Just before serving, transfer to a blender; cover and process for 2-3 minutes or until smooth.

❝You can make this frozen treat with many different kinds of fruit, and all you need is a blender. My mom used to prepare this all the time during the summer.❞

—PATRICIA HANCOCK HAWTHORNE, NJ

Butterscotch Bliss Layered Dessert

Four easy layers come together in one cool, delicious treat that's perfect for summer nights. Take this to a gathering, and you'll bring home an empty dish!

—**JANICE VERNON** LAS CRUCES, NM

PREP: 20 MIN. + CHILLING • **MAKES:** 24 SERVINGS

1½ cups graham cracker crumbs
    Sugar substitute equivalent to ½ cup sugar, divided
6 tablespoons butter, melted
2 packages (8 ounces each) reduced-fat cream cheese
3 cups cold fat-free milk, divided
2 packages (1 ounce each) sugar-free instant butterscotch pudding mix
1 carton (8 ounces) frozen reduced-fat whipped topping, thawed
½ teaspoon rum extract

1. In a small bowl, combine the cracker crumbs, ¼ cup sugar substitute and butter. Press into a 13-in. x 9-in. dish coated with cooking spray.
2. In a small bowl, beat the cream cheese, ¼ cup milk and the remaining sugar substitute until smooth. Spread over the crust.
3. In another bowl, whisk remaining milk with the pudding mix for 2 minutes. Let stand for 2 minutes or until soft-set. Gently spread over cream cheese layer.
4. Combine the whipped topping and rum extract; gently spread over the top. Refrigerate dessert for at least 4 hours before serving.

NOTE *This recipe was tested with Splenda no-calorie sweetener.*
PER SERVING *136 cal., 8 g fat (6 g sat. fat), 21 mg chol., 245 mg sodium, 12 g carb., trace fiber, 3 g pro.* **Diabetic Exchanges:** *1 starch, 1 fat.*

Blueberry-Pecan Crisp

This is the perfect marriage of cake and pie, and the toasted pecans give it an addicting crunch. Be prepared to serve seconds.

—**SHARON PARMA** VICTORIA, TX

PREP: 15 MIN. • **BAKE:** 40 MIN. • **MAKES:** 15 SERVINGS

1 can (20 ounces) unsweetened crushed pineapple, undrained
½ cup packed brown sugar
1 teaspoon ground cinnamon
1 can (21 ounces) blueberry pie filling
1 package yellow cake mix (regular size)
1 cup pecan halves, chopped
1 cup butter, melted
    Vanilla ice cream, optional

1. Pour pineapple into a greased 13-in. x 9-in. baking dish. Sprinkle with brown sugar and cinnamon. Top with pie filling. Sprinkle with the cake mix and pecans; drizzle with butter.
2. Bake at 350° for 40-50 minutes or until the filling is bubbly and topping is golden brown. Serve warm with ice cream if desired.

Frozen Chocolate Mint Dessert

This is adapted from my great-aunt's recipe for grasshopper pie. It came about by accident, as I put in too much mint extract. To cut the mint taste with something gooey and chocolaty, I ended up flipping the whole pie upside-down on top of a brownie crust.

—**SARAH NEWMAN** MAHTOMEDI, MN

PREP: 40 MIN. + FREEZING • **MAKES:** 24 SERVINGS

- 1 package fudge brownie mix (13x9-inch pan size)
- 2 egg whites
- ¼ cup unsweetened applesauce
- 2 teaspoons vanilla extract
- ½ cup baking cocoa
- 1½ cups fat-free milk
- 2 packages (16 ounces each) large marshmallows
- ½ teaspoon mint extract
- 1 carton (16 ounces) frozen reduced-fat whipped topping, thawed
- ⅔ cup Oreo cookie crumbs

1. In a large bowl, combine the brownie mix, egg whites, applesauce and vanilla. Spread into a 13x9-in. baking dish coated with cooking spray. Bake at 350° for 18-22 minutes or until a toothpick inserted near the center comes out clean. Cool on a wire rack.

2. In a Dutch oven, combine cocoa and milk. Cook and stir over medium heat until cocoa is dissolved. Stir in marshmallows until melted. Remove from the heat; stir in extract. Cool completely.

3. Fold in whipped topping. Spread over brownies. Sprinkle with cookie crumbs. Cover and freeze for at least 8 hours. Remove from freezer 10 minutes before serving.

Warm Chocolate Melting Cups

Described as over-the-top delicious, these rich, chocolaty desserts are surprisingly smooth and creamy. But what's even more surprising is that each one has fewer than 200 calories and only 6 grams of fat.

—**KISSA VAUGHN** TROY, TX

PREP: 20 MIN. • **BAKE:** 20 MIN. • **MAKES:** 10 SERVINGS

- 1¼ cups sugar, divided
- ½ cup baking cocoa
- 2 tablespoons all-purpose flour
- ⅛ teaspoon salt
- ¾ cup water
- ¾ cup plus 1 tablespoon semisweet chocolate chips
- 1 tablespoon brewed coffee
- 1 teaspoon vanilla extract
- 2 eggs
- 1 egg white
- 10 fresh strawberry halves, optional

1. In a small saucepan, combine ¾ cup sugar, cocoa, flour and salt. Gradually stir in water. Bring to a boil; cook and stir for 2 minutes or until thickened. Remove from the heat; stir in the chocolate chips, coffee and vanilla until smooth. Transfer to a large bowl.

2. In another bowl, beat eggs and egg white until slightly thickened. Gradually add remaining sugar, beating until thick and lemon-colored. Fold into chocolate mixture.

3. Transfer to ten 4-oz. ramekins coated with cooking spray. Place ramekins in a baking pan; add 1 in. of boiling water to pan.

4. Bake, uncovered, at 350° for 20-25 minutes or just until centers are set. Garnish with strawberry halves if desired. Serve immediately.

IRRESISTIBLE CHOCOLATE CUPS

The chocolate dessert cups recipe uses only 2 tablespoons of flour, which produces a very creamy and soft interior like a molten lava cake.

If you don't have 4-ounce ramekins, bake the batter in larger ramekins or in stoneware coffee cups for a longer time.

Store leftover chocolate cups, covered, in the refrigerator. Reheat them in the microwave before serving.

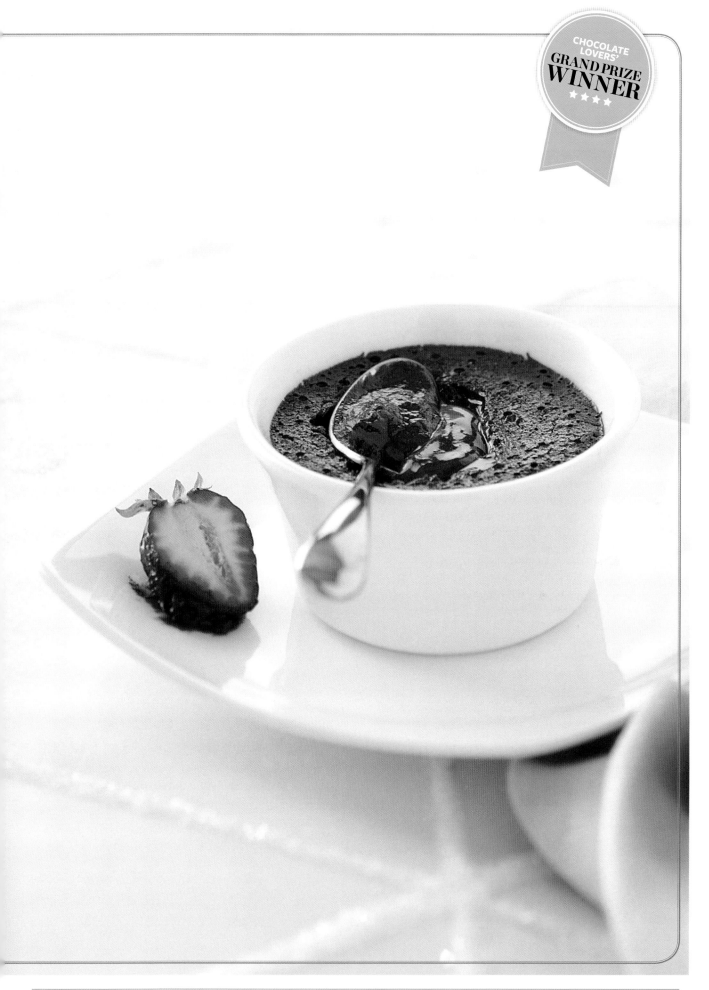

Berry & Cream Chocolate Cups

These cute chocolate cups are great for entertaining because you can make them ahead of time. They're yummy filled with the homemade pastry cream.

—AMY BLOM MARIETTA, GA

PREP: 50 MIN. + CHILLING
MAKES: 1 DOZEN

- 1 package (12 ounces) dark chocolate chips
- 2 ounces cream cheese, softened
- ½ cup sour cream
- ⅓ cup sugar
- 2 tablespoons cornstarch
- 1½ cups milk
- 2 egg yolks, lightly beaten
- 1½ teaspoons vanilla extract
- 1½ cups thinly sliced fresh strawberries

1. In a microwave, melt chocolate chips; stir until smooth. Spread melted chocolate over the bottoms and up the sides of 12 foil muffin cup liners. Refrigerate for 25 minutes or until firm.

2. In a small bowl, beat cream cheese until fluffy; beat in sour cream until smooth. Set aside.

3. In a small saucepan, combine sugar and cornstarch. Stir in milk until smooth. Cook and stir over medium-high heat until thickened and bubbly. Reduce heat to low; cook and stir for 2 minutes longer.

4. Remove from the heat. Stir a small amount of hot mixture into egg yolks; return all to the pan, stirring constantly. Bring to a gentle boil; cook and stir for 2 minutes. Remove from the heat; stir in vanilla and reserved sour cream mixture. Cool to room temperature, stirring occasionally. Refrigerate until chilled.

5. Carefully remove foil liners from chocolate cups. Fill cups with pastry cream and strawberries. Refrigerate until serving.

Strawberry Cheesecake Ice Cream

Light and refreshing, my dreamy, creamy ice cream is perfect for warm afternoons. It's great for scooping into cones, and it doesn't melt as fast as regular ice cream.
—**DEBRA GOFORTH** NEWPORT, TN

PREP: 10 MIN. + FREEZING • **MAKES:** 2 QUARTS

- 1 package (8 ounces) cream cheese, softened
- ⅓ cup refrigerated French vanilla nondairy creamer
- ¼ cup sugar
- 1 teaspoon grated lemon peel
- 1 carton (16 ounces) frozen whipped topping, thawed
- 2 packages (10 ounces each) frozen sweetened sliced strawberries, thawed

In a large bowl, beat the cream cheese, creamer, sugar and lemon peel until blended. Fold in whipped topping and strawberries. Transfer to a freezer container; freeze for 4 hours or until firm. Remove from the freezer 10 minutes before serving.

Easy Tiramisu

This recipe gives you the taste of traditional tiramisu in an instant. My husband and I love this dish, but because he has diabetes, I make it with sugar-free wafers and sugar-free pudding.
—**BETTY CLAYCOMB** ALVERTON, PA

START TO FINISH: 10 MIN. • **MAKES:** 2 SERVINGS

- 12 vanilla wafers, divided
- 1 teaspoon instant coffee granules
- 2 tablespoons hot water
- 2 snack-size cups (3½ ounces each) vanilla pudding
- ¼ cup whipped topping
- 1 teaspoon baking cocoa

1. Set aside two vanilla wafers; coarsely crush remaining wafers. Divide wafer crumbs between two dessert dishes.
2. In a small bowl, dissolve coffee granules in hot water. Drizzle over wafer crumbs. Spoon pudding into dessert dishes. Top with whipped topping; sprinkle with cocoa. Garnish with reserved vanilla wafers.

Gingerbread Pumpkin Trifle

I like to spice up special dinners with this towering dessert featuring two popular fall flavors. A delicious alternative to pumpkin pie, it's always my favorite potluck contribution.
—**DEBORAH HAHN** BELLE, MO

PREP: 1 HOUR + CHILLING • **MAKES:** 16 SERVINGS

- ½ cup shortening
- ⅓ cup sugar
- 1 cup molasses
- 1 egg
- 2⅓ cups all-purpose flour
- 1 teaspoon baking soda
- 1 teaspoon ground ginger
- 1 teaspoon ground cinnamon
- ¾ teaspoon salt
- ¾ cup hot water

FILLING/TOPPING
- 2 cups cold milk
- 1 package (3.4 ounces) instant vanilla pudding mix
- 1 can (15 ounces) solid-pack pumpkin
- ½ cup packed brown sugar
- 1 teaspoon vanilla extract
- ½ teaspoon ground cinnamon
- 2 cups heavy whipping cream
- ⅓ cup sugar
- 1 teaspoon rum extract

1. In a large bowl, cream shortening and sugar until light and fluffy. Beat in molasses and egg. Combine the flour, baking soda, ginger, cinnamon and salt; add to creamed mixture alternately with the hot water, beating well after each addition.

2. Pour into a greased 13-in. x 9-in. baking pan. Bake at 350° for 25-30 minutes or until a toothpick inserted near the center comes out clean. Cool on a wire rack. Cut gingerbread into ½-in. to 1-in. cubes; set aside.

3. In a large bowl, whisk the milk and pudding mix for 2 minutes. Let stand for 2 minutes or until soft-set. Combine the pumpkin, brown sugar, vanilla and cinnamon; stir into pudding. In another bowl, beat cream until it begins to thicken. Add sugar and extract; beat until stiff peaks form.

4. Set aside ¼ cup gingerbread cubes. In a 4-qt. trifle bowl or glass serving bowl, layer a third of the remaining gingerbread cubes; top with a third of the pumpkin mixture and whipped cream. Repeat layers twice. Crumble reserved gingerbread; sprinkle over top. Cover and refrigerate for at least 1 hour before serving.

Turtle Cheesecake

I always get compliments on this rich little cheesecake. With layers of caramel, chocolate and vanilla, it's an instant classic.
—**ERIN BYRD** SPRINGFIELD, MO

PREP: 20 MIN. • **BAKE:** 20 MIN. + CHILLING • **MAKES:** 2 SERVINGS

- ⅓ cup crushed vanilla wafers (about 10 wafers)
- 4 teaspoons butter, melted
- 4 ounces cream cheese, softened
- 2 tablespoons sugar
- ½ teaspoon vanilla extract
- 2 tablespoons beaten egg
- 2 tablespoons hot fudge ice cream topping, warmed
- 1 tablespoon caramel ice cream topping, warmed

1. In a small bowl, combine wafer crumbs and butter. Press onto the bottom and ½ in. up the sides of a greased 4-in. springform pan.

2. In a small bowl, beat the cream cheese, sugar and vanilla until smooth. Add egg; beat on low speed just until combined. Spread half of mixture into crust. Stir fudge topping into remaining batter; gently spread over cream cheese layer. Place pan on a baking sheet.

3. Bake at 350° for 20-25 minutes or until center is almost set. Cool on a wire rack for 10 minutes. Carefully run a knife around the edge of pan to loosen; cool 1 hour longer.

4. Refrigerate overnight. Remove sides of pan. Drizzle caramel topping over cheesecake..

Raspberry Chocolate Cheesecake

My layered no-bake cheesecake showcases red raspberries and heavenly dark chocolate. We love to celebrate special occasions with this homemade treat.
—**ROBINNE HURT** CROSSFIELD, AB

PREP: 40 MIN. + CHILLING • **MAKES:** 12 SERVINGS

- 2 **cups chocolate wafer crumbs (about 38 wafers)**
- ⅓ **cup sugar**
- ½ **cup butter, melted**
FILLING
- 1 **envelope unflavored gelatin**
- ¾ **cup cold water**
- 2 **cups heavy whipping cream**
- 3 **packages (two 8 ounces, one 3 ounces) cream cheese, softened**
- ⅓ **cup sugar**
- 4 **ounces semisweet chocolate, melted and cooled**
- 1 **cup fresh or frozen raspberries**
  Fresh raspberries and mint, optional

1. Combine the wafer crumbs, sugar and butter. Press onto the bottom and 1 in. up the sides of a greased 9-in. springform pan; set aside.
2. In a small saucepan, sprinkle gelatin over cold water; let stand for 1 minute. Heat over low heat, stirring until gelatin is completely dissolved; cool slightly.
3. In a large bowl, beat cream until stiff peaks form; set aside. In another large bowl, beat cream cheese and sugar; stir in cooled gelatin. Transfer half of the mixture to another bowl.

4. To one bowl, fold in melted chocolate and half of the whipped cream. Pour over prepared crust. To the other bowl, gently fold in the remaining whipped cream, then the raspberries. Pour over chocolate layer. Refrigerate for 6 hours or overnight.
5. Carefully run a knife around the edge of pan to loosen. Remove sides of pan. Garnish with berries and mint if desired.

Apple Raspberry Crisp

Dish up a warm serving of this sweet-tart crisp and top it with a scoop of vanilla ice cream for a classic treat that will make guests feel right at home.
—**GINGER PRICE** ELVERSON, PA

PREP: 35 MIN. • **BAKE:** 40 MIN. • **MAKES:** 12 SERVINGS

- 10 **cups thinly sliced peeled tart apples (about 10 medium)**
- 4 **cups fresh raspberries**
- ⅓ **cup sugar**
- 3 **tablespoons plus ¾ cup all-purpose flour, divided**
- 1½ **cups old-fashioned oats**
- 1 **cup packed brown sugar**
- ¾ **cup whole wheat flour**
- ¾ **cup cold butter**

1. Place the apples and raspberries in a large bowl. Add sugar and 3 tablespoons all-purpose flour; toss gently to coat. Transfer to a greased 13-in. x 9-in. baking dish.
2. In a small bowl, combine the oats, brown sugar, whole wheat flour and remaining all-purpose flour. Cut in butter until crumbly; sprinkle over top (dish will be full).
3. Bake, uncovered, at 350° for 40-50 minutes or until filling is bubbly and topping is golden brown. Serve warm.

Dessert Bruschetta with Nectarine Salsa

Here's a fresh no-cook dessert for hot summer days. The flavors work wonderfully together.
—**SALLY SIBTHORPE** SHELBY TOWNSHIP, MI

START TO FINISH: 15 MIN. • **MAKES:** 2 SERVINGS

- 1 medium nectarine, chopped
- ¼ cup fresh or frozen raspberries, thawed
- 1 tablespoon thinly sliced fresh mint leaves
- 2 slices pound cake
- 3 tablespoons Mascarpone cheese
- 2 teaspoons honey
   Whipped cream, optional

1. In a small bowl, combine the nectarine, raspberries and mint. Let stand for 5 minutes.
2. Spread cake slices with cheese; top with nectarine mixture. Drizzle with honey. Serve with whipped cream if desired.

Homemade cinnamon rolls are as easy as 1-2-3.

1   Fill and roll dough as directed, then slice. Place cut side down in greased pans.

2   Cover and let rise until doubled. Rolls will begin to touch each other.

3   Combine the glaze ingredients spoon in a thin stream over the warm rolls.

Streusel Pumpkin Sweet Rolls

My sons love anything pumpkin—including these yummy rolls. It wouldn't be fall without these irresistible, fragrant treats.
—**JULIE FEHR** MARTENSVILLE, SK

PREP: 45 MIN. + RISING • **BAKE:** 20 MIN. • **MAKES:** 2 DOZEN

- 1 package (¼ ounce) active dry yeast
- 1¼ cups warm 2% milk (110° to 115°)
- 1 cup solid-pack pumpkin
- ½ cup sugar
- ½ cup butter, melted
- 1 teaspoon salt
- 4¾ to 5¾ cups all-purpose flour

STREUSEL
- 1½ cups all-purpose flour
- 1 cup packed brown sugar
- 1 teaspoon ground cinnamon
- ½ teaspoon ground allspice
- ¾ cup cold butter, cubed

GLAZE
- 1 cup confectioners' sugar
- ½ teaspoon vanilla extract
- 1 to 2 tablespoons 2% milk

1. In a large bowl, dissolve yeast in warm milk. Add the pumpkin, sugar, butter, salt and 4¾ cups flour. Beat until smooth. Stir in enough remaining flour to form a soft dough (dough will be sticky).
2. Turn onto a floured surface; knead until smooth and elastic, about 6-8 minutes. Place in a greased bowl, turning once to grease top. Cover and let rise in a warm place until doubled, about 1 hour.
3. Punch dough down; divide in half. Roll each portion into a 12x10-in. rectangle. Combine the flour, brown sugar, cinnamon and allspice; cut in butter until crumbly. Set aside 1 cup. Sprinkle remaining streusel over dough to within ½ in. of edges; press down lightly. Roll up jelly-roll style, starting with a long side; pinch seams to seal.
4. Cut each into 12 slices. Place cut side down in two greased 13x9-in. baking pans. Sprinkle with reserved streusel. Cover and let rise until doubled, about 30 minutes.
5. Bake at 375° for 20-25 minutes or until golden brown. Combine glaze ingredients; drizzle over rolls. Serve warm.

Substitutions & Equivalents

EQUIVALENT MEASURES

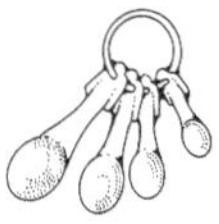

3 teaspoons	= 1 tablespoon	16 tablespoons	= 1 cup
4 tablespoons	= ¼ cup	2 cups	= 1 pint
5-1/3 tablespoons	= ⅓ cup	4 cups	= 1 quart
8 tablespoons	= ½ cup	4 quarts	= 1 gallon

FOOD EQUIVALENTS

GRAINS

Macaroni	1 cup (3½ ounces) uncooked	= 2½ cups cooked
Noodles, Medium	3 cups (4 ounces) uncooked	= 4 cups cooked
Popcorn	⅓ to ½ cup unpopped	= 8 cups popped
Rice, Long Grain	1 cup uncooked	= 3 cups cooked
Rice, Quick-Cooking	1 cup uncooked	= 2 cups cooked
Spaghetti	8 ounces uncooked	= 4 cups cooked

CRUMBS

Bread	1 slice	= ¾ cup soft crumbs, ¼ cup fine dry crumbs
Graham Crackers	7 squares	= ½ cup finely crushed
Buttery Round Crackers	12 crackers	= ½ cup finely crushed
Saltine Crackers	14 crackers	= ½ cup finely crushed

FRUITS

Bananas	1 medium	= ⅓ cup mashed
Lemons	1 medium	= 3 tablespoons juice, 2 teaspoons grated peel
Limes	1 medium	= 2 tablespoons juice, 1½ teaspoons grated peel
Oranges	1 medium	= ¼ to ⅓ cup juice, 4 teaspoons grated peel

VEGETABLES

Cabbage	1 head	= 5 cups shredded	Green Pepper	1 large	= 1 cup chopped
Carrots	1 pound	= 3 cups shredded	Mushrooms	½ pound	= 3 cups sliced
Celery	1 rib	= ½ cup chopped	Onions	1 medium	= ½ cup chopped
Corn	1 ear fresh	= ⅔ cup kernels	Potatoes	3 medium	= 2 cups cubed

NUTS

Almonds	1 pound	= 3 cups chopped	Pecan Halves	1 pound	= 4½ cups chopped
Ground Nuts	3¾ ounces	= 1 cup	Walnuts	1 pound	= 3¾ cups chopped

EASY SUBSTITUTIONS

WHEN YOU NEED...		USE...
Baking Powder	1 teaspoon	½ teaspoon cream of tartar + ¼ teaspoon baking soda
Buttermilk	1 cup	1 tablespoon lemon juice or vinegar + enough milk to measure 1 cup (let stand 5 minutes before using)
Cornstarch	1 tablespoon	2 tablespoons all-purpose flour
Honey	1 cup	1¼ cups sugar + ¼ cup water
Half-and-Half Cream	1 cup	1 tablespoon melted butter + enough whole milk to measure 1 cup
Onion	1 small, chopped (⅓ cup)	1 teaspoon onion powder or 1 tablespoon dried minced onion
Tomato Juice	1 cup	½ cup tomato sauce + ½ cup water
Tomato Sauce	2 cups	¾ cup tomato paste + 1 cup water
Unsweetened Chocolate	1 square (1 ounce)	3 tablespoons baking cocoa + 1 tablespoon shortening or oil
Whole Milk	1 cup	½ cup evaporated milk + ½ cup water

COOKING TERMS

BASTE To moisten food with melted butter, pan drippings, marinades or other liquid to add more flavor and juiciness.

BEAT A rapid movement to combine ingredients using a fork, spoon, wire whisk or electric mixer.

BLEND To combine ingredients until just mixed.

BOIL To heat liquids until bubbles form that cannot be "stirred down." In the case of water, the temperature will reach 212°.

BONE To remove all meat from the bone before cooking.

CREAM To beat ingredients together to a smooth consistency, usually in the case of butter and sugar for baking.

DASH A small amount of seasoning, less than ⅛ teaspoon. If using a shaker, a dash would comprise a quick flip of the container.

DREDGE To coat foods with flour or other dry ingredients. Most often done with pot roasts and stew meat before browning.

FOLD To incorporate several ingredients by careful and gentle turning with a spatula. Used generally with beaten egg whites or whipped cream when mixing into the rest of the ingredients to keep the batter light.

JULIENNE To cut foods into long thin strips much like matchsticks. Used most often for salads and stir-fry dishes.

MINCE To cut into very fine pieces. Used often for garlic or fresh herbs.

PARBOIL To cook partially, usually used in the case of chicken, sausages and vegetables.

PARTIALLY SET Describes the consistency of gelatin after it has been chilled for a short amount of time. Mixture should resemble the consistency of egg whites.

PUREE To process foods to a smooth mixture. Can be prepared in an electric blender, food processor, food mill or sieve.

SAUTE To fry quickly in a small amount of fat, stirring almost constantly. Most often done with onions, mushrooms and other chopped vegetables.

SCORE To cut slits partway through the outer surface of foods. Often used with ham or flank steak.

STIR-FRY To cook meats and/or vegetables with a constant stirring motion in a small amount of oil in a wok or skillet over high heat.

General Recipe Index

This handy index lists every recipe by food category, major ingredient and/or cooking method, so you can easily locate recipes to suit your needs.

✓ RECIPES INCLUDE **NUTRITION FACTS** AND **DIABETIC EXCHANGES**.

APPETIZERS
(*SEE SNACKS & APPETIZERS*)

ASPARAGUS
Asparagus and Sun-Dried Tomatoes, 166
Glazed Shrimp & Asparagus, 153
Radish Asparagus Salad, 36

AVOCADOS
Corn Cakes with Shrimp & Guacamole, 21
Southwest Egg Rolls & Avocado Dip, 21
Southwestern Burgers, 59

BACON
Apricot Turkey Sandwiches, 65
Bacon Cheeseburger Spaghetti, 96
Bacon Vegetable Quiche, 88
Bistro Breakfast Panini, 83
Chicken, Pear & Gorgonzola Tarts, 24
Chicken Pesto Clubs, 53
Italian BLTs, 54
Potato Bacon Casserole, 175
Stuffed Baby Red Potatoes, 10
Stuffed Burgers on Portobellos, 63
Turkey Sliders with Chili Cheese Mayo, 70

BANANAS
Banana Chip Pancakes, 80
Chocolate Ribbon Banana Loaf, 84
✓Monkey Muffins, 76
Peanut Butter Banana Bread, 172

BARS
Blondie Nut Bars, 178
✓Diamond Almond Bars, 179
Gooey Butterscotch Bars, 180
✓S'more Bars, 186

BEANS
✓Alfresco Bean Salad, 31
✓Black Bean Cakes with Mole Salsa, 153
✓Chicken Pita Salad, 31
Shaker Bean Soup, 63
✓Spicy Chicken Chili, 70

✓Spinach & Black Bean Egg Rolls, 8
✓Spinach Bean Salad with Maple Dressing, 46
Vegetarian Polka Dot Stew, 60

BEEF (*ALSO SEE GROUND BEEF*)
✓Cider Mushroom Brisket, 101
Creamy Reuben Soup, 68
Gone-All-Day Stew, 104
Hearty Beef and Noodles, 96
Italian Strip Steaks with Focaccia, 95
✓Moroccan Beef Kabobs, 99
Mushroom Beef Tips With Rice, 100
Peppered Filets with Tomato-Mushroom Salsa, 102
Santa Maria Roast Beef, 103
Savory Grilled T-Bones, 100
✓Special Pot Roast, 97
Thai Beef Pasta Salad, 38
Tuscan Steak Flatbreads, 95

BELL PEPPERS
Garden Tomato Relish, 174
✓Grilled Sweet Potato and Red Pepper Salad, 38
✓Olive & Roasted Pepper Bruschetta, 13
Orzo-Stuffed Peppers, 114
Peasant Peppers, 167
Roasted Red Pepper Soup, 51

BEVERAGES
Raspberry Mint Shakes, 215
Sparkling Kiwi Lemonade, 22

BISCUITS & BISCUIT MIX
Banana Chip Pancakes, 80
Cheeseburger Cups, 17
Cowboy Corn Bread, 175
Flatbread Tacos with Ranch Sour Cream, 103

BLACKBERRIES
Berry Delicious Rhubarb Crisp, 217
Cedar Plank Salmon with Blackberry Sauce, 147
Chocolate Berry Tarts, 211
Crumb-Coated Chicken & Blackberry Salsa, 125
Triple-Berry Crumb Pie, 203

BLUEBERRIES
Blueberry Bounty Cake , 201
Blueberry Cheesecake Flapjacks, 91
✓Blueberry Oat Pancakes, 77
Blueberry-Pecan Crisp, 219
Lemon Blueberry Tart, 208
Triple-Berry Crumb Pie, 203

BREADS, ROLLS & MUFFINS
(*ALSO SEE BISCUITS & BISCUIT MIX*)
Authentic Boston Brown Bread, 159
Blue Cheese & Shallot Bread, 167
Cappuccino Cinnamon Rolls, 88
Chocolate Chai Mini Loaves, 159
Chocolate Ribbon Banana Loaf, 84
Corn Bread with a Kick, 171
Cowboy Corn Bread, 175
✓Double-Chip Pumpkin Cinnamon Muffins, 83
Ginger Currant Scones, 74
Hot Buttered Rum Rolls, 74
✓Monkey Muffins, 76
Orange Nut Bread & Cream Cheese Spread, 165
Peanut Butter Banana Bread, 172
Peppery Cheese Bread, 165
Petite Sticky Buns, 91
Pina Colada Zucchini Bread, 160
Savory Dill and Caraway Scones, 170
Streusel Pumpkin Sweet Rolls, 227
Sweet Potato Bread & Pineapple Butter, 163
✓Sweet Potato Spice Bread, 168
Tomato & Brie Focaccia, 16
✓Tomato & Olive Bread, 171

BREAKFAST & BRUNCH RECIPES
(*ALSO SEE BREADS, ROLLS & MUFFINS*)
Bacon Vegetable Quiche, 88
✓Baked Blueberry & Peach Oatmeal, 80
Banana Chip Pancakes, 80
Bear's Breakfast Burritos, 75
Benedict Eggs in Pastry, 79
Bistro Breakfast Panini, 83
Blueberry Cheesecake Flapjacks, 91
✓Blueberry Oat Pancakes, 77
Butter Pecan French Toast, 85

Chocolate Peppermint Scones, 78
✓Fruit Salad with O.J. Reduction, 77
Ham & Cheese Breakfast Strudels, 87
Oatmeal Brulee with Ginger
    Cream, 89
PBJ-Stuffed French Toast, 84
Peanut Butter & Jelly Waffles, 76
Portobello Waffles with Balsamic
    Syrup, 82
Raspberry Cheese Blintz Bake, 82
Rhubarb Coffee Cake with Caramel
    Sauce, 87
Spiral Omelet Supreme, 79
Sunny Morning Doughnuts, 90
Tomato Onion Quiche, 155

BUTTERSCOTCH
✓Butterscotch Bliss Layered
    Dessert, 219
Gooey Butterscotch Bars, 180

CABBAGE & SAUERKRAUT
Creamy Reuben Soup, 68
Ginger Chicken Burgers with Sesame
    Slaw, 64

CAKES & CUPCAKES
Apricot-Raspberry Angel Torte, 197
Blueberry Bounty Cake , 201
Candy Bar Cupcakes, 200
Chocolate Bliss Marble Cake, 193
Chocolate Raspberry Tunnel
    Cake, 192
Chocolate Sour Cream Torte, 200
Chocolate Zucchini Cupcakes, 205
Grandma's Christmas Cake, 193
Hot Fudge Pudding Cake, 210
Holiday Walnut Torte, 197
Lemon-Mint Pound Cake with
    Strawberries, 194
Wonderful Carrot Cake, 202

CANDIES
✓Macadamia Nut Fudge, 188
✓Maple Nut Truffles, 189
✓Maple Walnut Crisps, 179
✓Peanut Butter Turtle Candies, 181
✓Trail Mix Clusters, 188

CARAMEL
Caramel Praline Tart, 216
Gooey Butterscotch Bars, 180
Hot Buttered Rum Rolls, 74
Petite Sticky Buns, 91
Rhubarb Coffee Cake with Caramel
    Sauce, 87
Turtle Bread Pudding, 208
Turtle Cheesecake, 224

CHEESE
(ALSO SEE CREAM CHEESE)
BREADS
Blue Cheese & Shallot Bread, 167
Peppery Cheese Bread, 165
Tomato & Brie Focaccia, 16
BREAKFAST & BRUNCH
Bacon Vegetable Quiche, 88
Bistro Breakfast Panini, 83
Raspberry Cheese Blintz Bake, 82
Tomato Onion Quiche, 155
MAIN DISHES
Bacon Cheeseburger Spaghetti, 96
Chicken Enchilada Bake, 135
Creamy Spinach Sausage Pasta, 108
Goat Cheese-Stuffed Chicken with
    Apricot Glaze, 128
Gorgonzola Pasta with Walnuts, 144
Italian Strip Steaks with Focaccia, 95
Lasagna Deliziosa, 126
Nacho Pizza, 99
Pecan Chicken with Blue Cheese
    Sauce, 135
Penne Gorgonzola with Chicken, 140
Pesto Chicken Mostaccioli, 131
Salads with Pistachio-Crusted Goat
    Cheese, 47
Sausage Calzones, 112
Shrimp & Macaroni Casserole, 147
Six-Cheese Lasagna, 94
Summer Squash Mushroom
    Casserole, 152
Tomato Onion Quiche, 155
SALADS
Fresh Mozzarella & Tomato Salad, 39
✓Greek-Inspired Quinoa Salad, 46
Hazelnut and Pear Salad, 36
Mediterranean Green Salad, 39
Orange Spinach Salad, 45
Salads with Pistachio-Crusted Goat
    Cheese, 47
SANDWICHES
Bistro Breakfast Panini, 83
Crab Toast, 69
Mini Muffuletta, 18
Portobello Burgers with Pear-Walnut
    Mayonnaise, 67
Turkey Sliders with Chili Cheese
    Mayo, 70
SIDE DISHES
Chili-Cheese Rice Bake, 163
Flavorful Red Potatoes, 169
✓Swiss-Onion Potato Bake, 161
SNACKS & APPETIZERS
Gorgonzola & Cranberry Cheese
    Ball, 11
Marinated Cheese, 20
Mediterranean Tomato Bites, 9

Mini Muffuletta, 18
Secret Ingredient Stuffed Eggs, 11
Stuffed Baby Red Potatoes, 10
Tomato & Brie Focaccia, 16
SOUP
Buttery Onion Soup, 56

CHEESECAKES
Miniature Peanut Butter
    Cheesecakes, 215
Nacho Party Cheesecake, 16
Raspberry Chocolate
    Cheesecake, 225
Turtle Cheesecake, 224

CHERRIES
✓Cherry Chocolate Chip
    Cookies, 178
Cherry Mocha Balls, 183

CHICKEN
MAIN DISHES
Barbecued Chicken Pizzas, 136
Chicken Enchilada Bake, 135
Chicken Saltimbocca with
    Mushroom Sauce, 129
Chicken with Rosemary Butter
    Sauce, 126
Crispy Chicken Fingers, 139
Crumb-Coated Chicken &
    Blackberry Salsa, 125
Fiesta Chicken Burritos, 139
✓Gingered Chicken Thighs, 140
Goat Cheese-Stuffed Chicken with
    Apricot Glaze, 128
✓Lemony Spinach-Stuffed Chicken
    Breasts, 130
Mango Chicken with Plum
    Sauce, 125
Maple Chicken 'n' Ribs, 131
Orange-Cashew Chicken and
    Rice, 130
Pecan Chicken with Blue Cheese
    Sauce, 135
Penne Gorgonzola with Chicken, 140
Pesto Chicken Mostaccioli, 131
✓Prosciutto Chicken in Wine
    Sauce, 133
Sesame Chicken with Ginger
    Shiitake Cream Sauce, 124
Southwest Chicken and Rice, 128
Swiss Chicken Rolls, 137
Thai Portobello Chicken
    Stir-Fry, 134
SALADS
Balsamic Chicken Pasta Salad, 33
✓Chicken Pita Salad, 31
Chicken Tostada Salad, 28

CHICKEN (*CONTINUED*)
✓Refreshing Grilled Chicken
   Salad, 30
Southwest Crunch Chicken Salad, 43
SANDWICHES
Chicken Pesto Clubs, 53
Cranberry Chicken Focaccia, 54
Ginger Chicken Burgers with Sesame
   Slaw, 64
Pepper & Jack Smothered
   Burgers, 53
SNACKS & APPETIZERS
Chicken, Pear & Gorgonzola
   Tarts, 24
Nacho Party Cheesecake, 16
Sesame Chicken Dip, 13
SOUP
✓Spicy Chicken Chili, 70

CHOCOLATE
BARS
Blondie Nut Bars, 178
✓S'more Bars, 186
BREADS
Chocolate Chai Mini Loaves, 159
Chocolate Peppermint Scones, 78
Chocolate Ribbon Banana Loaf, 84
Peanut Butter Banana Bread, 172
CAKES & CUPCAKES
Candy Bar Cupcakes, 200
Chocolate Bliss Marble Cake, 193
Chocolate Raspberry Tunnel
   Cake, 192
Chocolate Sour Cream Torte, 200
Chocolate Zucchini Cupcakes, 205
CANDIES
✓Macadamia Nut Fudge, 188
✓Maple Nut Truffles, 189
✓Trail Mix Clusters, 188
CHEESECAKES
Raspberry Chocolate
   Cheesecake, 225
Turtle Cheesecake, 224
COOKIES
✓Cherry Chocolate Chip
   Cookies, 178
Cherry Mocha Balls, 183
✓Chocolate Pistachio Biscotti, 181
Chocolate Shortbread, 189
✓Gooey Chocolate Cookies, 184
DESSERTS
Berry & Cream Chocolate
   Cups, 222
Chocolate Berry Tarts, 211
Frozen Chocolate Mint Dessert, 220
Hot Fudge Pudding Cake, 210
Strawberries with Chocolate Cream
   Filling, 216

Turtle Bread Pudding, 208
Warm Chocolate Melting Cups, 220
PIES
Frosty Coffee Pie, 205
German Chocolate Cream Pie, 199
Mayan Chocolate Pecan Pie, 192
SNACK
Chocolate Chip Dip, 14

CINNAMON
Cappuccino Cinnamon Rolls, 88
Greek Honey Nut Pie, 203

COCONUT
Ambrosia Fruit Salad, 45
German Chocolate Cream Pie, 199
Vermont Maple Oatmeal Pie, 199

COFFEE
Cappuccino Cinnamon Rolls, 88
Cherry Mocha Balls, 183
Easy Tiramisu, 223
Frosty Coffee Pie, 205

CONDIMENTS
Bread & Butter Peppers, 172
Garden Tomato Relish, 174
Triple Cranberry Sauce, 169

COOKIES
✓Cherry Chocolate Chip
   Cookies, 178
Cherry Mocha Balls, 183
Chewy Date Pinwheels, 184
✓Chocolate Pistachio Biscotti, 181
Chocolate Shortbread, 189
Eggnog Logs, 183
Finnish Pinwheels, 185
✓Gooey Chocolate Cookies, 184
Lemon Stars, 182
✓Nutty Orange Snowballs, 180
✓Oatmeal Surprise Cookies, 186
Whipped Shortbread, 185

CORN
Low Country Boil, 144
✓Spinach & Black Bean Egg
   Rolls, 8

CORNMEAL
Corn Bread with a Kick, 171
Cowboy Corn Bread, 175

CRANBERRIES
Cranberry Chicken Focaccia, 54
Gorgonzola & Cranberry Cheese
   Ball, 11
Triple Cranberry Sauce, 169

**CREAM CHEESE (*ALSO SEE
   CHEESECAKES*)**
Apricot-Raspberry Angel Torte, 197
✓Butterscotch Bliss Layered
   Dessert, 219
Candy Bar Cupcakes, 200
Chocolate Chip Dip, 14
Country-Style Tomatoes, 158
French Quarter Cheese Spread, 22
Gorgonzola & Cranberry Cheese
   Ball, 11
Greek Pinwheels, 12
Grilled Stuffed Jalapenos, 15
Hot Pepper Pleasers, 18
Marinated Cheese, 20
Orange Nut Bread & Cream Cheese
   Spread, 165
Peanut Butter Pies, 198
Raspberry Cream Pie, 195
Roasted Garlic & Tomato Spread, 19
Sesame Chicken Dip, 13
Strawberries with Chocolate Cream
   Filling, 216
Strawberry Cheesecake Ice Cream, 223
Strawberry Cheesecake Mousse, 212
Sun-Dried Tomato Dip, 14

**DESSERTS (*ALSO SEE BARS;
   CAKES & CUPCAKES; CANDIES;
   CHEESECAKES; COOKIES; ICE
   CREAM & FROZEN TREATS;
   PIES; TARTS*)**
Apple Raspberry Crisp, 225
Berry & Cream Chocolate Cups, 222
Berry Delicious Rhubarb Crisp, 217
Blueberry-Pecan Crisp, 219
✓Butterscotch Bliss Layered
   Dessert, 219
Dessert Bruschetta with Nectarine
   Salsa, 227
Easy Tiramisu, 223
Gingerbread Pumpkin Trifle, 224
Glazed Pear Shortcakes, 212
Hot Fudge Pudding Cake, 210
Hungarian Nut Rolls, 218
Pineapple Pecan Cups, 213
Raspberry Mint Shakes, 215
Strawberries with Chocolate Cream
   Filling, 216
Strawberry Cheesecake Mousse, 212
Streusel Pumpkin Sweet Rolls, 227
Sunny Morning Doughnuts, 90
Turtle Bread Pudding, 208
Warm Chocolate Melting Cups, 220

EGGS
Bear's Breakfast Burritos, 75
Benedict Eggs in Pastry, 79

Bistro Breakfast Panini, 83
Cucumber-Egg Salad Sandwiches, 65
Ham & Cheese Breakfast Strudels, 87
Secret Ingredient Stuffed Eggs, 11
Spiral Omelet Supreme, 79
Tomato Onion Quiche, 155

FISH (*SEE SEAFOOD*)

FRUIT (*ALSO SEE SPECIFIC LISTINGS*)
Ambrosia Fruit Salad, 45
Apple Raspberry Crisp, 225
✓Baked Blueberry & Peach Oatmeal, 80
Chewy Date Pinwheels, 184
Citrus-Melon Sorbet, 218
Dessert Bruschetta with Nectarine Salsa, 227
Finnish Pinwheels, 185
Fresh & Fruity Spinach Salad, 43
✓Fruit & Cream Layered Salad, 30
Fruit Salad with Lemon Dressing, 37
✓Fruit Salad with O.J. Reduction, 77
✓Fruited Turkey Salads, 40
Ginger Currant Scones, 74
Glazed Pear Shortcakes, 212
Jeweled Plum Tartlets, 210
Mango Chicken with Plum Sauce, 125
Marshmallow-Almond Key Lime Pie, 204
Mixed Nut 'n' Fig Pie, 195
Oatmeal Brulee with Ginger Cream, 89
✓Refreshing Grilled Chicken Salad, 30
Sparkling Kiwi Lemonade, 22
✓Trail Mix Clusters, 188
✓Vanilla-Lime Fruit Salad, 42

GRAND PRIZE WINNERS
Baked Blueberry & Peach Oatmeal, 78
Balsamic Chicken Pasta Salad, 33
Barbecue Pork and Penne Skillet, 119
Bread & Butter Peppers, 172
Dessert Bruschetta with Nectarine Salsa, 227
French Quarter Cheese Spread, 22
Gone-All-Day Stew, 104
Ham & Cheese Breakfast Strudels, 85
Holiday Walnut Torte, 197
Lasagna Deliziosa, 126
Lemon Blueberry Tart, 208
Miniature Peanut Butter Cheesecakes, 215
✓Oatmeal Surprise Cookies, 186

Orange Spinach Salad, 45
✓Peachy Shrimp Tacos, 150
Penne Gorgonzola with Chicken, 140
Peppery Cheese Bread, 165
Portobello Burgers with Pear-Walnut Mayonnaise, 67
✓Prosciutto Chicken in Wine Sauce, 133
✓Roast Pork Sandwiches with Peach Chutney, 56
Secret's in the Sauce BBQ Ribs, 112
Shaker Bean Soup, 63
Shrimp & Macaroni Casserole, 147
South-of-the-Border Caprese Salad, 40
Summer Veggie Subs, 50
Turkey Sliders with Chili Cheese Mayo, 68
Warm Chocolate Melting Cups, 220

GRILLED RECIPES
Asian-Style Baby Back Ribs, 115
Barbecued Chicken Pizzas, 136
Cedar Plank Salmon with Blackberry Sauce, 147
Fruit-Glazed Pork Chops, 111
Glazed Pork Chops, 120
Grilled Shrimp with Apricot Sauce, 154
Grilled Stuffed Jalapenos, 15
✓Grilled Sweet Potato and Red Pepper Salad, 38
✓Mango Shrimp Pitas, 61
✓Moroccan Beef Kabobs, 99
✓Mustard Turkey Cutlets, 136
Orange Roughy with Tartar Sauce, 154
Portobello Burgers with Pear-Walnut Mayonnaise, 67
✓Refreshing Grilled Chicken Salad, 30
Santa Maria Roast Beef, 103
Savory Grilled T-Bones, 100
Southwestern Burgers, 59
Tuscan Steak Flatbreads, 95

GROUND BEEF
Asian Burgers, 58
Bacon Cheeseburger Spaghetti, 96
Cheeseburger Cups, 17
✓Cheeseburger French Loaf, 52
Chili con Carne, 59
Creamy Beef Enchiladas, 102
Flatbread Tacos with Ranch Sour Cream, 103
Italian Meatball Tortes, 98
Lasagna Deliziosa, 126
Loaded Spaghetti Bake, 104

Macaroni Taco Bake, 101
Nacho Pizza, 99
Pepperoni Pizza Skillet, 94
Six-Cheese Lasagna, 94
Southwestern Burgers, 59
Stuffed Burgers on Portobellos, 63

HAM & CANADIAN BACON (*ALSO SEE PROSCIUTTO*)
Benedict Eggs in Pastry, 79
Grilled Shrimp with Apricot Sauce, 154
Ham & Cheese Breakfast Strudels, 87
Ham & Cheese Stuffed Potatoes, 109
Holiday Glazed Ham, 117
Muffuletta Pasta, 119
Shaker Bean Soup, 63

HERBS
Apricot-Glazed Salmon with Herb Rice, 150
Chicken with Rosemary Butter Sauce, 126
Lemon-Mint Pound Cake with Strawberries, 194
Raspberry Mint Shakes, 215
✓Roast Turkey Breast with Rosemary Gravy, 138
Roasted Citrus & Herb Turkey, 133
Savory Dill and Caraway Scones, 170

HONEY
Greek Honey Nut Pie, 203
Raspberry Mint Shakes, 215

HOT PEPPERS
Bear's Breakfast Burritos, 75
Bread & Butter Peppers, 172
Chili-Cheese Rice Bake, 163
✓Chipotle Sweet Potatoes, 166
✓Fresh Peach Salsa, 12
Grilled Stuffed Jalapenos, 15
Hot Pepper Pleasers, 18
Italian Sausage with Peppers, 67
Pepper & Jack Smothered Burgers, 53
✓Spicy Chicken Chili, 70
✓Tomato-Jalapeno Granita, 8

ICE CREAM & FROZEN TREATS
Citrus-Melon Sorbet, 218
Frosty Coffee Pie, 205
Frozen Chocolate Mint Dessert, 220
Peanut Butter Pies, 198
Strawberry & Wine Sorbet, 211
Strawberry Cheesecake Ice Cream, 223

LEMON
Blueberry Bounty Cake , 201
Lemon Blueberry Tart, 208
Lemon-Mint Pound Cake with
 Strawberries, 194
Lemon Stars, 182
Sparkling Kiwi Lemonade, 22

LETTUCE
Chicken Tostada Salad, 28
Mediterranean Green Salad, 39
Orange Spinach Salad, 45
✓Refreshing Grilled Chicken
 Salad, 30
Salads with Pistachio-Crusted Goat
 Cheese, 47

MAPLE
Maple Chicken 'n' Ribs, 131
✓Maple Nut Truffles, 189
✓Maple Walnut Crisps, 179
Spice Bread with Maple Butter, 158
✓Spinach Bean Salad with Maple
 Dressing, 46
Vermont Maple Oatmeal Pie, 199

MARSHMALLOWS
Frozen Chocolate Mint Dessert, 220
Marshmallow-Almond Key Lime
 Pie, 204
✓S'more Bars, 186

MEATLESS (*SEE VEGETARIAN*)

MINT
Chocolate Peppermint Scones, 78
Frozen Chocolate Mint Dessert, 220
Lemon-Mint Pound Cake with
 Strawberries, 194
Raspberry Mint Shakes, 215

MUSHROOMS
Italian Strip Steaks with Focaccia, 95
Portobello Burgers with Pear-Walnut
 Mayonnaise, 67
Portobello Waffles with Balsamic
 Syrup, 82
Sesame Chicken with Ginger
 Shiitake Cream Sauce, 124
Stuffed Asiago-Basil Mushrooms, 9
Stuffed Burgers on Portobellos, 63
Summer Squash Mushroom
 Casserole, 152
Thai Portobello Chicken
 Stir-Fry, 134

NUTS (*ALSO SEE PEANUTS &
 PEANUT BUTTER*)
BREADS
Orange Nut Bread & Cream Cheese
 Spread, 165
Petite Sticky Buns, 91
BREAKFAST & BRUNCH
Butter Pecan French Toast, 85
Petite Sticky Buns, 91
DESSERTS
Apricot-Raspberry Angel Torte, 197
Blondie Nut Bars, 178
Blueberry-Pecan Crisp, 219
Caramel Praline Tart, 216
Cherry Mocha Balls, 183
✓Diamond Almond Bars, 179
German Chocolate Cream Pie, 199
Greek Honey Nut Pie, 203
Holiday Walnut Torte, 197
Hungarian Nut Rolls, 218
✓Macadamia Nut Fudge, 188
✓Maple Nut Truffles, 189
✓Maple Walnut Crisps, 179
Marshmallow-Almond Key Lime
 Pie, 204
Mayan Chocolate Pecan Pie, 192
Mixed Nut 'n' Fig Pie, 195
✓Nutty Orange Snowballs, 180
✓Peanut Butter Turtle Candies, 181
Pineapple Pecan Cups, 213
✓Trail Mix Clusters, 188
Triple-Berry Crumb Pie, 203
MAIN DISHES
✓Fruited Turkey Salads, 40
Macadamia-Crusted Mahi Mahi, 148
Orange-Cashew Chicken and Rice, 130
Pecan Chicken with Blue Cheese
 Sauce, 135
Salads with Pistachio-Crusted Goat
 Cheese, 47
Southwest Crunch Chicken Salad, 43
SALADS
✓Fruited Turkey Salads, 40
Hazelnut and Pear Salad, 36
Salads with Pistachio-Crusted Goat
 Cheese, 47
Southwest Crunch Chicken Salad, 43
SANDWICHES
Asian Meatless Wraps, 61
SIDE DISH
Green Beans with Pecans, 170
SNACKS & APPETIZERS
French Quarter Cheese Spread, 22
Gorgonzola & Cranberry Cheese
 Ball, 11

Kickin' Snack Mix, 19
Secret Ingredient Stuffed Eggs, 11
Sweet & Spicy Nuts, 17

OATS
✓Baked Blueberry & Peach
 Oatmeal, 80
✓Blueberry Oat Pancakes, 77
✓Cherry Chocolate Chip Cookies, 178
Oatmeal Brulee with Ginger
 Cream, 89
✓Oatmeal Surprise Cookies, 186
Vermont Maple Oatmeal Pie, 199

OLIVES
Mini Muffuletta, 18
✓Olive & Roasted Pepper
 Bruschetta, 13
✓Tomato & Olive Bread, 171

ONIONS
Blue Cheese & Shallot Bread, 167
Buttery Onion Soup, 56
Garden Tomato Relish, 174
Gone-All-Day Stew, 104
✓Summertime Spaghetti Sauce, 111
Thai Portobello Chicken Stir-Fry, 134

ORANGE
✓Broccoli with Orange Sauce, 162
Cucumber & Spinach Tortellini
 Salad, 35
✓Nutty Orange Snowballs, 180
Orange Nut Bread & Cream Cheese
 Spread, 165
Sunny Morning Doughnuts, 90
Triple Cranberry Sauce, 169

PASTA
Bacon Cheeseburger Spaghetti, 96
Balsamic Chicken Pasta Salad, 33
Barbecue Pork and Penne Skillet, 119
Cabernet Marinara Pasta, 149
Creamy Spinach Sausage Pasta, 108
Cucumber & Spinach Tortellini
 Salad, 35
Glazed Shrimp & Asparagus, 153
Gorgonzola Pasta with Walnuts, 144
Hearty Beef and Noodles, 96
His Favorite Ravioli, 116
Italian Basil Pasta Salad, 34
Lasagna Deliziosa, 126
Loaded Spaghetti Bake, 104
Macaroni & Cheese Pizza, 116
✓Macaroni Coleslaw, 35

Macaroni Taco Bake, 101
Muffuletta Pasta, 119
Orzo-Stuffed Peppers, 114
Penne Gorgonzola with Chicken, 140
Pepperoni Pizza Skillet, 94
Pesto Chicken Mostaccioli, 131
Sausage Tortellini Soup, 58
Shrimp & Macaroni Casserole, 147
Six-Cheese Lasagna, 94
✓Summertime Spaghetti Sauce, 111
Szechuan Shrimp Noodles, 145
Thai Beef Pasta Salad, 38
Vegetarian Polka Dot Stew, 60

PEACHES
✓Fresh Peach Salsa, 12
Sour Cream Peach Pecan Pie, 198

PEANUTS & PEANUT BUTTER
Miniature Peanut Butter
    Cheesecakes, 215
✓Monkey Muffins, 76
PBJ-Stuffed French Toast, 84
Peanut Butter & Jelly Waffles, 76
Peanut Butter Banana Bread, 172
Peanut Butter Pies, 198
✓Peanut Butter Turtle Candies, 181

PEPPERONI
Bruschetta Pizza, 110
Hot Pepper Pleasers, 18
Muffuletta Pasta, 119
Pepperoni Pizza Skillet, 94

PEPPERS (*SEE BELL PEPPERS;*
    HOT PEPPERS)

PIES
Frosty Coffee Pie, 205
German Chocolate Cream Pie, 199
Greek Honey Nut Pie, 203
Marshmallow-Almond Key Lime
    Pie, 204
Mayan Chocolate Pecan Pie, 192
Mixed Nut 'n' Fig Pie, 195
Peanut Butter Pies, 198
Raspberry Cream Pie, 195
Raspberry-Lemon Pie, 202
Sour Cream Peach Pecan Pie, 198
Triple-Berry Crumb Pie, 203
Vermont Maple Oatmeal Pie, 199

PINEAPPLE
Blueberry-Pecan Crisp, 219
Fruit Salad with Lemon Dressing, 37

Pineapple Pecan Cups, 213
Sweet Potato Bread & Pineapple
    Butter, 163

PORK (*ALSO SEE BACON; HAM &
    CANADIAN BACON; PEPPERONI;
    PROSCIUTTO; SAUSAGE*)
✓Asian Barbecued Pork Loin, 108
Asian-Style Baby Back Ribs, 115
Barbecue Pork and Penne Skillet, 119
Chili Verde, 52
Fruit-Glazed Pork Chops, 111
Glazed Pork Chops, 120
Maple Chicken 'n' Ribs, 131
✓Pomegranate Pork Tenderloin, 120
✓Pork Burritos, 121
Pork Chops with Apple Rings, 114
Pork Tenderloin Panini with Fig Port
    Jam, 60
✓Roast Pork Sandwiches with Peach
    Chutney, 56
Sage Pork Chops with Cider Pan
    Gravy, 121
Secret's in the Sauce BBQ Ribs, 112
Sesame Pork Ribs, 117

POTATOES
Caramelized Onions in Mashed
    Potatoes, 162
Flavorful Red Potatoes, 169
Gone-All-Day Stew, 104
Ham & Cheese Stuffed Potatoes, 109
Low Country Boil, 144
Potato Bacon Casserole, 175
Stuffed Baby Red Potatoes, 10
✓Swiss-Onion Potato Bake, 161
Texas Garlic Mashed Potatoes, 160

PROSCIUTTO
His Favorite Ravioli, 116
✓Prosciutto Chicken in Wine Sauce, 133
Swiss Chicken Rolls, 137

PUMPKIN
✓Double-Chip Pumpkin Cinnamon
    Muffins, 83
Gingerbread Pumpkin Trifle, 224
Streusel Pumpkin Sweet Rolls, 227

RAISINS
Grandma's Christmas Cake, 193
✓Oatmeal Surprise Cookies, 186

RASPBERRIES
Apple Raspberry Crisp, 225

Apricot-Raspberry Angel Torte, 197
Chocolate Berry Tarts, 211
Chocolate Raspberry Tunnel
    Cake, 192
Oatmeal Brulee with Ginger
    Cream, 89
Raspberry Cheese Blintz Bake, 82
Raspberry Chocolate
    Cheesecake, 225
Raspberry Cream Pie, 195
Raspberry-Lemon Pie, 202
Raspberry Mint Shakes, 215

RHUBARB
Berry Delicious Rhubarb Crisp, 217
Rhubarb Berry Tart, 213
Rhubarb Coffee Cake with Caramel
    Sauce, 87

RICE
Apricot-Glazed Salmon with Herb
    Rice, 150
Chili-Cheese Rice Bake, 163
Mango Chicken with Plum
    Sauce, 125
Mushroom Beef Tips With Rice, 100
Orange-Cashew Chicken and Rice, 130
✓Pomegranate Pork Tenderloin, 120
Southwest Chicken and Rice, 128
Speedy Jambalaya, 109
Spicy Chorizo & Shrimp Rice, 149
Texas Confetti Rice Salad, 33

SALADS
MAIN DISHES
Balsamic Chicken Pasta Salad, 33
Chicken Tostada Salad, 28
Cucumber & Spinach Tortellini
    Salad, 35
✓Fruited Turkey Salads, 40
✓Refreshing Grilled Chicken
    Salad, 30
Salads with Pistachio-Crusted Goat
    Cheese, 47
Southwest Crunch Chicken Salad, 43
Texas Confetti Rice Salad, 33
Thai Beef Pasta Salad, 38
Turkey Waldorf Salad, 29
OTHER
✓Alfresco Bean Salad, 31
Ambrosia Fruit Salad, 45
✓Chicken Pita Salad, 31
Corn and Spinach Salad, 34
Fresh & Fruity Spinach Salad, 43
Fresh Mozzarella & Tomato Salad, 39

SALADS (*CONTINUED*)

✓Fruit & Cream Layered Salad, 30
Fruit Salad with Lemon Dressing, 37
✓Fruit Salad with O.J. Reduction, 77
✓Greek-Inspired Quinoa Salad, 46
✓Grilled Sweet Potato and Red
    Pepper Salad, 38
Hazelnut and Pear Salad, 36
Italian Basil Pasta Salad, 34
✓Macaroni Coleslaw, 35
Mediterranean Green Salad, 39
Orange Spinach Salad, 45
✓Radish Asparagus Salad, 36
South-of-the-Border Caprese
    Salad, 40
✓Spinach Bean Salad with Maple
    Dressing, 46
✓Vanilla-Lime Fruit Salad, 42
Zesty Crouton Salad, 28

SALSA

✓Black Bean Cakes with Mole
    Salsa, 153
Crumb-Coated Chicken &
    Blackberry Salsa, 125
✓Fresh Peach Salsa, 12
Peppered Filets with Tomato-
    Mushroom Salsa, 102
Salmon with Vegetable Salsa, 148

SANDWICHES, BURGERS & WRAPS

Apricot Turkey Sandwiches, 65
Asian Burgers, 58
Asian Meatless Wraps, 61
Bistro Breakfast Panini, 83
✓Breaded Eggplant Sandwiches, 68
✓Cheeseburger French Loaf, 52
Chicken Pesto Clubs, 53
Crab Toast, 69
Cranberry Chicken Focaccia, 54
Cucumber-Egg Salad Sandwiches, 65
Ginger Chicken Burgers with Sesame
    Slaw, 64
✓Italian BLTs, 54
Italian Sausage with Peppers, 67
✓Mango Shrimp Pitas, 61
Mini Muffuletta, 18
Pepper & Jack Smothered Burgers, 53
Pork Tenderloin Panini with Fig Port
    Jam, 60
Portobello Burgers with Pear-Walnut
    Mayonnaise, 67
✓Roast Pork Sandwiches with Peach
    Chutney, 56
Southwestern Burgers, 59
Stuffed Burgers on Portobellos, 63

Summer Veggie Subs, 51
Turkey Sliders with Chili Cheese
    Mayo, 70

SAUSAGE (*ALSO SEE PEPPERONI*)

Bear's Breakfast Burritos, 75
Chorizo-Stuffed Turkey Breast with
    Mexican Grits, 134
Creamy Spinach Sausage Pasta, 108
German Oktoberfest Pizza, 115
Italian Sausage with Peppers, 67
Lasagna Deliziosa, 126
Low Country Boil, 144
Macaroni & Cheese Pizza, 116
Mini Muffuletta, 18
Orzo-Stuffed Peppers, 114
Sausage Calzones, 112
Sausage Tortellini Soup, 58
Six-Cheese Lasagna, 94
Speedy Jambalaya, 109
Spicy Chorizo & Shrimp Rice, 149
✓Summertime Spaghetti Sauce, 111

SEAFOOD

Apricot-Glazed Salmon with Herb
    Rice, 150
Cedar Plank Salmon with Blackberry
    Sauce, 147
Corn Cakes with Shrimp &
    Guacamole, 21
Crab Cakes with Red Chili Mayo, 25
Crab Toast, 69
Glazed Shrimp & Asparagus, 153
Grilled Shrimp with Apricot
    Sauce, 154
Low Country Boil, 144
Macadamia-Crusted Mahi Mahi, 148
✓Mango Shrimp Pitas, 61
Orange Roughy with Tartar
    Sauce, 154
✓Peachy Shrimp Tacos, 150
Salmon with Vegetable Salsa, 148
Shrimp & Macaroni Casserole, 147
Spicy Chorizo & Shrimp Rice, 149
Spinach & Crab Dip, 24
Szechuan Shrimp Noodles, 145

SIDE DISHES

Asparagus and Sun-Dried
    Tomatoes, 166
✓Broccoli with Orange Sauce, 162
Caramelized Onions in Mashed
    Potatoes, 162
Chili-Cheese Rice Bake, 163
✓Chipotle Sweet Potatoes, 166
Country-Style Tomatoes, 158

Flavorful Red Potatoes, 169
Green Beans with Pecans, 170
Peasant Peppers, 167
Potato Bacon Casserole, 175
✓Swiss-Onion Potato Bake, 161
Texas Garlic Mashed Potatoes, 160

SLOW COOKER RECIPES

✓Cider Mushroom Brisket, 101
Fiesta Chicken Burritos, 139
Gone-All-Day Stew, 104
✓Pork Burritos, 121
Secret's in the Sauce BBQ Ribs, 112
Sesame Pork Ribs, 117
✓Special Pot Roast, 97

SNACKS & APPETIZERS

Cheeseburger Cups, 17
Chicken, Pear & Gorgonzola Tarts, 24
Chocolate Chip Dip, 14
Corn Cakes with Shrimp &
    Guacamole, 21
Crab Cakes with Red Chili Mayo, 25
French Quarter Cheese Spread, 22
✓Fresh Peach Salsa, 12
Gorgonzola & Cranberry Cheese
    Ball, 11
Greek Pinwheels, 12
Grilled Stuffed Jalapenos, 15
Hot Pepper Pleasers, 18
Kickin' Snack Mix, 19
Marinated Cheese, 20
Mediterranean Tomato Bites, 9
Mini Muffuletta, 18
Nacho Party Cheesecake, 16
✓Olive & Roasted Pepper
    Bruschetta, 13
Roasted Garlic & Tomato Spread, 19
Secret Ingredient Stuffed Eggs, 11
Sesame Chicken Dip, 13
Southwest Egg Rolls & Avocado
    Dip, 21
Sparkling Kiwi Lemonade, 22
✓Spinach & Black Bean Egg Rolls, 8
Spinach & Crab Dip, 24
Stuffed Asiago-Basil Mushrooms, 9
Stuffed Baby Red Potatoes, 10
Sun-Dried Tomato Dip, 14
Sweet & Spicy Nuts, 17
Tomato & Brie Focaccia, 16
✓Tomato-Jalapeno Granita, 8

SOUPS, STEWS & CHILI

Buttery Onion Soup, 56
Chili con Carne, 59
Chili Verde, 52

Creamy Reuben Soup, 68
Golden Squash Soup, 55
Gone-All-Day Stew, 104
Roasted Red Pepper Soup, 51
Sausage Tortellini Soup, 58
Shaker Bean Soup, 63
✓Spicy Chicken Chili, 70
Vegetarian Polka Dot Stew, 60
Yellow Tomato Soup with Goat
    Cheese Croutons, 69

SPINACH
Cucumber & Spinach Tortellini
    Salad, 35
Fresh & Fruity Spinach Salad, 43
✓Lemony Spinach-Stuffed Chicken
    Breasts, 130
Orange Spinach Salad, 45
Spinach & Crab Dip, 24
✓Spinach Bean Salad with Maple
    Dressing, 46

STRAWBERRIES
Berry & Cream Chocolate Cups, 222
Berry Delicious Rhubarb Crisp, 217
Lemon-Mint Pound Cake with
    Strawberries, 194
Rhubarb Berry Tart, 213
Strawberries with Chocolate Cream
    Filling, 216
Strawberry & Wine Sorbet, 211
Strawberry Cheesecake Ice
    Cream, 223
Strawberry Cheesecake Mousse, 212
Triple-Berry Crumb Pie, 203

SWEET POTATOES
✓Chipotle Sweet Potatoes, 166
✓Grilled Sweet Potato and Red
    Pepper Salad, 38
Sweet Potato Bread & Pineapple
    Butter, 163
✓Sweet Potato Spice Bread, 168

TARTS
Caramel Praline Tart, 216
Chocolate Berry Tarts, 211
Jeweled Plum Tartlets, 210
Lemon Blueberry Tart, 208
Rhubarb Berry Tart, 213

TOMATOES
Cabernet Marinara Pasta, 149
Chili con Carne, 59
Country-Style Tomatoes, 158
Creamy Spinach Sausage Pasta, 108

Fresh Mozzarella & Tomato Salad, 39
Garden Tomato Relish, 174
Mediterranean Tomato Bites, 9
Peppered Filets with Tomato-
    Mushroom Salsa, 102
Roasted Garlic & Tomato Spread, 19
South-of-the-Border Caprese
    Salad, 40
Speedy Jambalaya, 109
✓Spicy Chicken Chili, 70
✓Summertime Spaghetti Sauce, 111
Sun-Dried Tomato Dip, 14
Tomato & Brie Focaccia, 16
✓Tomato & Olive Bread, 171
✓Tomato-Jalapeno Granita, 8
Yellow Tomato Soup with Goat
    Cheese Croutons, 69
Zesty Crouton Salad, 28

TORTILLAS
Asian Meatless Wraps, 61
Bear's Breakfast Burritos, 75
Chicken Enchilada Bake, 135
Creamy Beef Enchiladas, 102
Fiesta Chicken Burritos, 139
✓Peachy Shrimp Tacos, 150
✓Pork Burritos, 121

TURKEY
Apricot Turkey Sandwiches, 65
Bruschetta Pizza, 110
Chorizo-Stuffed Turkey Breast with
    Mexican Grits, 134
✓Fruited Turkey Salads, 40
✓Honey-Brined Turkey Breast, 138
Lasagna Deliziosa, 126
✓Mustard Turkey Cutlets, 136
✓Roast Turkey Breast with
    Rosemary Gravy, 138
Roasted Citrus & Herb Turkey, 133
Summer Veggie Subs, 51
Texas Confetti Rice Salad, 33
Turkey Meat Loaf, 129
Turkey Sliders with Chili Cheese
    Mayo, 70
Turkey Waldorf Salad, 29

VEGETABLES (*ALSO SEE
    SPECIFIC LISTINGS*)
Asian Burgers, 58
Bacon Vegetable Quiche, 88
✓Breaded Eggplant Sandwiches, 68
✓Broccoli with Orange Sauce, 162
✓Chicken Pita Salad, 31
Chocolate Zucchini Cupcakes, 205
Corn and Spinach Salad, 34

Fiesta Chicken Burritos, 139
Golden Squash Soup, 55
Gone-All-Day Stew, 104
Green Beans with Pecans, 170
Italian Sausage with Peppers, 67
✓Macaroni Coleslaw, 35
Salmon with Vegetable Salsa, 148
Shaker Bean Soup, 63
✓Southwest Crunch Chicken
    Salad, 43
Speedy Jambalaya, 109
Summer Veggie Subs, 51
Szechuan Shrimp Noodles, 145
Thai Portobello Chicken Stir-Fry, 134
Tomato Onion Quiche, 155
Wonderful Carrot Cake, 202

VEGETARIAN
Asian Meatless Wraps, 61
✓Black Bean Cakes with Mole
    Salsa, 153
✓Breaded Eggplant Sandwiches, 68
Cabernet Marinara Pasta, 149
Cucumber-Egg Salad Sandwiches, 65
Gorgonzola Pasta with Walnuts, 144
Portobello Burgers with Pear-Walnut
    Mayonnaise, 67
Salads with Pistachio-Crusted Goat
    Cheese, 47
Spiral Omelet Supreme, 79
Summer Squash Mushroom
    Casserole, 152
Tomato Onion Quiche, 155
Vegetarian Polka Dot Stew, 60
Yellow Tomato Soup with Goat
    Cheese Croutons, 69

ZUCCHINI & **SUMMER SQUASH**
Pina Colada Zucchini Bread, 160
Summer Squash Mushroom
    Casserole, 152

Alphabetical Recipe Index

This index lists every recipe in alphabetical order.

✓ RECIPES INCLUDE **NUTRITION FACTS** AND **DIABETIC EXCHANGES**.

A

✓Alfresco Bean Salad, 31
Ambrosia Fruit Salad, 45
Apple Raspberry Crisp, 225
Apricot-Glazed Salmon with Herb Rice, 150
Apricot-Raspberry Angel Torte, 197
Apricot Turkey Sandwiches, 65
✓Asian Barbecued Pork Loin, 108
Asian Burgers, 58
Asian Meatless Wraps, 61
Asian-Style Baby Back Ribs, 115
Asparagus and Sun-Dried Tomatoes, 166
Authentic Boston Brown Bread, 159

B

Bacon Cheeseburger Spaghetti, 96
Bacon Vegetable Quiche, 88
✓Baked Blueberry & Peach Oatmeal, 80
Balsamic Chicken Pasta Salad, 33
Banana Chip Pancakes, 80
Barbecue Pork and Penne Skillet, 119
Barbecued Chicken Pizzas, 136
Bear's Breakfast Burritos, 75
Benedict Eggs in Pastry, 79
Berry & Cream Chocolate Cups, 222
Berry Delicious Rhubarb Crisp, 217
Bistro Breakfast Panini, 83
✓Black Bean Cakes with Mole Salsa, 153
Blondie Nut Bars, 178
Blue Cheese & Shallot Bread, 167
Blueberry Bounty Cake, 201
Blueberry Cheesecake Flapjacks, 91
✓Blueberry Oat Pancakes, 77
Blueberry-Pecan Crisp, 219
Bread & Butter Peppers, 172
✓Breaded Eggplant Sandwiches, 68
✓Broccoli with Orange Sauce, 162
Bruschetta Pizza, 110
Butter Pecan French Toast, 85
✓Butterscotch Bliss Layered Dessert, 219
Buttery Onion Soup, 56

C

Cabernet Marinara Pasta, 149
Candy Bar Cupcakes, 200
Cappuccino Cinnamon Rolls, 88
Caramel Praline Tart, 216
Caramelized Onions in Mashed Potatoes, 162
Cedar Plank Salmon with Blackberry Sauce, 147
Cheeseburger Cups, 17
✓Cheeseburger French Loaf, 52
✓Cherry Chocolate Chip Cookies, 178
Cherry Mocha Balls, 183
Chewy Date Pinwheels, 184
Chicken Enchilada Bake, 135
Chicken, Pear & Gorgonzola Tarts, 24
Chicken Pesto Clubs, 53
Chicken Pita Salad, 31
Chicken Saltimbocca with Mushroom Sauce, 129
Chicken Tostada Salad, 28
Chicken with Rosemary Butter Sauce, 126
Chili-Cheese Rice Bake, 163
Chili con Carne, 59
Chili Verde, 52
✓Chipotle Sweet Potatoes, 166
Chocolate Berry Tarts, 211
Chocolate Bliss Marble Cake, 193
Chocolate Chai Mini Loaves, 159
Chocolate Chip Dip, 14
Chocolate Peppermint Scones, 78
✓Chocolate Pistachio Biscotti, 181
Chocolate Raspberry Tunnel Cake, 192
Chocolate Ribbon Banana Loaf, 84
Chocolate Shortbread, 189
Chocolate Sour Cream Torte, 200
Chocolate Zucchini Cupcakes, 205
Chorizo-Stuffed Turkey Breast with Mexican Grits, 134
✓Cider Mushroom Brisket, 101
Citrus-Melon Sorbet, 218
Corn and Spinach Salad, 34
Corn Bread with a Kick, 171
Corn Cakes with Shrimp & Guacamole, 21
Country-Style Tomatoes, 158
Cowboy Corn Bread, 175
Crab Cakes with Red Chili Mayo, 25
Crab Toast, 69
Cranberry Chicken Focaccia, 54

Creamy Beef Enchiladas, 102
Creamy Reuben Soup, 68
Creamy Spinach Sausage Pasta, 108
Crispy Chicken Fingers, 139
Crumb-Coated Chicken & Blackberry Salsa, 125
Cucumber & Spinach Tortellini Salad, 35
Cucumber-Egg Salad Sandwiches, 65

D

Dessert Bruschetta with Nectarine Salsa, 227
✓Diamond Almond Bars, 179
✓Double-Chip Pumpkin Cinnamon Muffins, 83

E

Easy Tiramisu, 223
Eggnog Logs, 183

F

Fiesta Chicken Burritos, 139
Finnish Pinwheels, 185
Flatbread Tacos with Ranch Sour Cream, 103
Flavorful Red Potatoes, 169
French Quarter Cheese Spread, 22
Fresh & Fruity Spinach Salad, 43
Fresh Mozzarella & Tomato Salad, 39
✓Fresh Peach Salsa, 12
Frosty Coffee Pie, 205
Frozen Chocolate Mint Dessert, 220
✓Fruit & Cream Layered Salad, 30
Fruit-Glazed Pork Chops, 111
Fruit Salad with Lemon Dressing, 37
✓Fruit Salad with O.J. Reduction, 77
✓Fruited Turkey Salads, 40

G

Garden Tomato Relish, 174
German Chocolate Cream Pie, 199
German Oktoberfest Pizza, 115
Ginger Chicken Burgers with Sesame Slaw, 64
Ginger Currant Scones, 74
Gingerbread Pumpkin Trifle, 224
✓Gingered Chicken Thighs, 140
Glazed Pear Shortcakes, 212
Glazed Pork Chops, 120

Glazed Shrimp & Asparagus, 153
Goat Cheese-Stuffed Chicken with
    Apricot Glaze, 128
Golden Squash Soup, 55
Gone-All-Day Stew, 104
Gooey Butterscotch Bars, 180
✓Gooey Chocolate Cookies, 184
Gorgonzola & Cranberry Cheese
    Ball, 11
Gorgonzola Pasta with Walnuts, 144
Grandma's Christmas Cake, 193
Greek Honey Nut Pie, 203
✓Greek-Inspired Quinoa Salad, 46
Greek Pinwheels, 12
Green Beans with Pecans, 170
Grilled Shrimp with Apricot
    Sauce, 154
Grilled Stuffed Jalapenos, 15
✓Grilled Sweet Potato and Red
    Pepper Salad, 38

H
Ham & Cheese Breakfast Strudels, 87
Ham & Cheese Stuffed Potatoes, 109
Hazelnut and Pear Salad, 36
Hearty Beef and Noodles, 96
His Favorite Ravioli, 116
Holiday Glazed Ham, 117
Holiday Walnut Torte, 197
✓Honey-Brined Turkey Breast, 138
Hot Buttered Rum Rolls, 74
Hot Fudge Pudding Cake, 210
Hot Pepper Pleasers, 18
Hungarian Nut Rolls, 218

I
Italian Basil Pasta Salad, 34
✓Italian BLTs, 54
Italian Meatball Tortes, 98
Italian Sausage with Peppers, 67
Italian Strip Steaks with Focaccia, 95

J
Jeweled Plum Tartlets, 210

K
Kickin' Snack Mix, 19

L
Lasagna Deliziosa, 126
Lemon Blueberry Tart, 208
Lemon-Mint Pound Cake with
    Strawberries, 194
Lemon Stars, 182
✓Lemony Spinach-Stuffed Chicken
    Breasts, 130
Loaded Spaghetti Bake, 104
Low Country Boil, 144

M
Macadamia-Crusted Mahi Mahi, 148
✓Macadamia Nut Fudge, 188
Macaroni & Cheese Pizza, 116
✓Macaroni Coleslaw, 35
Macaroni Taco Bake, 101
Mango Chicken with Plum
    Sauce, 125
✓Mango Shrimp Pitas, 61
Maple Chicken 'n' Ribs, 131
✓Maple Nut Truffles, 189
✓Maple Walnut Crisps, 179
Marinated Cheese, 20
Marshmallow-Almond Key Lime
    Pie, 204
Mayan Chocolate Pecan Pie, 192
Mediterranean Green Salad, 39
Mediterranean Tomato Bites, 9
Mini Muffuletta, 18
Miniature Peanut Butter
    Cheesecakes, 215
Mixed Nut 'n' Fig Pie, 195
✓Monkey Muffins, 76
✓Moroccan Beef Kabobs, 99
Muffuletta Pasta, 119
Mushroom Beef Tips With Rice, 100
✓Mustard Turkey Cutlets, 136

N
Nacho Party Cheesecake, 16
Nacho Pizza, 99
✓Nutty Orange Snowballs, 180

O
Oatmeal Brulee with Ginger
    Cream, 89
✓Oatmeal Surprise Cookies, 186
✓Olive & Roasted Pepper
    Bruschetta, 13
Orange-Cashew Chicken and
    Rice, 130
Orange Nut Bread & Cream Cheese
    Spread, 165
Orange Roughy with Tartar
    Sauce, 154
Orange Spinach Salad, 45
Orzo-Stuffed Peppers, 114

P
PBJ-Stuffed French Toast, 84
✓Peachy Shrimp Tacos, 150
Peanut Butter & Jelly Waffles, 76
Peanut Butter Banana Bread, 172
Peanut Butter Pies, 198
✓Peanut Butter Turtle Candies, 181
Peasant Peppers, 167
Pecan Chicken with Blue Cheese
    Sauce, 135

Penne Gorgonzola with Chicken, 140
Pepper & Jack Smothered
    Burgers, 53
Peppered Filets with Tomato-
    Mushroom Salsa, 102
Pepperoni Pizza Skillet, 94
Peppery Cheese Bread, 165
Pesto Chicken Mostaccioli, 131
Petite Sticky Buns, 91
Pina Colada Zucchini Bread, 160
Pineapple Pecan Cups, 213
✓Pomegranate Pork Tenderloin, 120
✓Pork Burritos, 121
Pork Chops with Apple Rings, 114
Pork Tenderloin Panini with Fig Port
    Jam, 60
Portobello Burgers with Pear-Walnut
    Mayonnaise, 67
Portobello Waffles with Balsamic
    Syrup, 82
Potato Bacon Casserole, 175
✓Prosciutto Chicken in Wine
    Sauce, 133

R
✓Radish Asparagus Salad, 36
Raspberry Cheese Blintz Bake, 82
Raspberry Chocolate
    Cheesecake, 225
Raspberry Cream Pie, 195
Raspberry-Lemon Pie, 202
Raspberry Mint Shakes, 215
✓Refreshing Grilled Chicken
    Salad, 30
Rhubarb Berry Tart, 213
Rhubarb Coffee Cake with Caramel
    Sauce, 87
✓Roast Pork Sandwiches with Peach
    Chutney, 56
✓Roast Turkey Breast with
    Rosemary Gravy, 138
Roasted Citrus & Herb Turkey, 133
Roasted Garlic & Tomato Spread, 19
Roasted Red Pepper Soup, 51

S
✓S'more Bars, 186
Sage Pork Chops with Cider Pan
    Gravy, 121
Salads with Pistachio-Crusted Goat
    Cheese, 47
Salmon With Vegetable Salsa, 148
Santa Maria Roast Beef, 103
Sausage Calzones, 112
Sausage Tortellini Soup, 58
Savory Dill and Caraway Scones, 170
Savory Grilled T-Bones, 100
Secret Ingredient Stuffed Eggs, 11

Secret's in the Sauce BBQ Ribs, 112
Sesame Chicken Dip, 13
Sesame Chicken with Ginger
    Shiitake Cream Sauce, 124
Sesame Pork Ribs, 117
Shaker Bean Soup, 63
Shrimp & Macaroni Casserole, 147
Six-Cheese Lasagna, 94
Sour Cream Peach Pecan Pie, 198
South-of-the-Border Caprese
    Salad, 40
Southwest Chicken and Rice, 128
✓Southwest Crunch Chicken
    Salad, 43
Southwest Egg Rolls & Avocado
    Dip, 21
Southwestern Burgers, 59
Sparkling Kiwi Lemonade, 22
✓Special Pot Roast, 97
Speedy Jambalaya, 109
Spice Bread with Maple Butter, 158
✓Spicy Chicken Chili, 70
Spicy Chorizo & Shrimp Rice, 149
✓Spinach & Black Bean Egg Rolls, 8
Spinach & Crab Dip, 24
✓Spinach Bean Salad with Maple
    Dressing, 46
Spiral Omelet Supreme, 79
Strawberries with Chocolate Cream
    Filling, 216
Strawberry & Wine Sorbet, 211
Strawberry Cheesecake Ice
    Cream, 223
Strawberry Cheesecake Mousse, 212
Streusel Pumpkin Sweet Rolls, 227
Stuffed Asiago-Basil Mushrooms, 9
Stuffed Baby Red Potatoes, 10
Stuffed Burgers on Portobellos, 63
Summer Squash Mushroom
    Casserole, 152
Summer Veggie Subs, 51
✓Summertime Spaghetti Sauce, 111
Sun-Dried Tomato Dip, 14
Sunny Morning Doughnuts, 90
Sweet & Spicy Nuts, 17
Sweet Potato Bread & Pineapple
    Butter, 163
✓Sweet Potato Spice Bread, 168
Swiss Chicken Rolls, 137
✓Swiss-Onion Potato Bake, 161
Szechuan Shrimp Noodles, 145

T
Texas Confetti Rice Salad, 33
Texas Garlic Mashed Potatoes, 160
Thai Beef Pasta Salad, 38

Thai Portobello Chicken Stir-Fry, 134
Tomato & Brie Focaccia, 16
✓Tomato & Olive Bread, 171
✓Tomato-Jalapeno Granita, 8
Tomato Onion Quiche, 155
✓Trail Mix Clusters, 188
Triple-Berry Crumb Pie, 203
Triple Cranberry Sauce, 169
Turkey Meat Loaf, 129
Turkey Sliders with Chili Cheese
    Mayo, 70
Turkey Waldorf Salad, 29
Turtle Bread Pudding, 208
Turtle Cheesecake, 224
Tuscan Steak Flatbreads, 95

V
✓Vanilla-Lime Fruit Salad, 42
Vegetarian Polka Dot Stew, 60
Vermont Maple Oatmeal Pie, 199

W
Warm Chocolate Melting Cups, 220
Whipped Shortbread, 185
Wonderful Carrot Cake, 202

Y
Yellow Tomato Soup with Goat
    Cheese Croutons, 69

Z
Zesty Crouton Salad, 28